Three
week loan

Please return on or before the last
date stamped below.
Charges are made for late return.

UWCC LIBRARY,   PO BOX 430, CARDIFF CF1 3XT.

LF 56 / 1293

Other books in this series:

Volume IV. Sage Criminal Justice System Annuals

THE JURY SYSTEM
IN AMERICA

A CRITICAL OVERVIEW

RITA JAMES SIMON, *Editor*

SAGE Publications   *Beverly Hills* · *London*

For information address:

SAGE PUBLICATIONS, INC.
275 South Beverly Drive
Beverly Hills, California 90212

SAGE PUBLICATIONS LTD
St George's House / 44 Hatton Garden
London EC1N 8ER

Printed in the United States of America

International Standard Book No. 0-8039-0382-0 (cloth)
International Standard Book No. 0-8039-0504-1 (paper)

Library of Congress Catalog Card No. 72-82999

FIRST PRINTING

— CONTENTS

Part III: Perspectives on the Function and Value of the Jury in America

THE JURY SYSTEM IN AMERICA:
A CRITICAL OVERVIEW

INTRODUCTION

RITA JAMES SIMON

INTRODUCTION

RITA JAMES SIMON

The jury is enjoying a resurgence of interest on the part of the research community. Like the fashion industry, topics for research also seem to experience waves of ascension and decline; the jury system is clearly enjoying the former. Part of the resurgence of interest in the jury may be attributed to the important political trials that have occurred since the latter part of the 1960s and that have attracted national attention. All of those trials—the Chicago Seven, Huey Newton, Angela Davis, the Harrisburg Thirteen, Mitchell-Stans, and John Ehrlichman, to name some of the most sensational—have been jury trials; and in all of them the juries' behavior and verdicts have served to enhance the system in the eyes of the public and the press, as well as the bench and the bar.

Many judges and lawyers have traditionally held a jaundiced, or at best a skeptical attitude, concerning the worthwhileness of the jury; especially when it was called upon to hear complicated matters involving questions of constitutional importance. Jerome Frank, for example, emphasized the unpredictability of jury discretion and stressed the general incompetence and easy persuasability of jurors.

While the verdicts in the trials mentioned above were not all decided in the same direction, indicating thereby either a wave of support for the government or for the accused, in the main, each of the verdicts received positive and complimentary notices from the press and from a more critical audience —members of the bench and bar. The juries' performances in these nationally important trials evoked hardly any of the traditional complaints that laymen are neither competent nor motivated to deal with issues of constitutional law, and that such complex tasks should be delegated to experts. When the jury voted to acquit both Angela Davis, a member of the Communist Party, and Maurice Stans and John Mitchell, former Nixon Cabinet members, the verdicts in both actions were respected and considered legally acceptable, irrespective of popular sympathies and interests.

In this context, we note that two of the authors in this volume comment on a theme about jury behavior that is relevant. Both Kennebeck, who writes from the perspective of a juror (he served on the "Panther Thirteen" case in New York City), and Graham, who writes from the perspective of a member of the press, comment on the phenomenon that jurors "grow up to their office." Both of them believe that ordinary citizens sitting in their own homes might not have the wisdom and the interest to consider the issues, to weigh the arguments, and to debate the pros and cons of a particular case; but that these same citizens when selected by their government to serve as representatives of the public to the judiciary assume quite a different posture. Once they are selected for jury duty, their collective vision seems to expand and deepen, their reasoning takes on additional dimensions, and their ability and willingness to empathize and understand the feelings and life situation of others increases. Kennebeck quotes from G. K. Chesterton's essay, "Twelve Men,"

> Our civilization has decided, and very justly decided, that determining the guilt or innocence of men is a thing too important to be trusted to trained men. . . . When it wants a library catalogued, or the solar system discovered, or any trifle of that kind, it uses up its specialists. But when it wishes anything done which is really serious, it collects twelve of the ordinary men standing around.

Writing in the late 1950s, researchers at the University of Chicago Jury Project used the term "halo effect" to describe much the same phenomenon that Kennebeck and Graham describe in this volume. On the basis of their observations of the jury's performance, they concluded that individual jurors rise to the occasion and perform in representative roles. The jurors perceive themselves as representatives of the citizenry to the judiciary. The conclusions of the Chicago researchers were that the jury's performance is more responsible and more rational than one would expect from the sum of the individual performers. The jury takes its responsibility seriously; it checks many of its prejudices at the door of the jury room; it recognizes its special role as temporary members of the judiciary bound by rules of law and procedures not present in their business transactions or informal conversations. The fact is that ordinary citizens are willing to accept those trappings and are able to work within them. The fears voiced by critics that jurors are led by bias, incompetence, and irrelevant factors to make capricious decisions were not substantiated.

But the jury does not receive kudos from all the contributors to this volume. The chapter by Professor Watts describes how the jury fares at the pens of serious writers of American fiction who include the jury in their work (only relatively few of them do). In her chapter, the jury receives consistently negative reviews for its lack of intelligence, motivation and efficiency, and for its prejudices of mind and heart.

Singer and Barton describe the impact on the jury of newspaper stories which contain information about the defendant's previous criminal record and an alleged retracted confession. They conclude that jurors who are exposed to such types of information are prejudiced and that such exposure poses a serious problem for the impartiality of jury verdicts. Their findings suggest that "voir dire" examinations may be crucial in causing jurors to be less responsive to prejudicial information.

The American jury system is older than the United States. As an institution, we inherited the jury from the British. It came to American shores with the first group of English settlers. It was one of the important symbols during the struggle for independence; and it is prominently referred to in three of the first ten amendments to the Constitution. The right to trial by jury is one of the basic democratic institutions of American government and society. But its very democracy has made it a target for attack and ridicule. As the country has grown, as commercial and industrial activities and organizations have expanded and become more complex, the jury has come to be looked upon by some as unworkable. Like the "town hall" meetings of the New England colony days, the jury is perceived as part of an earlier era: it was important and it should be revered for the role it played in developing our sense of democracy; but by the twentieth century it has outgrown its usefulness.

Jerome Frank was one of the leading jurists in the 1930s and 1940s to attack the jury for its lack of competence and efficiency. But other important figures on the bench and bar since then have urged that the United States follow Great Britain in doing away with the jury in civil matters and retaining it only for criminal cases. That movement still has many supporters. There are those (for example see the reference to Zeisel in the chapter by Kessler) who see in the recent decisions by the Supreme Court, in support of nonunanimous verdicts and six-person juries, the court's interest in eventually discarding the jury system. In a recent article, Zeisel argued,

If the country wants to reconsider the desirability of the civil jury, it should be done in open and direct debate. Perhaps such debate should begin. But to pare the jury down and allow it to decay from the insufficiencies we impose is shabby treatment for an institution that has served the nation well.

Empirical research describing how the system works has consistently turned out to support continuance of the jury, even though the authors had no prior predilections in that direction. The 1930s saw the beginnings of work on how the jury actually functions: the importance of the deliberations, the types of jurors who are most influential, the allocation of time to various issues, and the importance of the attorneys and the judge in the jurors' considerations were some of the issues considered. But on the whole, not much was published about the jury during this period.

The real flowering of interest in the jury system developed in conjunction with a larger interest in developing research programs in law and the behavioral sciences. In 1953, the University of Chicago Law School received a grant from the Ford Foundation to begin a five-year research program in the newly termed area. The decision on the part of the research directors to select the jury system as one of its three major topics for research (commercial arbitration and the income tax were the other two) opened a new window on the jury and began a period of extensive research on that institution.

The American Jury by Kalven and Zeisel, published in 1966, cites some sixty articles that had been written at the time of publication about the jury stemming from the project. The other monographs that emerged from the project were Delay in the Court (Zeisel, Kalven, and Bucholz, 1959) and The Jury and the Defense of Insanity (Simon, 1967). The chapters in Part II of this volume all make some reference to the Chicago experience and describe some of the issues on which the Chicago project focused, as well as some of its major findings.

About a decade after the Chicago project officially ended its field operations, empirical work on the jury sprouted anew, this time not at any one center but at many universities and research institutes throughout the country. Some of the recent work is represented in this volume; for example, the chapters by Padawer-Singer and Barton, by Kessler, and by Fried, Kaplan, and Klein are segments of larger ongoing research projects concerned with the impact on juries' verdicts of pretrial publicity, the "voir dire" and juror selection, the size of the jury, and unanimous versus nonunanimous verdicts.

This volume examines and evaluates the jury from several perspectives. It contains contributions by historians, behavioral scientists, practicing attorneys, judges, journalists, literary critics and jurors—each of whom describes and evaluates the jury from his or her particular vantage point.

The volume has three major sections. The first provides a brief history of the American jury. In it Hyman and Tarrant characterize its British heritage and its American characteristics. They describe the role that the jury played during colonial times in the struggle for independence; and in the bitter years prior to the Civil War, especially when it became involved in the fugitive slave issues and in the personal liberty laws enacted by the free states. They review the debates that occurred on the issues of minority representation and the right to a jury of one's peers that began during the period of reconstruction following the Civil War, and continued for a century. Hyman and Tarrant emphasize the need for more work on the history of the jury. They provide a useful bibliography as possible take-off points for future authors.

The second section describes current research and reviews important prior research on the jury by behavioral scientists. The contributors to this section were selected by two criteria: one, each of the authors was currently involved in studying a specific aspect of jurors' behavior or of the jury system; and two, each of them agreed to write a chapter that would also summarize major related research that had been conducted on that same issue. Thus, for example, Professor Stephan's charge was to review the work on the social characteristics of jurors and litigants as they are believed to affect the juries' deliberations and verdicts. Fried, Kaplan, and Klein present a psychological model for the selection of juries during the "voir dire" of a criminal trial and provide a review of the relevant literature on the function of the "voir dire" in predicting or influencing juries' decisions. Their chapter offers a theoretical framework within which one can perceive the conflicting aims of the prosecuting and defense attorneys. Kessler reviews research on the social psychology of jury deliberations with special emphasis on the function of size and unanimity of verdicts. Padawer-Singer and Barton review the basic conflict between the rights of a defendant to a fair trial and freedom of the press; and they then describe the results of their work on the impact of pretrial publicity on juries' verdicts.

The third section of this volume sees the jury more subjectively and more impressionalistically. Each contributor writes about the jury from the particular vantage point from which he or she is most likely to see it function. Thus, the Honorable Charles Joiner describes his impressions of the jury from his position on the bench. Corboy and Friloux view the jury as practicing members of the bar. Joiner, Corboy, and Friloux each describe and evaluate the jury on the basis of their own experiences in a particular role. The jury system receives kudos from each of them.

Graham, currently a professor of journalism, but also a Pulitzer Prize reporter, evaluates the jury's performance from the perspective of a newsman. He reviews some of the trials he has covered and discusses the controversy between the rights of a free press and the rights of a defendant to a fair and speedy trial.

Professor Watts' focus differs somewhat from the other contributors to this section in that hers is less of a subjective account, and more of a disinterested analysis of how the jury has fared in the hands of serious writers of American literature. Professor Watts searched for references about the jury in major works of American fiction. She found them relatively infrequently; when she did, they were almost negative and depreciating. She notes that such major writers as Hawthorne, Melville, James, and Hemingway did not consider the jury at all. Theodore Dreiser, Mark Twain, James Fennimore Cooper, William Faulkner, and Robert Penn Warren—writers who did have juries in their novels, and who tended to represent the common man, the ordinary citizen, and down-and-outers—were usually suspicious and distrustful of juries. In their work, the jurors' impartiality was almost always compromised by prejudices, ignorance, manipulation by officers of the court, and wishy-washiness. They preferred to have the fate or fates of their heroes and heroines entrusted to the expert hands of a professionally trained jurist.

The last piece in the third section is the most impressionistic of all. Kennebeck describes how the jury works from the other side of the door. He writes about his experiences waiting to be accepted or rejected by prosecuting and defense attorneys, and about how jurors respond to the judge, to the attorneys and to each other. He tells how it feels to be sitting in the jury box watching a lawyer put on a show, or a judge look bored, or a defendant confused. He describes and evaluates the system from the vantage point of a juror.

Putting the three sections together, this volume provides the reader with the opportunity to trace the role that the jury has played in American history as well as the history of that institution in the United States; to observe its functioning and performance along specific dimensions; and to evaluate critically others' impressions of the jury's performance as well as of its usefulness.

Part I

A HISTORICAL PERSPECTIVE

1

ASPECTS OF
AMERICAN TRIAL JURY HISTORY

HAROLD M. HYMAN and
CATHERINE M. TARRANT

The history of the present jury system antedates by several hundred years the charter granted to the Virginia Company in 1606. This charter guaranteed to the colonists all the rights of Englishmen, including trial by jury. In bestowing these rights, King James I set an example that was followed in all of the other English colonies, as well as their conquests, in North America during the seventeenth and eighteenth centuries.

American jurisprudence, examined in terms of the jury, reflects the necessary compromises involved in the everyday administration of property rights and criminal justice. Most important, while defining this system as a sometimes uneasy balance between the ideals of justice and liberty and the realities of human prejudices and passion, the jury is seen to represent a fundamental commitment to the federal system, embodying a concept of laws as rules of government and not as mere whims or dictums of men.

Chapter 1

ASPECTS OF AMERICAN TRIAL JURY HISTORY

HAROLD M. HYMAN and
CATHERINE M. TARRANT

In 1961, according to the United States Justice Department, 92 federal courts employed 92 differing methods for selecting jurors. Far greater variations existed in state and local courts (Murphy, 1972: 413n). Odds are that this multiplicity has not lessened substantially during the intervening fifteen years.

Persons who deplore such diversity, and who seek to replace trial jury methods, procedures, and standards with some relatively more uniform alternatives, face rugged impediments. The first obstacle is American federalism. Jury pluralism is only one aspect of the almost incredible diversity obtaining in the more than 110,000 governments—local, state, and national—which today operate America.

This intensely local-horizoned federalism was already tenaciously rooted in the hearts, minds, and institutional arrangements of George Washington's countrymen 200 years ago, to the discomfiture of King George III and his imperceptive, Oxbridge-graduate Cabinet ministers. For good and ill, federalism has increased its hold on the habits and affections of Americans since 1776. It is very unlikely that modern would-be improvers of the jury "system" who fail to take into account the many ways that juries developed within the context of federalism, from the beginnings of America's history to the present, have much chance for success.

Another obstacle against immediate success is a factor of the very thin body of American legal history concerning juries. Most unfortunately, research into American jury history has been far from adequate, systematic, or synthetic. Scholars who have attended to juries, by and large, have done so incidentally as they pursued other themes. The result is that any attempt to survey jury history, especially in brief form, as in the following essay, is necessarily impressionistic, discursive, and tentative.

Within these sobering, indeed, depressing limitations, an overview of aspects of trial (or petit) jury history, based upon the best secondary scholarship, may pay certain dividends. Hopefully, it can suggest to court officers the plastic, imprecise nature of knowledge on major configurations of their institutions, leading to caution in the exercise of power. Perhaps this essay will also illuminate some jury history configurations that will serve those who aim to improve jury operations. And it may be that, if only out of irritation, the inadequacies of this survey will impel persons who are involved in legal research, to look hard at jury history. Few areas of legal history need attention more.

I.

Ironically, the English common law tradition, aspects of which stressed uniformity more than diversity, found snug harbors in American colonial legal arrangements, which, like every other institution in the colonies, were federalistic. The jury, perhaps more than any other common law institution as it developed in England, retained intimate connections to local customs and procedures. Therefore, diverse jury practices and the plural governments of federalism, as they developed here, meshed surprisingly well.

Yet, at the same time, federalism allowed unifying threads to develop in jury operations. To a surprising extent, colonial Americans perceived and acted on a common principle: that every accused person—white person, at least—had a right to a jury trial, which adequately protected him while he was before the law. In this manner, juries helped substantially to link "nationally" the colonies with individuals. Considering the imperial expanses of the American land, the lack of other connectives such as an established church (except in Virginia and in a few counties of New York and New Jersey), and the multiplicity of ethnic ancestries, races, and languages of the inhabitants, this was no mean contribution.

The jury system was an old and revered institution in England by 1606, when King James I granted a Charter to the Virginia Company. The following year, the company established the community of Jamestown along the marshy banks of the James River in Virginia. The Charter guaranteed to the colonizers all the rights of Englishmen, including trial by jury. So doing, the Virginia Charter set a pattern emulated in the establishment and governance of the other English colonies in North America during the seventeenth and eighteenth centuries. In the small number of colonies acquired by conquest, such as New York, and governed initially by royal orders rather than by charter, juries were authorized very early, and developed thereafter in ways parallel to the commerical colonies. The result was that an assumption favoring the right to trial by jury was common in all the British North American colonies (Scott, 1930: 86; Heller, 1969: 14).

But a declaration of rights and their firm practice were not always synonymous. In instructions which accompanied the Charter of the Virginia Company, James I ordered that all capital cases be tried by a jury. Nevertheless, in the early days of the Jamestown settlement, a few individuals were put to death without jury trials. Their offenses were considered rebellious, during periods when martial law operated. Under Crown government in Virginia, which was established in 1624, jury trial was provided for in all civil and criminal cases where demanded (Scott, 1930: 86).[1] After 1727, however, jury trial was abolished in the Virginia Courts where the money penalty was less than £5 (Scott, 1930: 87).

Great jury practice diversity grew not only between the colonies and between a colony and England, but also within a colony. James I's instructions, and similar orders by his successor dynasts, were that England's laws be introduced and implemented in their transatlantic possessions. But these orders were frequently disobeyed or incorrectly followed, often less from defiance than from ignorance. Law books, manuals, and reports were scarce, expensive, and irregularly available. Legal education was, simultaneously, highly ritualized, yet intensely personalized. England's law institutions provided almost no ongoing oversight. Very few colonists studied law in England. Colonial distances were vast and interior communications awful, with frequent interruptions from epidemic diseases, inclement weather, or hostile Indians.

With respect to jury development, the upshot was not the frontier democratization of Frederick Jackson Turner's imagery. As example of contrary effects, the enmeshment of Negroes and some Indians into Virginia's property law, as chattel slaves, affected jury practices in tragically and undemocratic ways. Opportunities to be jurymen, or to offer self-defensive testimony to a jury, were not enjoyed by Negroes or Indians in Virginia or in other states with slave property codes.

Virginia, the first successful, permanent, English-speaking colony on the continent of North America, became both a prototype and a deviant with respect to jury development. As noted earlier, this hodge-podge patternlessness is deceptive, however. A confusing, complex feature of federalism here was (and is) the coexistence of surprising degrees of uniformity within diversity in many aspects of colonial life, including jury institutions. Virginia's jury history possesses features that were relatively common along the string of colonies that, by the mid-eighteenth century, stretched between Massachusetts and Georgia. In order to avoid excessive repetition and hoppings, this account will concentrate its sparse coverage of the prerevolutionary century-and-a-half on jury history in the Old Dominion, with attention elsewhere as indicated.

II.

Generally, petit juries in Virginia courts were composed of 12 men, although early records of the General Court (colonial assembly) show that some juries were composed of 13, 14, or, in one instance, 24 men (Chitwood, 1905: 67; Scott, 1930: 91, n. 129). At first Virginia attempted to follow the common law practice of drawing jurors from the vicinage (i.e., neighborhood; later, county) of Jamestown. Until the mid-1650s, all capital crimes were tried in Jamestown, and all jurors in those trials were drawn from that community. But as the population spread into interior Virginia, such efforts proved to be very inconvenient and expensive. Therefore, in 1655, Virginia enacted a law permitting capital trials to be held in other counties. However, the law was repealed the following year, and the previous practice was resumed. Then, in 1662, the Virginia legislature passed a law requiring juries of twelve men in all capital cases. Six of the jurors had to be summoned from the locality where the crime had been committed, but the other six could be selected from temporary residents there (Chitwood, 1905: 67; Scott, 1930: 87-88; Heller, 1969: 19-20).

In general, felony trials were held in one day. When the case was given to the jury, it was locked up without food or water until it reached a verdict. A juryman could not leave his fellows until a verdict was reached, which, as one writer has noted, made prolonged disagreements practically unknown. Practice required that the jury deliver its verdict in open court in the presence of the accused (Scott, 1930: 101).

Juries in Virginia seem to have had great discretion in fact-finding and rendering of verdicts. They could return general verdicts of guilty or not guilty, or find a special verdict which recited facts particular to the case, and leave points of law for the court (i.e., the judge), to decide.[2] Juries could also bring in verdicts for offenses less than those originally charged, but they had to arrive at these lesser verdicts in such a fashion that the judge could derive the law arising from the facts (Scott, 1930: 101-102).[3] The jury foreman was required to sign all verdicts, and acquittal meant permanent discharge for the defendant regarding the particular offense. Once acquitted, the defendant could continue to be held until he paid the jailor's fees, although he could not be held if he failed to pay the cost of food and lodging (Scott, 1930: 102).

Juror selection bedeviled courts and troubled the consciences of persons sensitive to the adequacy of justice, throughout the colonial period, as would be true throughout our history. Jury selection in the colonial decades was, almost universally, related to property ownership. In Virginia, under a 1699 law, jurors in the General Court, and in the higher criminal courts of Oyer and Terminer under a 1734 law, had to be freeholders who possessed at least £100 in property. In the county courts, jurors were also required to be freeholders, but they had to possess only £50 worth of property. However, no juror once sworn, could be challenged for an insufficient estate (Scott, 1930: 89).

Litigants were usually allowed any number of general challenges but only twenty peremptory challenges. In some instances, the Virginia legislature provided that if more than twenty peremptory challenges were made, the defendant was convicted. Under a 1734 law, when a jury panel was challenged on the King's behalf, good cause for displacing a juror had to be demonstrated. County sheriffs selected the jury, which occasionally posed problems for the even-handed administration of justice (Scott, 1930: 59; Heller, 1969: 19).

As illustration of these problems, consider the famous 1735 John Peter Zenger criminal libel case in New York. Zenger, a newspaper publisher, editorialized against the incumbent royal governor, William Cosby. Jailed, Zenger secured as counsel the prominent Philadelphia lawyer Andrew Hamilton. In the trial, the judges insisted that the common law's concern in libel allegations was not with the truth or falseness of the statements, but only with the fact that a defendant had made them. All that a jury could do was find the fact, and the guilty verdict must follow. Hamilton insisted that in America, a jury had a right to take a great leap forward, and inquire both into the fact of the allegedly libellous writing, and its truth or falsity. If an allegation was true, no criminally punishable libel existed. The presiding judge interrupted him, intending to override Hamilton's novel position by adverse ruling. But, appealed to directly by Hamilton, the New York jury in effect overrode the judges; and notwithstanding the fact, punishable under common law, that Zenger had written the defamatory statements, declared him not guilty because the editorials were true. Freed, Zenger became New York's official printer. Freedom to publish was enlarged in the colonies by reason of the New York jury's brave and sensitive frontiersmanship.

As the most important student of the Zenger trial, Levy (1960: 131) noted, "At a time when judges were dependent instruments of the crown, a jury of one's peers and neighbors seemed to be a promising bulwark against the tyrannous enforcement of the law of seditious libel by the administration and its judges." The jury, a popular institution, could sometimes protect political critics of the royal administration. Ironically, juries which adopted libertarian positions in famous instances, were as susceptible as judges to prejudice against litigants who expressed opinions that were unpopular in the community.

One measure of the deep affection the colonists had developed by the mid-1770s for their jury arrangements is in their resistance to the increasingly determined efforts of Crown officers to dominate those arrangements.

In 1763, for example, young Virginia lawyer Patrick Henry addressed a jury on behalf of the defendant, in the famous Parson Maury's case against the colony. The parson considered the jury panel, and the bench, packed. As one writer described the situation, "The sheriff had deliberately chosen a number of poorer persons, including some New-Light dissenters. The Court [Henry's father] overruled objections to them, and as a result there were only two 'Gentlemen' in the jury box" (Scott, 1930: 91).

The "Parson's Case" gave young Henry a transcolonial reputation as a defender of colonial rights. At issue was the justice of a switch made by Virginia in the salary of the Anglican priest, Maury, a colonial-imperial official in the state-church apparatus (Meade, 1957: 4-6). The capacity of Virginia's jurymen to withstand the divinity that, to paraphrase Claudius in *Hamlet,* surrounds a king, even when it is delegated to a priest, helped to increase feelings of colonial maturity.

Distinguished historians, including Bernard Bailyn and Julius Goebel, have described struggles between the Crown and colonists for control of judicial administration. Prior to the Glorious Revolution (1689), the creation of courts and the appointment of judges were part of the King's prerogative powers. The postrevolution settlement and subsequent parliamentary acts largely took away these powers. However, it remained a point of controversy whether the King's powers vis-à-vis the colonies were limited in the same fashion as in England. Royal instructions to colonial governors after 1690, were predicated on the assumption that the King retained power in these areas; and as the eighteenth century advanced, the royal governors intended to use them (Bailyn, 1968: 68-69).

But by the 1760s, the colonies' courts had become, in fact, largely autonomous of the homeland's. Appeals from a colonial judgment were slow, expensive, and uncertain. Paradoxically, colonists who were concerned particularly with exalting the independence of their courts learned to extol England's common law's traditions and aspirations. It was in this common law system that the powers and duties of the jury process, independent from central, especially royal, direction, had been most clearly established and consistently maintained. As tensions increased in the 1760s between England and her fractious North

American offspring, jury independency in America became an essential aspect of colonial rights.

Admiralty courts did not require juries. It was through expansions of the Admiralty court system at crucial points in time, that the Crown attempted to enforce what became the most abrasive aspects of its imperial policy, the Navigation Acts. Through fact-finding and appellate procedures, the Admiralty jurisdictions enjoyed great latitude in inquiries into the conduct of colonists' affairs.

Two examples illustrate the symbolic, political importance of colonial juries in events leading to the American Revolution. Prior to the early 1770s in Massachusetts, judges were paid by annual grants from the legislature. However, by royal orders, the Massachusetts Charter was changed so that the judges' salaries would be paid by the Crown. This order inspired great objections in towns throughout Massachusetts. The colonial legislature demanded that the judges state whether they would accept the new salary arrangement. Four of the justices declined it. The Chief Justice, Peter Oliver, accepted. A clamor rose for his impeachment. At the insistence of John Adams, the House voted a resolution of impeachment in mid-1773, but the royal governor and his council rejected the resolution.

When Judge Oliver went on circuit, grand and petit jurors refused to take the jurors' oath from him. According to Adams, one juror told Oliver, in the course of refusing to take the oath, that "The Chief Justice of this Court stands impeached, by the representatives, of high crimes and misdemeanors, and of a conspiracy against the charter privileges of the people. I, therefore, cannot serve as a Juror, or take the oath." Oliver encountered similar resistance wherever he went. Only when he did not sit at the Worcester court, in September 1773, did the jurors take the oath (F.W.G., 1927: 34-44).

In 1764 and 1765, New York's royal governor and colonists fought over whether cases could be taken by appeal from the colony's supreme court to the council and governor. The immediate cause for the confrontation was an action of trespass for assault and battery. The jury, finding for the plaintiff, awarded him £100. The defendant's attorney applied to Lieutenant Governor Cadwallader Colden, for an appeal to bring the case before the governor and council, which was granted. This was the first time that such an appeal was sought and granted in New York in a common law case.

Colden's action seemed to imperil the jury's fact-finding and to intrude executive powers into the judicial arena. The ordinary channel for a loser in a case was to seek a writ of error from a higher court. But in common law the writ of error permitted review only of defective interpretations of the law in lower courts, as they appeared in the record. Colden allowed the appeal in 1764-1765, in order to strengthen the Crown's hand in colonial jury deliberations. It permitted Colden to review not only the colony's laws, but also the merits and facts in the original controversy as affected by those laws. In short, Colden had discerned a way to short-circuit colonial juries in courts of first resort, or at least to reverse their abrasive floutings of the spirit of royal orders, even when colonists stayed within the letter of those orders.

Colden had made the basis of his action the fact that instructions from the King in 1753, and since, regarding review of judicial decisions had omitted from appeal matters the words, "in case of error only." However, the colonial council ruled in 1765 that, nevertheless, under the King's instructions there could be only an appeal in error. New York Justice Horsmanden, who prepared an opinion on the matter, as one writer put it, "saw beneath the innocent and just design [of Acting Governor Colden] of having an appellate review, which would inquire into the merits of an adjudicated case and not merely of errors on the record, a villainous thrust at the jury." The New York legislature, as perceptive as the judge in discerning the governor's action as an attack on the jury system, affirmed by resolution the right of trial by jury, praised the justices for their perception, and reprimanded Colden (Goebel, 1969: 274-275).

III.

Intermittently from 1607 through the 1760s, then with augmented pace, frequency, and intensity during the early 1770s, colonists had concerned themselves with defining colonies' and individuals' rights and jury prerogatives. Accumulated anxieties, including those about juries' autonomy from imperial direction, became causes for revolution. Colonists created in their Declaration of Independence a catalog of grievances, justifying revolt, in which the jury question was prominent. Americans from Maine to Georgia who might not feel deep concern, as example, for punishments levied by England on Boston tea-destroyers, could respond to this appeal to jury sanctity. By their very intensely local ways, juries involved close-to-home, law-and-order principles and practices that helped greatly to create a spirit of American nationality.

In the Declaration year, when protest became a transcolonial revolution, five colonies transformed themselves into would-be states, enshrining juries and other precious intracolonial institutions in the new states' constitutions. According to one writer, these constitutions contained "a jarring but exciting combination of ringing declarations of universal principles with a motley collection of common law procedures in order to fence them off from the rulers' power." Constitution-writers in other states, however, believing that they had sufficiently circumscribed state powers, especially of governors, declined to write such guarantees into their new constitutions (Wood, 1969: 270-271).

Meanwhile, during the long, uncertain course of America's Revolution, these innovators of governments, in the midst of a civil war which they were losing, transformed the "temporary" forum of concerted protest, the Continental Congress, into a permanent forum for conducting the new nation's business. In 1781 the ad hoc Continental Congress gave way to the Articles of Confederation national government. Then, in 1789, the Confederation exited in turn, without a coup d'état, in favor of the still newer experiment sketched in the 1787 Constitution.

Believing that they had safeguarded states and individuals adequately, the framers of the 1787 Constitution did not include a separate listing of constraints on the national government they were creating. Certainly the 1787 Constitution incorporated novel, indeed, unique features, well designed to frustrate the accumulation of power. It achieved protections by allowing avarice to counter avarice, as John Adams explained it. These innovative safeguards included power and functional separations, mixed with checks and balances (functional sharings), between the proposed national branches.

These constraints on their new nation failed fully to satisfy antifederalists (opponents to the Constitution) in the states, and even many persons who had voted to have their states ratify the Constitution.

Constituents' pressures evoked from the first Congress under the 1787 Constitution ten proposed amendments, which limited further the arenas in which the nation could function and the powers it could exercise. These amendments, ratified by 1791, were winnowed out from among a large number of proposals the first congressmen received from constituents or worked out themselves (Yankwich, 1948: 1-28; Warren, 1923: 111-131). They formed a bill of wrongs which the national government was not to commit, more than a decalog of positive rights.

The fifth, sixth, and seventh amendments are insights into prevailing ideas and practices concerning justice, trial procedures, and the jury. The portions of these amendments that pertain to juries ratified practices that had developed during the century-and-a-half of colonial status since Virginia's founding, and affirmed basic principles for which the colonists had contended in their long struggle against the British.

The fifth amendment declares in part that a person cannot be tried for a crime unless he is indicted by a grand jury, "except in cases arising in the land or naval forces, or in the Militia, when in actual service in time of war or public danger."[4] The other two amendments discuss the petit jury in civil and criminal cases. The sixth amendment guarantees to each person a speedy and public trial in all criminal cases. The trial must be held in the state in which the offense is alleged to have been committed.[5] The seventh amendment provides that in all cases at common law where the amount in controversy exceeds twenty dollars, "the right of trial by jury shall be preserved...." The amendment stipulates further that no fact determined by a jury can be reexamined in a national court except by "the rules of the common law." [6]

Americans' choice and content of the first ten amendments to the 1787 Constitution were strongly influenced by the fact that the congressmen were considering simultaneously, the composition, jurisdiction, and procedures of the United States courts. As in the Constitution itself, and in many other expedients resorted to by these remarkable men, the 1789 Judiciary Act represented an effort to construct and initiate an effective national government, while constraining its powers in order to sustain local liberties and interests.

The 1789 Judiciary Act remains today the legislative base of the national court structure. In 1789, the Senate drafted the judiciary bill, while the House concerned itself with the amendments. But their admixtures are clear and numerous (Warren, 1923: 49-111). With one predictable exception, admiralty jurisdiction,[7] the framers of the 1789 Judiciary Act demonstrated a marked concern for preserving trial by jury in the course of establishing the judiciary system.

Congressmen demonstrated their concern for preserving the jury system in the debates on the jurisdiction of the federal district and circuit courts, and over the extent and scope of the Supreme Court's appellate review and original jurisdictions. The Judiciary Act provided that the circuit and district courts try all issues of fact by a jury in all cases, except, as noted, those arising under admiralty and maritime jurisdiction. This requirement meant that issues of fact in equity proceedings, as well as in those tried under common law, required a jury (Warren, 1923: 75).

Subsequently, as a result of this provision, the Supreme Court determined that it could not review judgments from the lower federal courts in cases where the trial had been without jury, even when the parties consented, since, as one writer put it, "no statute authorized a writ of error or appeal based on such a proceeding; and it was not until the passage of the Act of 1865, allowing jury-waived trials, that the Supreme Court took appellate cognizance of such suits" (Warren, 1923: 90).

With respect to the Supreme Court, the 1789 Judiciary Act excluded questions of fact-determination (a trial jury's function) from its appellate jurisdiction, even in cases at common law. This represented a victory for those who feared that the Constitution's provision granting the Supreme Court appellate jurisdiction as to law and to fact, meant an undermining of jury trials and an institution of a system of juryless civil (i.e., Roman, as distinguished from common) law appeals.

Most opponents of this provision of the Constitution had conceded that juryless review was necessary in equity and admiralty litigation, and that permitting it in those cases would not threaten the common law jury system. But such was their concern for the jury that they prohibited review of facts in all classes of actions by allowing appeals to the Supreme Court from the circuit courts, and from the highest court of the states, by writ of error. As noted with respect to Colden, this mode permitted review only of questions of law. This tight jurisdiction in the 1789 Judiciary Act was instituted, although the Continental and Confederation Congresses had permitted appeals as to facts in admiralty cases, and states which had Chancery Courts had recognized appeals as to facts in equity cases. (Congress, in 1803, recognizing the inconvenience which prohibition of appeals in equity and admiralty cases had caused, removed the prohibition and even went so far as to permit the introduction of new evidence on appeal [Warren, 1923: 103-105] .)

Section 19 of the 1789 Judiciary Act defined the scope of the evidence that could be sent up to the Supreme Court from the federal Circuit Courts in equity and admiralty cases. As enacted, this section limited Supreme Court review of such facts as appeared on the face of the record. During the course of debates on this section, an effort was made to substitute the word "evidences" for "facts," which some saw as a plot to introduce civil law principles and to determine the case without aid of a jury (Warren, 1923: 98-99). In exercise of its original jurisdiction, the Supreme Court was required to submit issues of fact to a jury in cases at law brought against citizens, but not against foreigners, since it would be inappropriate for foreigners to face a domestic jury (Warren, 1923: 94-95).

In the original draft of Section 26 of the Act, the jury would determine whether the breach or forfeitures had occurred, and the judge would assess damages. The section, as enacted, however, mixed equity habits in the predominantly common law procedures. It left the determination of the breach and damage assessment to the judge, except when there was a doubt as to the amount of damages, which the jury would determine if either party requested such determination (Warren, 1923: 101).

Perhaps the bitterest debate occurred over defining the locale from which federal court jurors would be selected in capital cases. The debate points up the tension that has been evident many times in our history, between a reverence for legal tradition and awareness of the need to cope with the diverse situations and standards implicit in a federal system.

At the time of the writing the Constitution, strong opposition was expressed to a provision (Article III, section 2, clause 2), requiring that a trial be held in the state in which the offense was committed. Opponents argued that this provision violated the common law right to a jury from the vicinage of the offense. Attempts to cure this defect included abortive constitutional amendments. The judiciary bill as enacted required that juries in capital cases be drawn from the county in which the offense was committed, regardless of whether the trial was actually held in that county, and that federal juries in each of the states, in all other cases, be chosen according to the laws of the respective states (Warren, 1923: 105-106).

Proposed requirements that juries in all cases be drawn from the county where the offense occurred were defeated. James Madison explained the reasons for defeat to a correspondent:

> The truth is that in most of the States, the practice is different, and hence the irreconcilable difference of ideas on the subject. In some States, jurors are drawn from the whole body of the community indiscriminately; in others, from larger districts comprehending a number of counties, and in a few only from a single county [Warren, 1923: 106].

Under the 1789 Judiciary Act, the Supreme Court judges were assigned to ride circuits. The purpose of this provision, one writer has explained, was to keep them in touch with the local communities. Through these circuit-riders the people became acquainted with the natioanl judiciary. Members of the Supreme Court, on circuit, created opportunities to lecture to state citizens on nationhood. When instructing grand and petit jurors on points of law, the jurists educated the public about the new Constitution and national judiciary. The *Farmer's Weekly Museum,* (Walpole, New Hampshire) pointed out in June 1799, that "In these useful addresses to the jury, we not only discern sound legal information conveyed in a style at once popular and condensed, but much political and constitutional knowledge" (Warren, 1922: I, 59-60).

During the 1790s, internal pressures spinning off from the French Revolution, generated political party organizations, building on state bases, in the not-terribly-united states. Some U.S. judges were passionately anti-French Revolution. They partisanly favored the Federalist Party. Federalists, pro-British, supported the Washington and Adams administrations' internal security improvisations, as they would be labelled today, especially the Sedition and the Alien Acts. These judges were equally ardent in their detestation of the Republican Party organizations (also called Democratic in localities), which enjoyed as chief spokesmen Thomas Jefferson (Adams' Vice President) and James Madison.

Circuit-riding federal judges were one of the very few visible national government presences inside the states. Republicans alleged that judges' charges to grand juries were pernicious, turning the jury boxes into political arenas. One Republican writer asserted that:

judges [were] itinerating through their Circuits and converting the holy seat of law, reason and equity into a rostrum from which they could harangue the populace under the artful pretence of instructing a grand jury, and excite an alarming fanaticism among them under cover of legal authority [Warren, 1922: I, 165, n.2].

No doubt many of these charges of judges' partisanship had merit. Judges Pickering's and Chase's anti-Republican harangues before grand juries are infamous, and provided the basis for the first impeachments under the new Constitution (Warren, 1922: I, 276-282).

The federal bench's performance became less overtly Federalist after Jefferson's accession to the Presidency and John Marshall became Chief Justice (1801). Instead, the federal courts and juries helped greatly to stabilize interstate commercial exchanges and intrastate property sanctity, when federal questions were involved. Concerns over juries shifted again to the states. There, after all, rather than in the jurisdictionally fettered national courts, the primary arenas existed, in form of state and local courts, where person and property were placed at risk.

IV.

Through the unique device of federal territories serving as incubators of future free-and-equal states, as well as through diplomacy, purchase, and conquest, the number of states swiftly increased. In states old and new, democratizing trends continued during the 1800-1850 decades. Sharp reductions occurred in property, residence, and religious qualifications for state citizenship, suffrage, office-holding, and militia and jury service. Catholics, Jews, and, in one northern state, Negroes, were admitted to jury duty (Williamson, 1960: 208-209; Litwack, 1961: 94, 96; Hurst, 1956: 30-31).

More technical legal questions sporadically but recurrently engaged the attention of politically sensitive state legislators and their constituents. It had become a fact of American life, long before de Tocqueville arrived here to comment on it, that ordinary men considered themselves as qualified as lawyers to argue about (that is, to politicize) technical legal matters (Miller, 1965: 102). In Massachusetts, as example, moderates and conservatives contested bitterly the question whether juries should find facts only, leaving questions of law to the judge (Ellis, 1971: 190-191, 197-203; and see Friedman, 1973: 251-252). In the ages of Jackson and Lincoln, more and more state and local judges were popularly elected rather than appointed. Therefore, the fact-versus-law issue for juries possessed implications well-calculated to stir hearts and disturb financially interested litigants.

As they did with so many matters, men, and institutions, the fugitive slave issue and the personal liberty laws of some free (i.e., nonslave property) states involved juries. The 1789 Constitution and a 1793 statute required the return of fugitive slaves. States defined property, including slaves. Federal fugitive slave-return laws, which under slave state pressures in Congress became increasingly coercive, were a rare bridge across the federal system. On it, the property laws of slave states intruded within free states, to pluck out alleged runaway slaves, and, without trial and jury decision by ordinary free state procedures, returned black residents to servitude and punishment. The slaveless quality of the free states' laws could not go the reverse direction and have effect inside slave states. When runaway slaves—no instance is known of a free state Negro voluntarily becoming a slave; no "fugitive-free law" was ever needed —reached free states, the rough grasp of federal slave-catchers, buttressed by national military power, was terribly visible.

Some free states enacted personal liberty laws in the 1830s, less under abolitionist pressures than out of generalized anger at the Orwellian priorities enjoyed by southern slave state property laws in the federal system. In general, these efforts to make a jury trial mandatory failed in cases where persons apprehended under the federal fugitive statute were alleged to be slaves in the state from which they had fled.

Those who supported such efforts were divided among themselves as to the rationale for making the demand. Some abolitionists wanted to use a jury trial as a means of striking at slavery. Others, whose concern was more with northern states' rights, believed that the jury trial requirement would be the best way of assuring that only those who in fact were runaway slaves would be returned. The jury would play a fact-finding role to determine whether the person, always a black, claimed to servitude, was the runaway. As one writer put it, "The objective was to secure the personal liberty of free blacks and not to infringe upon the legitimate rights of claimants" (Morris, 1974: 93).

Whichever reason obtained, the desire for free state jury trials in instances of runaways who came under the federal fugitive slave rendition statute, became almost academic in the 1840s and 1850s. The U.S. Supreme Court's *Prigg vs. Pennsylvania* decision (1842), and the Congress's new 1850 fugitive slave law (the latter a part of the misnamed "compromise" of 1850), seriously undercut the pacific options open to the opponents to the return of slaves.

In the Prigg decision, the Court, citing the 1793 fugitive slave law as a proper exercise of constitutional national power and functions, held that the federal action excluded state action, even to the extent of augmenting federal return procedures. Of course, the federal exclusiveness did not oust slave state property law. Only free state trial and jury procedures were delimited.

During the later 1850s, violence against slave-catchers and the refusal of juries to convict persons who aided escaping slaves effectively nullified the federal fugitive law in several free states (White, 1965: 527-529). Then the Civil War and Reconstruction made the fugitive return-jury issues obsolete. First by new statutes which forbade federal civil and military officers to return runaways, then by terms of the Emancipation Proclamation (1863) and the thirteenth amendment to the Constitution (1865), state property laws which legitimized human servitude, became war casualties (Hyman, 1973: 414-432).

The derivative question, whether the freedmen were now fully free-and-equal men before their states' laws, enjoying the same rights and responsibilities as whites, including jury trial and service, became central in post-Appomattox Reconstruction. Juries in southern states "reconstructed" by President Andrew Johnson's lily-white formulas, were little inclined to decide fairly cases in which blacks were accused of crimes, in which whites were accused of crimes against blacks, or in which testimony of black witnesses was called for (Tarrant, 1972: 334-345).

These all-white, predominantly ex-Confederate jurymen, pardoned or amnestied by President Johnson, dominated federal as well as state courts in the South. Their presence made justice impossible, as federal prosecutors learned who attempted to try Jefferson Davis for treason. In 1868, the government decided not to pursue the matter, and Davis went free (Tarrant, 1972: 333; 439-440, n.15).

The question whether Negroes could receive justice from all-white juries, expanded into a determination by Republican leaders that blacks should serve on juries in federal and state courts. Increasingly, amenability to color-blind jury service was considered to be a civil right of national and state citizens, as defined in the new fourteenth and fifteenth amendments (1868, 1870) and in several national civil rights and enforcement acts, 1866-1872. The civil rights laws provided, in essence, that race must not be a basis for disqualification from jury service in state or national courts. Plaintiffs alleging disqualification from jury service for reasons of race, could remove their suits from state to national tribunals. It was assumed that appointed federal judges and interracial juries there would provide more even-handed justice.

But the assumption misfired. The "civil rights cases" of the 1870s and early 1880s centered on particular litigations, avoiding the general principles incorporated into the statutes favoring color-blind, undiscriminatory jury selection. Black litigants' lawyers found it all but impossible to prove that their particular clients had suffered exclusion from jury service by reason of generalized racial prejudice (Beth, 1971: 202).

Of course, if a state or local subdivision *legislated* specifically against black jurors, that was another matter. In 1880, the U.S. Supreme Court struck down a West Virginia law which excluded blacks from jury service [*Strauder v. West Virginia,* 100 U.S. 803 (1880)]. In another decision that year, the Court held that rulings of a state judge who allowed only whites on juries in his courtroom constituted state action forbidden by the fifteenth amendment and the civil rights enforcement laws [*Ex parte Virginia,* 100 U.S. 339 (1880)]. But in a third decision the same year, the Court decided that the absence of blacks from particular juries was not conclusive proof of state discrimination [*Virginia v. Rives,* 100 U.S. 313 (1880)]. Therefore, the plaintiff could not remove his case from the state's to the nation's courts before a jury was chosen in his case. The burden of proof, expense, and risk of appeal were his (Beth, 1971: 202).

Southern advocates of enlarging the areas of white superiority, grew louder from the 1870s through the century's turn. Alert to implications in the Supreme Court's civil rights decisions, segregationists arranged voting and jury service laws and precedures which appeared superficially to be racially nondiscriminatory. The victory of segregationists strategy concerning juries came in 1898 in *Williams vs. Mississippi.* The Supreme Court held that since Mississippi's voting laws were constitutional under the fifteenth amendment, its law restricting jury service to voters (in effect, whites only) was constitutional despite the fact that Mississippi had gone to great lengths to deny blacks the vote (Beth, 1971: 203).

The South achieved these rulings by avoiding gross appearances of official discrimination. In many states, jury lists contained the names of Negroes, but state judges' bailiffs and marshals called none for jury service. This practice was not challenged until the Supreme Court in *Norris vs. Alabama* [294 U.S. 587 (1935)] struck it down as a violation of the fourteenth amendment. In that historic decision, the Court overturned the conviction of a Negro when it was shown that blacks were consistently barred from service on state grand and petit juries.

But as in many matters, the Court's rulings over the years have been inconsistent on black representation on juries. Nine years after the *Norris* decision, the Court [*Akins v. Texas,* 325 U.S. 398 (1944)], as one writer put it, held that "no race is entitled to proportional representation on a jury" (Cushman, 1966: 243). Six years later, however, the Court found discrimination in one case despite the *presence* of Negroes on the jury list [*Cassell v. Texas,* 339 U.S. 282 (1950)]. In 1965 the Court refused to invalidate state provisions for peremptory challenges, even though the prosecutor used them to exclude Negroes from jury service [*Swain v. Alabama,* 380 U.S. 202 (1965)]. The Court has held [*Avery v. Georgia,* 345 U.S. 559 (1953)], however, that the use, by state court officers, of color-coded cards in impanelling a jury in order to distinguish race, which results in the exclusion of Negroes, is not permitted (Cushman, 1966: 242-243; Swindler, 1970: 462).

It was not until 1968, precisely a century after the ratification of the fourteenth amendment, that the Supreme Court applied one of the Bill of Rights, affecting jury protections through the fourteenth amendment, as a restraint on state options. The Court declared that the states had to guarantee the sixth amendment right to a speedy and public trial, in misdemeanor, criminal contempt, and possibly even in petty offense cases [*Duncan v. Louisiana*, 391 U.S. 145 (1968); *Bloom v. Illinois*, 391 U.S. 194 (1968); *Dyke v. Taylor Implement Co.*, 391 U.S. 216 (1968)]. A more recent case indicates, however, that the Court is still hesitant to interfere with state standards as to what constitutes a fair trial insofar as the composition of the jury is concerned. In 1970 the Court held that a Florida law permitting a jury of six to try certain cases, was not a violation of the fourteenth amendment [*Williams v. Florida*, 399 U.S. 78 (1970)].

The Court's decision has provoked campus and law journal controversy as to whether a jury of six substantively provides an adequately representative cross-section of the defendant's community, so that justice will be achieved. At the time of this writing, the weight of opinion is that such state juries do not violate fair trial principles, at least in civil cases and in criminal cases involving minor offenses (Zeisel, 1972: 367-370). A number of the federal courts have employed six-person juries in civil cases (Fisher, 1973: 507-542).

This issue is only one of many jury questions that have captured the attention of scholars and legal professionals, as indicated in the *Index to Legal Periodicals* during the past several years. A great variety of jury-focused questions have been raised in diverse areas of litigation.

Unfortunately, however, this upsurge in interest in the jury has not yet generated equivalent interest in the history of that troublesome, often vexing, irreplaceable institution. As noted, the historical work that has been done has been only a part of larger studies, concerned primarily with other issues.

This slighting of jury history is particularly unfortunate now. The preeminent importance of local communities in shaping attitudes and values has become increasingly recognized in the past few years. Juries offer essential insights into the ways in which these attitudes and values are shaped by public policies and shape policies.

Perhaps this brief survey suggests the fertility of jury history research. The jury has been and is a symbol of the enduring desire for human liberty. It reflects also the more mundane necessities and compromises involved in the workaday administration of property rights and criminal justice. Moreover, it demonstrates that a frequently uneasy, often unsatisfactory balance exists between the desire for liberty and the realities of human prejudices and passions. As with life itself, this balance is easier to upset than to maintain. The jury continues, nevertheless, to be a compelling and durable reminder of the fundamental American commitment to the federal system of and to a rule of law by government. Little more than a hundred years ago a French commentator—a lawyer and jurist—perceptively summed up the essence and meaning that the jury has for the American system of justice:

> The Americans consider and value the jury otherwise than as a judicial institution; they think that the jury constitutes the best political school in a popular government. Its operation puts the people in repeated contact with the elite of democratic countries, the lawyers and magistracy. In this instructive business, he [i.e., the juror] is initiated into the ideas of law and of justice; he develops respect for the laws and for the feeling of dignity and individual responsibility [Helbronner, 1872: 10].

To whatever degree the Frenchman's outlook was colored by his national origins, he expressed, nevertheless, sentiments with which few Americans would disagree in theory, however much they might ignore them in practice. These sentiments embody the American commitment to the ideals of law and justice about which each citizen, through his service on a jury, is educated. Thus, through the jury, these ideals are constantly reaffirmed in timeless, yet somehow timely, fashion.

NOTES

1. Also the practice in Massachusetts. See Wolford, 1969: 164.

2. In Massachusetts, this practice caused so much trouble in civil cases that it was abolished in 1657 (Wolford, 1969: 165, n. 87).

3. In Massachusetts juries had much the same discretion. In matters of fact if the jury could not decide the main issue it was required to find as much of it as it could (Wolford, 1969: 165).

4. Article V: "No person shall be held to answer for a capital, or otherwise infamous crime, unless on a presentment or indictment of a Grand Jury, except in cases arising in the land or naval forces, or in the Militia, when in actual service in time of War or public danger; nor shall any person be subject for the same offense to be twice put in jeopardy of life or limb; nor shall be compelled in any criminal case to be a witness against himself, nor be deprived of life, liberty, or property, without due process of law; nor shall private property be taken for public use, without just compensation."

5. Article VI: "In all criminal prosecutions, the accused shall enjoy the right to a speedy and public trial, by an impartial jury of the State and district wherein the crime shall have been committed, which district shall have been previously ascertained by law, and to be informed of the nature and cause of the accusation; to be confronted with the witnesses against him; to have compulsory process for obtaining witnesses in his favor, and to have the Assistance of Counsel for his defense."

6. Article VII: "In Suits at common law, where the value in controversy shall exceed twenty dollars, the right of trial by jury shall be preserved, and no fact tried by a jury, shall be otherwise re-examined in any Court of the United States, than according to the rules of the common law."

7. The exception was in section 9 of the Act which conferred admiralty and maritime jurisdiction exclusively on the district courts. The section provided that such jurisdiction included "seizures under laws of impost, navigation or trade of the United States" which was not granted to the admiralty courts in England. Some of the admiralty courts in the colonies had tried such cases, although trials in such courts were not by jury (Warren, 1923: 74-75). Warren notes that the federal courts were given no jurisdiction for seizures made elsewhere than on the high seas, but placed jurisdiction for such seizures under common law (i.e., nonadmiralty or equity law).

REFERENCES

ANDERSON, R. A. (1957) Wharton's Criminal Law and Procedure (5 vols.). Rochester, N.Y.: Lawyers Co-operative.

AVINS, A. (1967) "The fourteenth amendment and jury discrimination: the original understanding." Federal Bar Journal 27 (Summer): 257-290.

BAILYN, B. (1968) The Origins of American Politics. New York: Alfred A. Knopf.

BETH, L. P. (1971) The Development of the American Constitution, 1877-1917. New York, Evanston, San Francisco, and London: Harper & Row.

CHADBOURN, J. H. (1943) "Trial by jury under the seventh amendment." University of Pennsylvania Law Review 92 (September): 92-101.

CHITWOOD, O. P. (1905) Justice in Colonial Virginia. Baltimore: Johns Hopkins University Studies in Historical and Political Science, Series XXIII.

CLARK, T. D. (1939) The Rampaging Frontier: Manners and Humors of Pioneer Days in the South and the Middle West. New York: Bobbs-Merrill.

Columbia Law Review (1973) "United States v. Dionisio [(93 Sup. Ct. 764)] : The grand jury and the fourth amendment." Volume 73 (May): 1145-1167.

Connecticut Bar Journal (1948) "Choosing the twelve: the selection of Connecticut jurors since 1744 [a report]." Volume 22 (December): 316-332.

CUSHMAN, R. E. [ed.] (1966) Leading Constitutional Decisions. New York: Appleton-Century-Crofts.

DAVIS, W. W. (1914) "The Federal Enforcement Acts," pp. 205-228 in Studies in Southern History and Politics. New York: Columbia University Press.

DEMPSEY, E. J. (1948) "Law and lawyers in American colonial days." Nevada State Bar Journal 13 (October): 190-193.

EASTMAN, A.E.W. (1945) "History of trial by jury." National Bar Journal 3 (June): 87-113.

ELLIS, R. E. (1971) The Jefferson Crisis: Courts and Politics in the Young Republic. New York: Oxford University Press.

FARRAND, M. (1913) The Framing of the Constitution of the United States. New Haven and London: Yale University Press.

FISHER, H. R. (1973) "The seventh amendment and the common law: no magic in numbers." Federal Rules Decisions 56 (January): 507-542.

FLAHERTY, D. H. [ed.] (1969) Essays in the History of Early American Law. Chapel Hill: University of North Carolina Press.

FRIEDMAN, L. M. (1973) A History of American Law. New York: Simon and Schuster.

F. W. G. (1927) "Hitherto unpublished manuscript account by Judge [Edmund] Trowbridge relating to Chief Justice [Peter] Oliver and the juries in 1773-1774." Massachusetts Law Quarterly 13 (April): 34-44.

GOEBEL, J., Jr. (1969) "The courts and the law in colonial New York," pp. 245-277 in D. H. Flaherty (ed.) Essays in the History of Early American Law. Chapel Hill: University of North Carolina Press.

GOULD, E.R.L. (1886) Local Government in Pennsylvania. Baltimore: Johns Hopkins University Studies in Historical and Political Science, Vol. 1, No. 3.

GRANT, J.A.C. (1959) "What areas of exploration of legal history are appropriate?" American Journal of Legal History 3 (October): 370-378.

GRIFFITH, E. S. (1938) History of American City Government: The Colonial Period. New York: Oxford University Press.

GRUBB, I. C. (1897) "The colonial and state judiciary of Delaware." Papers of the Historical Society of Delaware 17: 3-70.

HAMILTON, J.G.deR. (1914) "Southern legislation in respect to freedmen, 1865-1866," pp. 137-158 in Studies in Southern History and Politics. New York: Columbia University Press.

HELBRONNER, H. (1872) Le Pouvoir Judiciaire Aux Etats-Unis: Son Organisation et Ses Attributions. Paris: Imprimerie de A. Parent. [H. Hyman, trans.]

HELLER, F. H. (1969) The Sixth Amendment to the Constitution of the United States: A Study in Constitutional Development. New York: Greenwood.

HENRY, H. M. (1914) The Police Control of the Slave in South Carolina. Emory, Virginia: n.p.

HOGAN, J. C. (1958) "Joseph Story on juries." Oregon Law Review 37 (April): 234ff.

HUGHES, C. (1905) The Law of Instructions to Juries in Civil and Criminal Actions and Approved Forms with References to Analogous Precedents. Indianapolis: Bobbs-Merrill.

HURST, J. W. (1956) Law and the Conditions of Freedom in the Nineteenth-Century United States. Madison, Milwaukee, and London: University of Wisconsin Press.

HYMAN, H. M. (1973) A More Perfect Union: The Impact of the Civil War and Reconstruction on the Constitution. New York: Alfred A. Knopf.

LEVY, L. W. (1960) Legacy of Suppression: Freedom of Speech and Press in Early American History. Cambridge: Harvard University Press.

LITWACK, L. F. (1961) North of Slavery: The Negro in the Free States, 1790-1860. Chicago and London: University of Chicago Press.

McKINLEY, A. E. (1905) The Suffrage Franchise in the Thirteen English Colonies. Philadelphia: Lippincott.

Massachusetts Law Quarterly (1935) "The function of a judge at a jury trial under American Constitutions as defined by the Supreme Court of the United States." Volume 20 (May): 41-48.

MEADE, R. D. (1957) Patrick Henry: Patriot in the Making. Philadelphia and New York: Lippincott.

MILLER, P. (1965) The Life of the Mind in America from the Revolution to the Civil War. New York: Harcourt, Brace, & World.

Minnesota Law Review (1927) "Jury—effect of constitutional provision that jury is to determine the law." Volume 11 (April): 472-474.

——— (1931) "Constitutionality of statute giving jury in criminal case right to determine law as well as facts." Volume 15 (June): 830-831.

MORRIS, T. (1974) Free Men All: The Personal Liberty Laws of the North, 1780-1861. Baltimore and London: Johns Hopkins University Press.

MURPHY, P. L. (1972) The Constitution in Crisis Time, 1918-1969. New York, Evanston, San Francisco, and London: Harper & Row.

POPE, J. (1961) "The jury." Texas Law Review 39 (April): 426-447.

SCOTT, A. P. (1930) Criminal Law in Colonial Virginia. Chicago: University of Chicago Press.

SPIVOCK, A. (1946) "American tradition of a democratic jury." Insurance Law Journal 1946 (September): 611-615.

SURRENCY, E. C. (1967) "Courts in the American colonies." American Journal of Legal History 11 (July-October): 253-276; 347-376.

SWINDLER, W. F. (1970) Court and Constitution in the Twentieth Century: The New Legality, 1932-1968. Indianapolis and New York: Bobbs-Merrill.

TARRANT, C. M. (1972) "A Writ of Liberty or A Covenant With Hell: Habeas Corpus in the War Congresses, 1861-1867." Ph.D. dissertation. Houston: Rice University.

WARNER, H. C. (1959) "Development of trial by jury." Tennessee Law Review 26 (Summer): 459-467.

WARREN, C. (1923) "New light on the history of the Federal Judiciary Act of 1789." Harvard Law Review 37 (November): 49-132.

——— (1922) The Supreme Court in United States History. 3 volumes, Boston: Little, Brown.

——— (1913) A History of the American Bar. Boston: Little, Brown.

WESTWOOD, H. C. (1971) "Getting justice for the freedmen." Howard Law Journal 16 (Spring): 492-537.

WHITE, L. D. (1965) The Jacksonians: A Study in Administrative History, 1829-1861. New York: Free Press.

WILLIAMSON, C. (1960) American Suffrage: From Property to Democracy. Princeton, N.J.: Princeton University Press.

WOLFORD, T. L. (1969) "The laws and liberties of 1648," pp. 147-185 in D. H. Flaherty (ed.) Essays in the History of Early American Law. Chapel Hill: University of North Carolina Press.

WOOD, G. S. (1969) The Creation of the American Republic, 1776-1787. Chapel Hill: University of North Carolina Press.

YANKWICH, L. R. (1948) "Background of the American Bill of Rights." Georgetown Law Journal 37 (November): 1-28.

YOUNGER, R. D. (1963) The People's Panel: The Grand Jury in the United States, 1634-1941. Providence: American History Research Center.

ZEISEL, H. (1972) "The waning of the American jury." American Bar Association Journal 58 (April): 367-370.

Part II

EMPIRICAL STUDIES OF THE JURY

2

JUROR SELECTION:
AN ANALYSIS OF VOIR DIRE

MICHAEL FRIED,
KALMAN J. KAPLAN and
KATHERINE W. KLEIN

A psychological model is developed to describe the selection and influence of prospective jurors by (P) and (D) attorneys during the first phase of a criminal trial. Called "voir dire" or "to see, to tell," the questioning process has three major purposes: (1) it is used as an information-gathering technique upon which to base jury selection; (2) it facilitates communication between the (P) and (D) attorneys and the prospective jurors; and (3) it enables both sides to attempt to exert some influence over how the jury will process the evidence that will be heard during the trial.

In addition, voir dire optimally makes each juror aware of his/her own prejudices. If impaneled, individual jurors are confronted with their own stereotypic thinking; it is hoped they will be forced to act in a positive fashion during deliberation. Finally, voir dire may be used to educate the prospective jury with regard to the burden of proof (on the accuser) and the elements of the crime on trial prior to hearing the evidence.

This chapter examines the often contradictory aims of (P) and (D), differentiated in terms of the jurors' prior susceptibility to conformity pressure; juror predisposition to side with authority; juror openness of cognitive set; juror perception of the weight of evidence; and juror criteria for conviction. The prosecutor will, of course, always endeavor to raise the jurors' perceptions of evidence level and lower the standard for conviction; conversely, the defense will attempt to decrease the estimate of evidence level and increase the standard for acquittal.

Chapter 2

JUROR SELECTION:
AN ANALYSIS OF VOIR DIRE

MICHAEL FRIED,
KALMAN J. KAPLAN and
KATHERINE W. KLEIN

It is perhaps instructive to begin this chapter with a statement of what we will not do. This chapter is not intended to be a systematic or exhaustive review of literature on voir dire *per se*. Rather, we intend to develop a psychological model regarding the selection and influence of jurors during the voir dire of a criminal trial. Research will be cited when relevant. We should, however, not lose sight of the major purpose of the chapter: namely, to provide a much needed theoretical framework within which to understand the conflicting aims of prosecution (P) and defense (D) during voir dire. This is aimed at improving our insights into their respective behaviors and at leading to the development of productive empirical research into this critical portion of a trial.

Voir dire, literally "to see, to tell," is the first phase of a trial in which prospective jurors are questioned and selected to sit on the impaneled jury. Depending on the court, prospective jurors are questioned by the judge alone, by prosecution and defense without the judge, or by all three.

Typically, a twelve-person prospective jury panel is randomly selected from a large group of assembled prospective jurors and questioned by the judge on their

AUTHORS' NOTE: *This chapter has drawn to some degree upon two earlier papers (cf. Fried, 1973; Kaplan, Klein, and Fried, 1973). The authors would like to thank Marguerite Walker for her invaluable aid in library research for this paper.*

general fitness to serve. The judge may excuse a juror at this time. Following this initial questioning P and D are allowed to question the temporarily impaneled jurors as a group or individually.

If P or D object to the impaneling of a juror, then they can challenge the objectional juror(s). Challenges fall into three categories: (1) *to the array,* if counsel feels the entire panel has been irregularly selected; (2) *for cause,* when a juror is deemed unable to render an impartial verdict because of his experience, occupation, personal or financial interests, or preconceived bias; and (3) *peremptory,* if counsel feels for any reason that the juror is undesirable. Challenges to the array are primarily procedural and extremely rare, while those for cause typically involve legal objections to a specific juror in a specific case. In peremptory challenges, however, P and D often follow their instinctive reactions, some of which will be discussed later in this chapter. Challenges to the array or for cause are unlimited in number, but subject to the discretion of the judge who may overrule the challenge and allow the juror(s) to remain seated. Peremptory challenges, in contrast, are not subject to such judicial discretion, but are limited in number. This number is fixed by law or court rule and increases with the seriousness of the charge. In general, D has more peremptory challenges than P.

When a challenge for cause is accepted by the judge or when a peremptory challenge is employed, the prospective juror is excused and a new candidate is randomly chosen from the remaining group to reconstitute the panel. At this point, questioning begins again. This process continues until both P and D are satisfied with the impaneled jury or have exhausted their peremptory challenges and all challenges for cause are refused.

Voir dire has three major purposes. First, it is used as an information-gathering technique upon which to base jury selection. Prospective jurors are questioned and information obtained is then used by P and D as a basis of selection. A second purpose of voir dire is to enable P and D to develop rapport with jurors and thereby facilitate communication. Finally voir dire gives P and D an opportunity to influence jurors to change their attitudes or values and to affect the way in which they will process the evidence they will hear. These latter two purposes are closely related and often overlap. For the purposes of the present chapter, no distinction is made between the aim of developing rapport and that of influencing the jury, both falling under the category of social influence. Jury selection and influence, however, will be treated as distinct categories.

Our basic thesis is that P and D attempt to select jurors who are likely to be susceptible to their influence attempts, that these influence attempts can be conceptualized as pertaining to the way jurors process evidence (to reach likelihood of guilt) and the values jurors place on the possible trial outcomes, and that—as P and D have conflicting goals at trial—they also have conflicting strategies at voir dire.

DIFFERENTIAL AIMS IN VOIR DIRE: SPECIFIC MEANS

The differential aims of P and D in the selection and influence of jurors are presented in Table 1. They are differentiated in terms of (a) juror susceptibility to conformity pressure; (b) juror predisposition to side with authority figures; (c) juror openness of cognitive set; (d) juror estimate of guilt; and (e) juror criterion for conviction. The first three aims will be discussed in social-psychological terms and the latter two will be investigated by use of a statistical decision theoretic model of juror decision-making.

A. Predisposition to Side with Authority

The first assumption presented in Table 1 is that P should select jurors predisposed to side with authority. This factor becomes important to the extent P represents himself as the voice of society rather than as the complaint of a single victim. Authoritarians, by definition, identify with authorities currently in power, especially if the positive authority figures are perceived as high-status sources of information (Ehrlich and Lee, 1969). The practical consequences of this reliance on authority figures may be that authoritarian jurors are more likely to heed P's arguments than D's, because of the association of P with legitimized government authority. Furthermore, authoritarians are also more likely to favor P because of their acceptance of societal norms of behavior.

Table 1. DIFFERENTIAL AIMS OF P VERSUS D IN THE SELECTION
AND INFLUENCE OF JURORS

	Prosecution (P)	Defense (D)
Specific Means		
(a) predisposition to side with authority	select authoritarian jurors	select egalitarian jurors
(b) susceptibility to conformity pressure	attempt to maximize interjuror conformity	select jurors predisposed to individual dissent
(c) openness of cognitive sets	select jurors with a closed or rigid cognitive set	select jurors willing to consider conflicting information
Ultimate Goals		
(d) estimate of guilt	convince jurors of high probability of guilt	convince jurors of low probability of guilt
(e) criterion for conviction	establish in jurors a low criterion for conviction	establish in jurors a high criterion for conviction

However, an authoritarian's susceptibility to P's persuasive arguments also depends on the nature of the defendant. Authoritarians are sensitive to ingroup-outgroup distinctions, and are intolerant of deviation from accepted norms (cf. Adorno et al., 1950). Therefore, if the defense attorney (D) or the defendant is noted for supporting radical political causes, authoritarian jurors would be particularly biased toward P. However, when the defendants are high-status authority figures themselves, as in the Watergate trials, low authoritarian jurors may actually be a better choice for P.

Demographic guidelines. Our assumption is implicitly expressed by legal writers espousing rules of thumb for jury selection. They suggest many demographic clues to reliance on authority. Groups traditionally believed to favor P as an agent of society include (1) men; (2) Republicans; (3) upper income groups; (4) occupational groups such as bankers (Adkins, 1968-1969), engineers and certified public accountants (Katz, 1968-1969), and others with positions of petty respectability (Campbell, 1972); and (5) members of the Teutonic ethnic groups, particularly Germans (Campbell, 1972).

The same authors recommend the following groups as more likely to be egalitarians: (1) women; (2) Democrats (Hayes, 1972); (3) middle and lower economic groups such as butchers (Katz, 1968-1969); (4) certain occupational groups, such as social scientists; and (5) minority racial or ethnic groups, such as Latins or Jews (Campbell, 1972).

Similarity and empathy. Complicating the formula relating personality characteristics to a predisposition to side with authority, however, is the juror's perception of the similarity of the defendant to himself. Chaiken and Darley (1972) found that in judgments of responsibility for an accident, subjects who had been assigned a supervisor role blamed chance for the mistake, while subjects assigned to be workers blamed the supervisor. A juror who identifies with the victim will be more likely to assume the vantage point of P, who can offer society's protection against further transgressions. A juror who feels himself similar to the accused will be more ready to accept the egalitarian view that each individual must be judged in terms of his own motives and circumstances, rather than in the framework of larger societal rights.

On a demographic level, similarity is usually operationalized in terms of ethnicity, occupation, and sex. In general, D should try to obtain jurors similar to his client, but many exceptions and clauses complicate this truism. Similarity to the defendant is not a ubiquitous rule of thumb. For example, if the evidence is overwhelmingly in favor of conviction, P may obtain a more severe verdict by choosing juror members who are ethnically similar to the defendant such that they might have special knowledge of his circumstances and be less gullible to his protestations of innocence. One illustration is Belli's (1963) warning that Jewish jurors are harsher on Jews accused of a crime. Another illustrative anecdote involves a jury of black Detroit welfare mothers convicting a black welfare defendant when her alibi (grocery shopping) was denounced by the jurors who shopped at the same market and refuted her claims of the time involved in making a week's purchases. Such demographic similarities at the same time may evoke a sense of empathy with the defendant. If D's case is reasonably strong, he may exploit this with the aim of seducing the jurors into assuming the individual's reference point throughout the trial.

Ethnic dissimilarity is also a two-edged sword. On the one hand, Byrne and Wong (1962) report that subjects are more tolerant of racially dissimilar individuals who hold sissimilar attitudes than of racially similar persons holding dissimilar attitudes. Such charitable excusing of people demographically unlike oneself can be of considerable value to D, especially when he has a weak case. At the same time, however, dissimilarity may prevent the emergence of the emotional empathy necessary for the jurors to see the situation from the defendant's viewpoint. Such a societal orientation is invaluable to P.

Occupational interactions with type of crime are also important. Courtroom folklore advises P to favor bankers in cases of theft or robbery; but bankers are better jurors for D in securities, fraud, or white-collar crime (Campbell, 1972)—presumably because the banker can identify or see himself as similar to the defendant. This relationship between similarity and attribution of guilt has been called situational or personal relevance (Evenbeck, 1974). When relevance is high—that is, when the juror has some real or potential experience with a similar situation or is very similar to the defendant—he will be more likely to exonerate the defendant. This defensive attribution, or blaming the situation rather than the perpetrator, may cognitively protect the juror from an imaginary similar fate.

Sex interactions also emerge in evaluating the effects of juror-defendant similarity. Female jurors, for example, are reported (Karcher, 1969) to be more sympathetic in general *unless* the defendant is a more attractive female, in which event women jurors are often more punitive. In addition, Fishman and Izett (1974) found that when the defendant is attractive, crimes in which the defendant's beauty is irrelevant are judged more leniently, presumably because expectancies of jurors are violated when an attractive defendant is implicated.

This same type of reasoning explains why D is often reluctant to allow an overly unattractive defendant to testify in his own behalf. If jurors cannot identify with the defendant, they are far more likely to accept a societal viewpoint, with P as its legitimate authority, without the pangs of conscience they might experience for a sympathy-eliciting defendant.

B. Susceptibility to Conformity Pressure

The second assumption of our model presented in Table 1 is that P will strive for greater interjuror conformity than will D. P should try to select jurors who will be susceptible to conformity pressure during both the trial and juror deliberations. D, on the other hand, should try to select on tendencies toward individual dissent in the jury.

There are two major reasons for differential conformity needs of P and D. First, the prospects of a hung jury are far more damaging for P than for D. Though it is true that unanimity of juror opinion is necessary to attain either conviction or acquittal, it is likewise true that in practice P will almost never push a case beyond two hung juries, but in fact will typically drastically reduce its charges after a single "hung jury" outcome. Thus, the possibility of a nonconforming juror is more detrimental to P than to D.

A second reason involves the covariation between conformity tendencies and authoritarianism. High conformists are likely to side with authority, a tendency typically favoring P as was noted before.

True conformity. Two types of conformity have been identified by social psychologists. True conformity (McGuire, 1968), involves yielding to another even in the absence of persuasive arguments, but simply in acquiescence to the presumed expertise or authority of the source. In a trial, such conformity pressure may be applied to less intelligent jurors who fail to comprehend abstruse expert witness testimony or complicated examinations. During deliberations, a true conformity situation will arise when a juror is intimidated by another, perhaps the foreman, so that he will acquiesce to the group decision regardless of his personal convictions.

Suggestibility. The second type of conformity, perhaps better labeled "suggestibility," involves yielding to the persuasive message of a source, as opposed to agreement simply because the source is a respected authority. Suggestibility becomes an important variable during the trial itself, when a juror is presumably swayed by the arguments of P or D.

In general, P should attempt to select jurors who are true conformists or are at least predisposed to suggestibility, while D should choose jurors with the opposite predispositions. The social-psychological literature suggests that both authoritarianism and self-esteem are personality variables underlying conformity and suggestibility.

Relation to authoritarianism. Authoritarianism, as originally conceived by Adorno et al. (1950) is a tendency toward oversimplified categorization of people on the evaluative dimension into a few extreme groups—the very good (the ingroup) and the very bad (the outgroup). Authoritarians have strong dependencies for ingroup authority figures and great intolerance and punitive tendencies for outgroup members. In a true conformity situation, especially an ambiguous one such as may occur during jury deliberations, authoritarians are more influenced by high-status sources than by low-status ones (Vidulich and Kaiman, 1961). Thus, if a foreman is selected because of his leadership ability or presumed expertise, an authoritarian juror should be more likely to conform to the foreman's judgment than to lower-status peers. Secret balloting during deliberations may thwart some of this dependence on the foreman. However, when the situation becomes one of suggestibility in which jury members openly support their opinions, an authoritarian is most likely to agree with a clique of his peers who provide him with social reality, in the sense of a shared outlook (Hollander and Julian, 1967).

Relation to self-esteem. A second personality variable, self-esteem, should also be noted by P and D in their attempts to select a favorable jury. Self-esteem is a large determinant of suggestibility, with low self-esteem individuals being the most suggestible. Low self-esteem jurors can favor either prosecution or defense, unlike high authoritarians who generally favor prosecution. Susceptibility should have its greatest impact during deliberations, in which the influence of an eloquent foreman or a nearly unanimous group should be greatest for the highly susceptible juror. If the case is not clearcut, the vacillations of a suggestible, low self-esteem juror may end with him under the influence of a stronger fellow juror, rather than with his deciding independently on some facet of the evidence itself.

Courtroom folklore: demography revisited. In the search for personality predispositions such as those discussed above, counsellors will often resort to demographic heuristics. There exists a considerable folklore regarding the use of such variables, much of which has not been systematically investigated or only partially supported. Females are generally believed to be more susceptible to social influence (Janis and Field, 1959), a social-psychological dictum often noted by legal authors (MacGutman, 1972). An older person, because of his experience, is often viewed as more tolerant of human frailty than a younger juror. Such an individual orientation, however, might be offset by an older person's greater respect for authority.

Conformity and interjuror homogeneity. Interjuror homogeneity is likely to be an important determinant of conformity. Adkins (1968-1969) suggests that the selection of a leader and eleven followers will lead to a single decision. Presumably, P or D can then concentrate their efforts on this leader who will then function as an opinion leader for the rest of the jurors (Hayes, 1972). It should be far easier to achieve the "group sense" and strong opinion leader necessary for either conviction or acquittal if the jurors are similar in personality or at least demographic characteristics. Selection of a homogenous group capable of consensus should be especially important to P according to our model, even if they are all low authoritarians.

On the other hand, D, particularly if he has a weak case, might actively seek interjuror heterogeneity. D's intent might be to work on a small number of jurors to create a hung jury. Thus, he would want to minimize the conformity pressures that high interjuror homogeneity would occasion. D should also avoid the selection of any juror with relevant expertise, if the trial is of a technical nature in which such a person is likely to emerge as a strong opinion leader. He should avoid him unless he were absolutely certain that he would prove to be favorable. P on the other hand, should push for such a juror, if he thinks there is a reasonable chance that he will be favorably inclined. In other words, consensus works for P and against D in the absence of a strong case on either side.

A qualification should be offered at this point. If D has a very strong case, he too should press for juror homogeneity. Generally however, he can far better afford and even encourage interjuror disagreement. In practice, then, we assume that P must attempt to influence all of the jurors even with a weak case. He must avoid actions which would antagonize any jurors, such as the overuse of peremptory challenges. D in contrast, unless he has a strong case, may direct his appeal to a small minority of jurors—in fact, even to a single member. Thus, it would behoove prosecution to maximize conformity pressure within the jury, while defense should glorify the integrity of individual dissent.

C. Openness of Cognitive Set

A third assumption presented in Table 1 is that P and D have differential aims in choosing jurors who are predisposed to certain cognitive styles. P should welcome a juror with a closed cognitive set who has difficulty processing conflicting information. D should seek jurors who are open to new information, even though it may be incongruent with their own beliefs or in conflict with other trial-produced evidence.

This is the case because, during the trial, P attempts to present evidence which is consistent and complete in order to evoke certainty and closure. D on the other hand, will want to present evidence which shows the situation is complex, many-sided and filled with doubt. Such differential styles in presentation will prove most beneficial if jurors have been selected for these particular cognitive sets.

Courtroom folklore. As with conformity pressure, practicing lawyers use a variety of techniques to select jurors with certain cognitive sets. A social-psychologist's admonition that P should choose closed cognitive sets is reflected in Hayes' suggestions that jurors who "sharpen" during an argument are those who exaggerate the salience of particular data and may overlook other aspects of the evidence. The juror who claims strong opinions on any topic is more likely to be dogmatic and less able to bring various facts together for comparison purposes. Military men and persons in mid-level positions in an organizational hierarchy are assumed to be good prosecution jurors because of their previous experiences in following and transmitting essential and rational information.

D, however, will want jurors who are open to dissonant information and who can withhold judgment until defense has presented its case. Hayes suggests that younger people are the most open in this regard, and Katz recommends jurors with a wide variety of experience as being more flexible in their thinking.

Cognitive set and relationship to authoritarianism. In P's attempt to choose jurors with closed cognitive sets, authoritarians again appear to be good candidates. The ideal prosecution juror should focus on P's opening statements and thereafter process information using P's theory of the case. Long and Ziller (1965) found that authoritarians spend less time than do egalitarians in making decisions and fail to reserve judgment or seek further information. This tendency to restrict cognitive input should favor prosecution, especially when a juror's original set of beliefs are congruent with those of authority figures, as an authoritarian's presumably are.

There is also social-psychological evidence to support the contention that highly authoritarian persons are more rigid in their thinking (Brown, 1953). This lack of flexibility further assists P in its attempt to solicit favorable votes from authoritarian jurors. Rigidity will prevent vacillation during deliberations and will be particularly valuable to P if the foreman is a pro-prosecution authoritarian.

DIFFERENTIAL AIMS IN VOIR DIRE: ULTIMATE GOALS

Up to this point we have discussed social-psychological factors in the selection and influence of jurors. We have concentrated on three factors: (a) predisposition to side with authority, (b) susceptibility to conformity pressure, and (c) openness of cognitive set. These factors have been discussed both in terms of setting pretrial biases in jurors' decisions and also in their susceptibility to various influence attempts by P and D.

This section will primarily focus at a more abstract level on two specific aims of P and D: (d) estimate of guilt and (e) criterion for conviction. To conceptualize these latter aims we shall first develop a statistical decision theoretic model of juror decision-making and relate this model to the behavior of P and D in their attempts to influence and select jurors during voir dire.

The decision theoretic model will guide us to analyze juror selection and influence in terms of (1) the utilities a juror implicitly assigns to outcomes

—which in time determine his criterion for conviction, and (2) the way he processes the evidence—which determines his probability of the defendant's guilt.

Statistical Decision Theory Model of Jury
Decision-Making and its Relationship to Voir Dire

A statistical decision model of jury decision making (Kaplan, 1967; Fried, 1973) assumes that the juror makes his decision to vote for a defendant's conviction or acquittal on the basis of two variables: (1) the juror's probability calculation, based upon the evidence presented, that the defendant actually is guilty of the crime of which he is accused; and (2) the juror's values or utilities for voting for conviction or acquittal, given the possible true states of the world. In the most simple circumstance, the juror can be conceived of as being able to make two decisions: a vote for conviction or a vote for acquittal. Further, there are two possible states of the world: guilt or innocence. (In actual practice a juror may have more than two alternatives open to him, such as conviction on a lesser included offense. Likewise there may be more than two states of the world.) The possible actions available to the juror and true states of the world are presented in a payoff matrix in Table 2. Each row of the matrix represents an option available to the juror and each column represents a possible state of the world. The matrix illustrates the simple situation we have already identified.

Each cell in the matrix represents an outcome defined by an action and a state of the world. Cell 1 represents the outcome of a juror vote for conviction and the defendant actually being guilty. Cell 2 represents the outcome of a juror vote for conviction and the defendant being innocent. Cell 3 represents the outcome if the juror votes for acquittal and the defendant actually is guilty. Cell 4 represents the outcome if the juror votes for acquittal and the defendant is actually innocent.

The decision theoretic model assumes that associated with each outcome is a

Table 2. MATRIX OF UTILITIES FOR OUTCOMES

| | | State of the World | |
		Guilty	Innocent
Decision	Convict	U_{CG} Cell 1	U_{CI} Cell 2
	Acquit	U_{AG} Cell 3	U_{AI} Cell 4

value or utility to a juror for that outcome. In this instance we should expect that the value of convicting a guilty person should be greater than the value of convicting an innocent person. We call these values utilities which can be represented symbolically by:

U_{CG}:   Utility of convicting a guilty person

U_{CI}:   Utility of convicting an innocent person

U_{AG}:   Utility of acquitting a guilty person

U_{AI}:   Utility of acquitting an innocent person

Where do the utilities come from? Utilities that a juror conceptionally assigns to a given outcome are a function of many factors including the juror's attitude toward the defendant, the juror's assessment of the likely sentencing outcomes and his attitudes towards those outcomes. For example, a juror who feels that the expected penalty for conviction, even if the defendant were guilty, was far too great might even be conceived of as assigning a low or even negative utility to convicting a guilty person. An illustration of this might be a situation where the state has a law making the possession of any amount of marijuana a major felony and the juror feels that, even if the defendant were guilty of marijuana possession, he should not be convicted. Here would be a case where, under the model, a juror's utilities would be affected by considerations of whether the punishment fits the crime.

The probability of guilt. The model assumes that the juror can be described as assessing the evidence presented in the trial and, based on that evidence, developing a probability that the defendant is guilty. If a juror were absolutely certain the defendant were guilty, then the probability of guilt would be 1. If he were absolutely sure the defendant were innocent, the probability of guilt would equal 0. If he were completely uncertain as to the defendant's guilt or innocence, then the probability of guilt would equal .5. The model assumes that, at the end of the trial, the juror has arrived at some probability estimate of the defendant's guilt.

How the decision is made to vote for conviction or acquittal. Jurors are told to vote for conviction if they are sure beyond a reasonable doubt that the defendant is guilty of the crime with which he is charged. Based on this instruction, the juror must decide how to vote. A major assumption of the model we are describing is that the juror should vote for conviction if the expected utility of convicting the defendant is greater than the expected utility of acquittal. The expected utility for conviction and for acquittal are calculated in the following manner.

(1) $EU(C) = pU_{CG} + (1 - p)U_{CI}$

(2) $EU(A) = pU_{AG} + (1 - p)U_{AI}$

Where

$EU(C)$ = the expected utility of conviction

$EU(A)$ = the expected utility of acquittal

p = probability of guilt

$1 - p$ = probability of innocence

U_{CG} = utility of conviction given guilt

U_{CI} = utility of conviction given innocence

U_{AG} = utility of acquittal given guilt

U_{AI} = utility of acquittal given innocence

Examining Formula (1) we can see that the expected utility for conviction increases with the probability of guilt, the utility of convicting a guilty person, and the utility of convicting an innocent person (a decrease in disutility). In a similar manner, Formula (2) shows that the expected utility for acquitting a person increases with the probability of innocence (which is one minus the probability of guilt), the utility of acquitting an innocent person, and the utility of acquitting a guilty person (a decrease in disutility). One can see from the formulae that both the probability of guilt or innocence and the utility of the possible outcomes play separate and independent roles in the development of a final decision.

Measuring "beyond reasonable doubt." According to the decision theoretic model the juror should vote for conviction if and only if the expected utility of conviction is greater than the expected utility of acquittal. Expressing this rule mathematically, a juror should vote to convict if and only if

(3) $EU(C) > EU(A)$

or

(4) $pU_{CG} + (1 - p)U_{CI} > pU_{AG} + (1 - p)U_{AI}$

Algebraically, we can derive a juror's decision rules as follows. He should vote to convict if

(5) $p(U_{CG} - U_{AG}) + (1 - p)(U_{CI} - U_{AI}) > 0$

(6) $p(U_{CG} - U_{AG}) + (U_{CI} - U_{AI}) + p(U_{AI} - U_{CI}) > 0$

(7) $p(U_{CG} - U_{AG} + U_{AI} - U_{CI}) > U_{AI} - U_{CI}$ and

$$(8) \quad p > \frac{U_{AI} - U_{CI}}{U_{CG} - U_{AG} + U_{AI} - U_{CI}}$$

The right half of equation (8), of course, indicates the standard or criterion value for the probability estimate of guilt. Let us denote this criterion value by p^*. In other words,

$$(9) \quad p^* = \frac{U_{AI} - U_{CI}}{U_{CG} - U_{AG} + U_{AI} - U_{CI}}$$

To convict, then, as indicated in equation (8), the obtaining or actual probability of guilt value, p, must exceed this criterion, p^*. Thus

$$(10) \quad p > p^*.$$

p^* then is the criterion or standard beyond which there is no longer reasonable doubt.

In other words, a juror should vote for conviction whenever his probability of guilt, p, is greater than p^* as defined in equation (9). For example, imagine yourself a juror in a trial of a defendant charged with possession of marijuana. If you felt that the likely sentence for possession of marijuana was much too severe and should perhaps be decriminalized, then your utility matrix might look like that presented in Table 3. Then your criterion value p^* would be

$$p^* = \frac{100 - (-5000)}{10 - 0 + 100 - (-5000)} = \frac{5100}{5110} = .998$$

You would have to have a probability estimate of guilt greater than .998 before you would be willing to convict (i.e., $p = .998$).

Consider a very different type of example, however. Imagine that there were a wave of rapes in a small city. You are sitting on a jury in a trial where the defendant is charged with one of the rapes. In contrast to the previous example,

Table 3. UTILITY MATRIX FOR HYPOTHETICAL JUROR
WHO THINKS PUNISHMENTS ARE OVERLY SEVERE

		State of the World	
		Guilty	Innocent
Decision	Convict	10	−5000
	Acquit	0	100

Table 4. UTILITY MATRIX FOR HYPOTHETICAL JUROR
WHO FEARS RELEASE OF A GUILTY DEFENDANT

		State of the World	
		Guilty	Innocent
Decision	Convict	100	−1000
	Acquit	−200	+300

you would now be much more concerned about a guilty man going free. Your utility matrix might be characterized by Table 4. In this situation your probability estimate of the defendant's guilt would only have to reach .82 in order to vote for conviction:

$$p^* = \frac{300 - (-1000)}{100 - (-200) + 300 - (-1000)} = \frac{1300}{1600} = .82$$

These two examples graphically illustrate how changes in the relative utilities assigned by jurors to trial outcomes can affect the criterion for proof beyond reasonable doubt.

The decision theoretic model points to two facets of decision-making that should be of particular interest to attorneys at voir dire. The first aspect is reasonable doubt in the desired direction. In addition, P and D will want to influence the values of the juror during voir dire to affect their criterion (p*). The other area P and D should concentrate on during voir dire is choosing jurors who will process the evidence in such a way as to lead to higher or lower levels of probability estimates (p).

Estimate of Guilt and Criterion for Conviction

The fourth and fifth assumptions of the model presented in Table 1 point to the differential aims of P and D in selecting jurors on their criteria for conviction and their estimate of guilt from evidence.

To understand this one should recall that the statistical decision theoretic model assumes that a juror has a probability criterion for reasonable doubt. If the evidence for guilt is above this criterion, he will vote to convict; if below, to acquit. This criterion varies directly with the utilities associated with acquittal and inversely with those associated with conviction. In other words, as acquittal of either innocent or guilty parties becomes more valuable or less harmful, the level of evidence needed to convict increases. As conviction of either guilty or innocent parties is judged as less valuable or more harmful, the level of evidence demanded by conviction increases.

Prosecutor (P) should work toward lowering this standard in the mind of jurors and/or increasing their perception of the obtaining strength of evidence. Defense (D) should do the opposite—that is, work toward raising the standard in the mind of jurors and/or decreasing the perception of the obtaining strength of evidence. In other words, P should employ tactics designed to (1) raise the utilities for conviction, (2) lower the utilities for acquittal, and (3) raise the estimate of the strength of the actual evidence. D should attempt the opposite: to (1) lower the utilities for conviction, (2) raise the utilities for acquittal and (3) lower the estimate of the strength of the actual evidence.

Considering the tactics discussed in Table 1 from this vantage point, encouraging group conformity on the part of P should specifically work to diffuse responsibility for a false conviction—that is to lessen the negative utility associated with convicting an innocent man. Encouraging individual dissent is a tactic of D which should serve to increase an individual juror's sense of responsibility for a false conviction—that is, to exaggerate the negative utility associated with such an error. It does not seem to us that the utility associated with acquitting a guilty man will be likewise affected. Responsibility, in this case, whether individual or shared, does not seem to be as germane or sensitive.

Given this assumption, it follows that encouraging group conformity decreases one's criterion for conviction while encouraging individual dissent increases it. Encouraging conformity may also depend on social pressure to exaggerate one's judgment of actual obtaining evidence. That such judgments in the "objective" physical realm are influenced by conformity pressures has been amply demonstrated in the social-psychology literature (e.g., Asch, 1951).

Promoting identification with society has the obvious advantage for P of increasing the utilities associated with conviction and decreasing those of acquittal, both lowering the standard for conviction. Promoting identification with the individual defendant on the part of D should do the opposite—i.e., decrease the utilities associated with conviction and increase those associated with acquittal, both raising the standard for conviction. To put it another way, given a societal vantage point, the worst possible outcome would be acquitting a guilty man. Given the defendant's vantage point, the worst possible outcome would derive from convicting an innocent man.

Creating closed versus open sets on the part of the juror is likely to affect perception of the obtaining level of guilt. P should attempt to create a closed set, blocking the input of contradictory material likely to decrease the estimate of the obtaining evidence level. D should attempt to create an open set, because in this case the input of conflicting information will lower the judgment of the strength of the evidence. Although this effect is likely to be very sensitive to factors such as presentation order, it seems generally true that the above effects will hold.

CONCLUSION

Implicit in our entire discussion has been the concept that the voir dire behavior of P and D is a function of their respective theories of juror decision-making. We have proposed a statistical decision theoretic model as one normative model, providing ultimate goals against which P and D can measure their strategies.

It would seem useful, in closing this chapter, to recast Table 1 in a slightly different framework. Table 5 presents such a framework. Variables such as those discussed in (a) to (c) differentially affect (d) juror perceptions of defendant guilt, which are then compared to (e) juror standards for conviction. This comparison generates a decision for conviction or acquittal.

P will always work to raise the estimate of the obtaining evidence level and lower the standard for conviction; D will do the opposite: attempt to lower the estimate and raise the standard.

This model thus provides the beginnings of an integrating theoretical framework on research regarding voir dire. The three "means" variables offered in this paper are not exhaustive. The point to be made, however, is that all such independent variables be classified against their effects on probability estimates of guilt, utility values, and subsequent criteria for acquittal versus conviction.

Table 5. MODEL OF THE RELATIONSHIP BETWEEN INPUT VARIABLES, MEDIATING VARIABLES, AND OUTCOME VARIABLES

Input Variables	Mediating Variables	Outcome Variables
Predisposition to side with authority	utilities ⟶ criterion for conviction (p^*)	If $p > p^*$ convict
Susceptibility to conformity pressure	estimate of guilt (p)	If $p < p^*$ acquit
Openness of cognitive set		

REFERENCES

ADKINS, J. C. (1968-1969) "Jury selection: an art? a science? or luck?" Trial Magazine (December-January): 37-39.

ADORNO, T. W., E. FRENKEL-BRUNSWICK, D. J. LEVINSON, and R. N. SANFORD (1950) The Authoritarian Personality. New York: Harper.

ASCH, S. E. (1951) "Effects of group pressure upon the modification and distortion of judgments," pp. 177-190 in H. Guetzkow (ed.) Groups, Leadership and Men. Pittsburgh: Carnegie Press.

BELLI, M. M. (1963) Modern Trials (abridged ed.) Indianapolis: Bobbs-Merrill.

BROWN, R. W. (1953) "A determinant of the relationship between rigidity and authoritarianism." Journal of Abnormal and Social Psychology 48: 469-476.

BYRNE, D. and T. J. WONG (1962) "Racial prejudice, interpersonal attraction, and assumed dissimilarity of attitudes." Journal of Abnormal and Social Psychology 65: 246-253.

CAMPBELL, S. (1972) "The multiple functions of the criminal defense voir dire in Texas." American Journal of Criminal Law 1 (October): 255.

CHAIKEN, A. L. and J. M. DARLEY (1972) "Victim or perpetrator: defensive attribution of responsibility and the need for order and justice." Journal of Experimental and Social Psychology: 268-275.

EHRLICH, H. J. and D. LEE (1969) "Dogmatism learning and resistance to change: a review and a new paradigm." Psychological Bulletin 71: 241-260.

EVENBECK, S. (1974) "Observer's attributions of causality." Presented at the annual meeting of the Midwestern Psychological Association, Chicago.

FISHMAN, L. and R. R. IZZETT (1974) "The influence of a defendant's attractiveness and justification for his act on the sentencing tendencies of subject-jurors." Presented at the annual meeting of the Midwestern Psychological Association, Chicago.

FRIED, M. (1973) "Models of juror decision making." Presented at the annual meeting of the American Psychological Association, Montreal.

HAYES, H. B. (1972) "Applying persuasive techniques to trial proceedings." South Carolina Law Review 24: 380.

HOLLANDER, E. P. and J. W. JULIAN (1967) "Contemporary trends in the analysis of leadership process." Psychological Bulletin 71: 387-397.

JANIS, I. L. and P. B. FIELD (1959) "Sex differences and personality factors related to persuasibility," pp. 55-58 in I. L. Janis and C. I. Hovland (eds.) Personality and Persuasibility, New Haven: Yale University Press.

KAPLAN, J. (1967) "Decision theory and the fact-finding process." Stanford Law Review 20: 1065-1092.

KAPLAN, K. J., K. W. KLEIN, and M. FRIED (1973) "General aims of prosecution and defense in the selection and influence of jurors in a criminal trial." Presented at the annual meeting of the American Psychological Association, Montreal; to appear in Journal of Social and Behavioral Sciences, Winter 1975.

KARCHER, J. T. (1969) "Importance of voir dire." Practicing Lawyer 15 (December): 59.

KATZ, L. S. (1968-1969) "The twelve man jury." Trial Magazine (December-January): 39-42.

LONG, R. E. and R. C. ZILLER (1965) "Dogmatism and predecisional information search."
    Journal of Applied Psychology 49: 376-378.
MacGUTMAN, S. (1972) "Attorney-conducted voir dire of jurors: a constitutional right."
    Brooklyn Law Review 39 (Fall): 290.
McGUIRE, W. (1968) "Personality and susceptibility to social influence," pp. 1130-1187 in
    E. F. Borgatta and W. W. Lambert (eds.) Handbook of Personality Theory and Research.
    Chicago: Rand McNally.
VIDULICH, R. N. and I. P. KAIMAN (1961) "The effects of information source status and
    dogmatism upon conformity behavior." Journal of Abnormal and Social Psychology 63:
    639-642.

3

THE SOCIAL PSYCHOLOGY OF
JURY DELIBERATIONS

JOAN B. KESSLER

A survey of relevant research on small group behavior is coupled with a survey of the limited jury product and process research especially emphasizing group size research, which is an unresolved issue currently under investigation. Although the recording of the deliberations of real juries is impossible, some researchers have used jurors from jury pools deliberating in mock juries; others have used student jurors.

Current research methodology, including the use of videotaped trial dramatization, is discussed.

Most jury research has involved examination of the product of jury deliberations because information is easy to collect and there is much interest in this area in the legal community. The author, however, stresses the need for more process jury research to more fully understand the workings of the jury and to contribute to the creation of a formalized theory of jury behavior.

Chapter 3

THE SOCIAL PSYCHOLOGY OF
JURY DELIBERATIONS

J O A N   B.   K E S S L E R

The mystique of jury deliberations has long fascinated lawyers and laymen and more recently social scientists. Jury deliberations are secret and there is great curiosity about what goes on in the juryroom.[1] Communication researchers interested in studying small group interaction have used the jury as one small problem-solving group. But the jury is a specialized small group, and generalizations of small group findings from other contexts to the jury must be made in a guarded manner. This chapter summarizes relevant general small group research and the limited jury deliberation product and process research. Directions for further needed jury research are suggested.

THE WHYS OF JURY RESEARCH

The first systematic empirical study of the jury was conducted by the University of Chicago. The major focus of this interdisciplinary study

> was to bring together into a working partnership the lawyer and the social scientist; . . . the hope was to marry the research skills and fresh

AUTHOR'S NOTE: *Research for this chapter was assisted by a faculty research grant from Loyola University of Chicago.*

perspectives of the one to the socially significant problems of the other, and in the end to produce a new scholarship and literature for both. . . . It was the intention . . . that new data be collected about old legal institutions [Kalven and Zeisel, 1966: v].

The Chicago study did collect new data, and the heuristic function that the project played is evidenced by the more than sixty articles which have been published as extensions of results from the study.

The book *The American Jury* represents the central focus of the civil section of the study: it analyzes the extent to which the judge and jury disagree on the verdict reached. The study consisted of judges in 3,576 cases responding to a questionnaire and relating their judgment on each case before the jury reached its verdict. In about 80% of the cases the same decision was reached by both judge and the jury. This section of the Chicago Project has implications for the continuation of the jury system (Kalven and Zeisel, 1966). If judges and juries arrive at the same decisions, the question arises as to whether the expensive jury system should be maintained.

Further analysis of the verdicts by Kalven (1958) showed that the first ballot vote by juries has a strong relationship to their final verdict. In about 90% of cases when the majority said "not guilty" on the first ballot, the jury found the defendant "not guilty" on the final vote. Moreover, in an earlier study (Weld and Roff, 1938), experimenters read scripts of a trial to mock juries and found that jurors came to their decision even before all the evidence was presented.

In addition to this question of the value of the jury's deliberation, actual study of these deliberations has been very difficult. In the Chicago Project, one phase dealt with actually recording live jury deliberations in Wichita, Kansas. The American Bar Association sanctions and federal law[2] which followed have closed the door to further recordings of actual jury deliberations. Jury deliberations are shrouded in secrecy, and the courts are resistant to any infringement on their privacy.

If the value of deliberations is in question, and if the study of actual deliberations is impossible, the questions of the why and how of jury deliberation studies may be raised. Researchers have stressed the need for evaluation of the deliberation process as the jury is a major part of our justice system. Kalven and Zeisel question their own jury studies and asked if they had studied the wrong things by not studying the jury's deliberations. These researchers and others have stressed the need for studies of jury deliberations (Kalven and Zeisel, 1966; Erlander, 1970; Zeisel, 1973).

Many questions have been raised in the literature about jury deliberations. For instance, some of the issues researchers want to find out about include how foremen are chosen, how jury size affects deliberations, how the requirement of unanimous-versus-nonunanimous verdicts affects deliberations, how personal traits of the litigants and jurors affect deliberations (see chapter 4 by Stephan for a discussion of research in these areas), how judge's instructions affect deliberations, and how videotaping affects the deliberations. Analyses of simulated jury deliberations have begun to answer some of these questions about the jury; and although general studies of the small group's decision-making process are quite common in the social-psychological literature and may answer other jury-related questions, further studies of specialized decision-making processes of the jury are needed to give an accurate picture of the jury deliberation process.

THE HOWS OF JURY RESEARCH

Types of Stimuli and Types of Juror Subjects

As this chapter will demonstrate, research on jury deliberation is limited. One reason is the difficulty in using real trials and real jurors for experimentation. However, though taping of real deliberations is unlawful, variations are possible. Strodtbeck (1962) reports having no problem obtaining assistance from judges in Chicago, St. Louis, and Minneapolis who provided space and jurors from jury pools for use in his experiment. Forston (1968) used jurors from the county courts of Minneapolis and Chicago in analyzing various methods of jury research. Simon and Mahan (1971) used both real and student jurors to find out how jurors compare with judges in defining "burden of proof" in probability terms. They found that students were more defendant-prone than real jurors, but both groups of jurors defined "burden of proof" in a more similar manner than the judges did, especially in civil actions. Forston (1972) has also used student jurors; and in comparing eight groups of real jurors and eight groups of student jurors, he found that the monetary rewards were slightly higher with student jurors, that somewhat more time was spent in the discussion of personal experiences with the real jurors, and that the student jurors seemed to have a better understanding of the judge's instructions. The cost and problems involved with using actual jurors may not equal the benefits of using them in experimentation, Forston concluded. Kessler (1973a and 1973b) and Kulka and Kessler (1973) used student jurors in view of the time and money they had available.

The motivation of subjects that is needed in order to create the feeling of importance in their decision-making process may be difficult in laboratory simulations. Realistically portrayed trials and carefully delivered judge's instructions to the jury can help to approach a real-life situation. Merely reading sections of trial testimony or lawyer's closing statements may not supply enough realistic simulation to the subjects, yet many studies have used this inexpensive and convenient method of presentation. The Chicago Project, however, relied on audiotapes of edited trial transcripts which more closely approximate a realistic simulation. Although both audio- and videotape enable more than one group of jurors to decide the same case and thereby allow for comparisons between jury decisions, the added video treatment creates a more realistic situation and enhances motivation.

Experimentation with videotaping actual trials has already begun. For instance, in the chambers of Judge Sam Street Hughes of Ingham County Court, Mason, Michigan, criminal trials were videotaped during December, 1971. The recording equipment and crew were paid for by the Michigan Bar Association under a grant from the National Law Enforcement Assistance Association for an experiment in modernizing trial apparatus (*New York Times,* 1971: 5). This experiment represents a departure from the American Bar Association's 1937 policy against use of electronics in the courtroom. Chief Justice Thomas M. Kavanagh of Michigan ordered an exception to this ABA policy as part of an attempt to bring the Michigan courts into the "space age" (*New York Times,* 1971: 24). Judge John B. Wilson, Jr., of Marion criminal court in Indianapolis, Indiana, is taping a real criminal trial with the agreement of defense and prosecution (*Daily Herald,* 1974), and similar experiments have been conducted around the country under the supervision of the National Center for State Courts in Denver (see *Chicago Tribune,* 1974).

Currently jury researchers at Michigan State University (Miller, et al., 1974) are using a videotaped dramatization of an edited trial transcript of a civil case under a National Science Foundation grant. Miller and Siebert, the principal investigators, are studying the effects of stricken testimony on jurors' verdicts and on perceptions of attorneys' credibility; the effect of videotape on jurors' retention of evidence; the effect of black-and-white versus color taping in relation to jurors' retention of information and on perceptions of witness credibility; and the differences, if any, in response of jurors to live and taped trials. Barton and Padawer-Singer at Columbia University have been studying the six- and twelve-member unanimous and nonunanimous criminal jury under a National Science Foundation grant. They are using a videotaped dramatization of a trial and showing it to 80 mock juries made up of actual jurors.

Forston (1968) utilized three methods of case presentation in his study of the differences in jury experimentation. He employed live mock trials, audiotaped trials and reading of edited transcripts. He concluded that although there were some differences among the methods and problems within each method, all three were viable alternatives in conducting jury research. Forston is currently attempting to use videotaped trials in jury research. This method seems to be more realistic than any of those previously used.

Kessler (1973a and 1973b) produced a two-and-one-half hour videotaped trial involving an automobile negligence case that had been settled out of court. The actual plaintiff and defendant agreed to portray themselves. Kulka and Kessler (1973) used an edited audiotape version of Kessler's (1973a and 1973b) videotaped trial along with slides (see chapter 4 in this volume). In this case a videotape would not have been workable to manipulate appearance of plaintiff and defendant in various conditions; therefore, an audiotape and slides were used.

Thus, the techniques used in jury research may depend on the resources available and the manipulation necessary. The use of a laboratory setting and student jurors is far less costly in time and money; but generalizability is limited, as in most communication studies, to the college population from which the sample was drawn.

Product and Process Research

Jury deliberation research has analyzed both product and process[3]. Most jury studies only examine the variables affecting the product of deliberations —i.e., verdicts (criminal cases) or verdicts and amount of damages (civil cases)—rather than evaluating variables affecting the process of deliberations —i.e., leadership, content and participation. The reasons for few process studies are that members of the bench and bar may be less interested in the process used by the jurors than the product reached[4], and that such studies involve more expense in both money and time for the researcher. Process studies involve the time for deliberations to take place, require the use of many subjects, and the necessity to record, transcribe and analyze deliberations. In addition, researchers (Kalven and Zeisel, 1966; Simon, 1967) have suggested that deliberations may not change the juror's initial verdict. Because of the expense and questionable value of process research, many product studies have been conducted.

Recently, more interest in studying process has arisen in both the general small group research and the specific area of jury research. Some instruments have been created to study the process of decision-making. Bales (1950 and 1970), a major contributor in the area of analyzing group interaction, has created a system for tabulation and evaluation of group discussions.[5] Simon (1967) used some content analysis of mock deliberations, but found less systematic analyses more productive. Forston (1968) and Kessler (1973a) created instruments to evaluate the specialized jury decision-making process.

One method of analyzing deliberations is to audiotape (James-Simon, 1959; Kessler, 1973b) or videotape (Forston, 1968) the deliberations and then content analyze them. Simon (1967) states that a formal content analysis was attempted, but was not very "fruitful or interesting." She suggests that a less systematic technique of analysis through observation yielded a better understanding of the process (Simon, 1967: 132).[6]

THE WHATS OF JURY RESEARCH

Research on Deliberation Product

In the early days of group communication research there was a strong emphasis on the product rather than the process of group interaction. Various factors were shown to have some effect on group product, but no formal theory of group productivity has yet been developed. Cohesion (individuals liking for or attraction to a group), for example, may lead to a stronger social influence of a group and, therefore, greater conformity to group goals (Shaw, 1971). The type of communication network within a group has also been shown to effect group productivity to some extent. A centralized group network where everyone communicates only with the leader and with no one else in the group seems to be more productive when simple tasks are involved because extraneous information is eliminated. With difficult tasks, such restrictive networks may lead to errors and lower efficiency (Cartwright and Zander, 1968).

Group size has also been shown to affect productivity in some cases, because larger groups may have more trouble reaching consensus, cliques may form, quantity of ideas may increase and conflict resolution may become more difficult (Hare, 1952). There are conflicting results on the relationship of group size and time required for task completion (Taylor and Faust, 1952; South, 1927). Other research has found that as responsibility becomes more dispersed, larger groups were more willing to take risks than smaller groups (Teger and Pruitt, 1967; Bem et al., 1965).

Other studies have compared the product of the group working together with that of an individual working alone. Researchers have found the group superior in speed and accuracy over individuals in solving the problems (Triplett, 1897; Shaw, 1932; Taylor and Faust, 1952). As mentioned above, judges working alone end up with the same verdict as the jury approximately 80% of the time (Kalven and Zeisel, 1966).

Simon and Mahan (1971) have studied the juror's definition of "burden of proof" ("beyond a reasonable doubt" in criminal cases and "by a preponderance of the evidence" in civil cases) through constructing a probability scale. Student jurors, real jurors, and judges were asked to indicate on a 0.0—10.0 scale the probability of guilt of the defendant after listening to edited trials. While half or more of those in all three groups (students, jurors and judges) translated "beyond a reasonable doubt" into an 8.6 out of 10 chance of guilt, there was a disagreement on civil matters. Judges saw "by a preponderance of the evidence" as a 5.5 probability, while both students and real jurors saw it as about a 7.5 probability. Thus, jurors and judges may disagree on the distinctions in the civil definitions of burden of proof used by the judge (Simon and Mahan, 1971: 325).

Examining general group literature can provide some perspective on the jury. But because the jury is a specialized group with a specialized task, valid conclusions about its productivity can be drawn only by studying its particular product. Some researchers have begun to assess the affect of various factors on the jury's product; but like the general small group data, many confounding variables may affect the study results and generalizability of results is limited.

The use of statistical models is one way of studying the jury's product. Zeisel (1971), in opposition to the Supreme Court decision on the constitutionality of the use of six-member juries in criminal cases (*Williams v. Florida,* 1970) used a statistical model to reach his conclusion that because six-member juries can be shown to differ in composition from twelve-member juries, the smaller jury does not offer a "jury of your peers" as guaranteed in the Constitution. There would be statistically less chance for a minority member, more variance in awards of damages, and fewer hung juries. Further, a change to small juries in criminal cases as in Britain, Zeisel contends, would lead to "fewer hung juries, more findings of guilt, and among them relatively fewer convictions for lesser included offenses" (Zeisel, 1971: 721) than with twelve-member juries in similar cases. He discusses a statistical model to support his theory of how deliberating juries might behave.

Walbert (1971), like Zeisel, bases his argument against the reduction of jury size on statistical models. He constructed a model based in part on small group research findings on group pressure to conformity (Walbert, 1971: 543) and suggests that in *Williams v. Florida* the Court's conclusion that six-member juries and twelve-member juries would return the same verdicts was "unsupportable" (Walbert, 1971: 553). Rather, Walbert suggests that "A proper treatment of representation, in conjunction with a description of the deliberation process, shows that the six-man jury convicts different persons" (Walbert, 1971: 554). Walbert cautions that much of his statistical model upon which he bases the above is from small group research on tasks other than jury deliberations and from the Broeder (1959) study on jury behavior. Walbert suggests that

more experimentation might be desirable to further investigate the deliberation process . . . *[and the studies he cites to support his model on the prevalence of majority persuasion were]* . . . performed outside the actual trial context . . . and are not necessarily conclusive in jury situations . . . *[Walbert also assumes in his model]* . . . that each juror has some type of predilection that provides a basis for classification. Thus, the guilty-prone plus the innocent-prone jurors total 100 percent. . . . This assumption is not contradicted by any evidence, but it could be better corroborated [Walbert, 1971: 554, n. 60; italics added].

Walbert's model neglects the continuum of gradations of guilt a juror might feel and the different personality types which lead to different group dynamics within each jury. These statistical models give great insight into the probable occurrences within the jury, but analysis of deliberations can lead to more accurate conclusions about human interaction.

Many other methods have also been used to evaluate the effect of size on jury product. Pabst (1972 and 1973) examined the records of 147 civil jury trials in the District Court for the District of Columbia during 1971. The use of six-member juries was begun midyear, so an automatic comparison was possible. Unfortunately, there was no separation in the court's records of time spent during the trial and during the deliberations. The results of this study indicate "virtually no difference in voir dire or trial time, and only from 12 to 20 percent difference in overall juror manpower requirements" (Pabst, 1973: 6).

Powell (1971) argues that in order to compare accurately the deliberation time of the six- and twelve-member juries, both groups would need to see the same trial.

This of course, would be virtually impossible, because precisely the same case would be unlikely to arise in two jurisdictions—one of which used twelve jurors and the other using fewer. Even if it did, the participants would be different, and therefore no accurate comparison could be made [Powell, 1971: 100, n. 80].

Some research has attempted experiments to minimize the problem suggested by Powell. Gordon (1968) presented a filmed dramatization of a trial to three juries each of six, nine and twelve students. He found no differences in the verdicts. All the juries that reached a decision favored the defendant. There were, however, two hung juries in the six-member condition, caused by female jurors who maintained their position in favor of the plaintiff. The researcher used a very small sample (n = 3), and this weakens the impact of his findings. Additionally, he evaluated only product aspects with little mention of process. Gordon (1968) found no significant differences in the deliberation times of student juries of six, nine, and twelve members. Ahern (1971) examined the question of jury size by having groups of four, eight, and twelve read the same sections from a law board preparation text. He found no significant differences among the verdicts of the different-sized juries.

The following four studies on jury size (Mills, 1973; Kessler, 1973b; Institute . . ., 1972; Bermant and Coppock, 1973) were cited in a recent

Supreme Court decision (*Colgrove v. Battin,* 1973) allowing the use of six-member juries in civil cases. The *Colgrove* decision, which referred to the following empirical studies, was a departure from the *Williams* case, which lacked any reference to empirical studies (see Kessler, 1973a: 714). But, researchers opposed to the use of six-member juries (Pabst, 1973; Zeisel and Diamond, 1974) have strongly criticized these studies for various procedural and methodological problems. As with all small group research, each piece of research cited in this chapter seems to be weak in some respect—whether it be the mathematical models which may be based on laboratory research of different group tasks, the methodological problems with arise in laboratory research, or the confounding factors possible in the analysis of actual trial data.

Mills (1973) studies the effect of jury size on verdicts and awards of damages by collecting data from Wayne County, Michigan, Circuit Court records during the six months before six-member juries were used (March 1, 1969–August 31, 1969) and a six-month period after six-member juries were used (March 1, 1971–August 31, 1971). There were 193 cases in the six-member sample and 292 cases in the twelve-member sample. Mills found no significant differences in verdicts, awards, or duration of trials between the two different-sized juries. But these results may have been confounded by two other court changes also instituted around the time when jury size was reduced. Mills indicates that a mediation board of two attorneys and a judge was instituted to be available for cases where probable liability is admitted and the sole question is amount of award. Mills states that

> this pretrial settlement activity in automobile negligence cases resulting from the availability of mediation may have influenced the nature of the cases reaching trial stage during the six-member jury sampling period [Mills, 1973: 681].

In addition, the discovery of insurance policy limits was permitted by a general court rule revision in April 1971. Zeisel and Diamond (1974) suggest that if the two procedures led to an increased proportion of settled cases (Mills documents this in at least the mediation board situation), and if "the largest cases are less likely to be settled . . .,[*then*] the average size of cases reaching trial [*in the six-member sample*] would be increased" (Zeisel and Diamond, 1974: 289; italics mine).

Although the actual case used by Kessler (1973a) for her videotaped recreation was actually settled out of court in the plaintiff's favor, all sixteen juries either found for the defendant or were unable to arrive at a verdict.[7] Zeisel and Diamond (1974) criticize this study's use of what they termed a one-sided case, which led to a preponderance of defendant verdicts. The cause of the discrepancy between the actual out-of-court settlement for the plaintiff and the verdicts of the student juries for the defendant may have been the result of several factors. The defendant's demeanor appeared to be more informal and, therefore, more appealing to student jurors than was the plaintiff's demeanor on the witness stand. (See Kulka and Kessler, 1973, for the follow-up study of effect of appearance on verdicts.) Also, the defendant's counsel was a more eloquent speaker than was the plaintiff's counsel. A further explanation might be that the defendant's insurance company might have been willing to settle this case rather than risk losing in court. Zeisel and Diamond (1974) also suggest that initial vote distribution (there were six twelve-member juries and only four six-member juries at the five-sixths majority needed for verdict before deliberations began) may have accounted for the six-member juries deliberating somewhat longer in the Kessler study.

A 1972 New Jersey study (Institute . . ., 1972) states that nonunanimous verdicts (five-sixths majority) were found in 20.2% of six-member juries and 45.0% of twelve-member juries. The experimenters caution, however, that because the option of using a six-member or twelve-member jury was available, the twelve-member juries were requested in more difficult cases than were six-member juries (Institute . . ., 1972: 7). The study stated that 50% of the six-member juries completed deliberations in 55 minutes, while 50% of the twelve-member juries required 75 minutes. But six-member and twelve-member juries deliberated as long when damages ran over $10,000 (Institute . . ., 1972: 29). This study presents a distorted view because the twelve-member juries were requested for complicated cases which would take longer to deliberate under any circumstances. (See Zeisel and Diamond, 1974: 284-286, and Pabst, 1973, for a discussion of the problems in this study.)

Bermant and Coppock (1973) examined 128 Workmen's Compensation Act cases heard by 33 six-member and 95 twelve-member juries in the State of Washington during 1970. Like the New Jersey study, lawyers chose the jury size. Of the 128 cases, there was no significant difference between plaintiff or defendant decisions between the two different-sized juries; in fact, the proportions were virtually identical (Bermant and Coppock, 1973: 595). The authors suggest the increased use of six-member juries, "if we may properly assume that the assignment of jury size was essentially random in respect to the merits of the cases" (Bermant and Coppock, 1973: 595). Their surveys of the records revealed no "obvious interaction" of kind of case and size of jury used. Zeisel and Diamond (1974: 283-284) criticize this study for lack of random assignment of cases to the two different-sized conditions.

Bermant and Coppock emphasize that the similarity in verdicts they indicated in the study does not assure similarity of process for "as Wiehl and others have suggested, members of small panels may feel greater individual responsibility than members of large panels" (Bermant and Coppock, 1973: 596). Wiehl (1968: 35, 40), however, does not analyze the process of decision-making, and the authors suggest that experiments in social psychology "will answer the question of the process involved."

After two Supreme Court decisions (*Williams v. Florida,* 1970, and *Colgrove v. Battin,* 1973), the issue of the use of six-member and twelve-member juries is yet to be resolved. Barton and Padawer-Singer are presently studying the issue of size and unanimous versus nonunanimous verdicts by evaluating 80 mock juries that are deliberating the reenactment of a criminal case. The House of Representatives is still undecided on the size issue (Hearings on H.R. 8285, 1974).

Other issues have also been investigated in studying the jury's product. One part of the Chicago Project was Simon's (1967) study of the relationship between judge's instructions on insanity and the jury's verdict. Two audiotaped edited trials, one of a house-breaking case and the other of an incest case, were played to 98 mock juries, each varying instructions on how to treat insanity (M'Naghten rule, Durham rule, or no rule; see Simon, 1967: 66-77, for jurors' reaction to these rules). The jurors were all selected randomly from real jury pools.[8] The results showed a definite effect caused by the varying of instructions. The juries hearing the M'Naghten rule had lower acquittal rates than the juries who heard the Durham rule or the no rule version. The latter two versions were close in their higher rates of acquittals due to insanity than either was to the M'Naghten version. This study combined the analysis of both jury product and process since the deliberations were also analyzed.

Other experimenters have researched the effect of the one-sided versus two-sided message variable. Studies of this type compare the relative persuasibility of presenting one-sided arguments as opposed to presenting both sides of the issue to the receiver. The results of these studies suggest that two-sided jury arguments possess a significant advantage over one-sided presentations. (See Rosnow and Robinson, 1967: 71-99, and Lawson, 1970, for discussion of this area of research.)

One major area in communication research that lends itself to legal comparisons is the "primacy-recency" controversy. Studies of these phenomena generally compare the persuasiveness of arguments heard first (primacy) with those arguments heard last (recency) by the receiver. Lawson (1969), who surveys much of the literature upholding the primacy effect, states that there is a direct correlation between the primacy effect and prior information on the topic. If facts are first received by the juror during the prosecutor's (or plaintiff's) and then the defendant's presentation of the evidence, and prior to the persuasive or inferential communication (during the defendant's and then the prosecutor's closing arguments), then the primacy effect of the communication will increase. Lawson contends that because prior opinions may be formed by the jury during the factual periods, a stronger *primacy* effect will occur when the persuasive speeches of closing statements begin, thus giving the defendant a decided advantage. The wide variance in experimental results might be attributed to the fact that the researchers viewed the jury process differently. For instance, Lund (1925) and Hovland et al. (1957) saw primacy effects favoring the prosecutor who speaks first during the opening statement and witness examinations. Lawson (1969), however, saw these sections only as factual and not persuasive in nature. He saw a primacy effect in favor of the defendant who speaks first during the closing statements which are, he feels, the only real examples of persuasion in the trial process.

A further problem with the experimental data surveyed by Lawson (Lund, 1925; Hovland et al., 1957; Lana, 1964) was that they pertain to laboratory studies unrelated to the legal research area, which Lawson believes are not directly comparable to the jury process. However, some researchers have demonstrated the effect of *both* primacy and recency on persuasion of jurors (Weld and Danzig, 1940). Another experimenter challenged the primacy effect in jury trials on the ground that prior commitments rather than order of presentation affect the juror's decisions (Stone, 1969). Other studies showed recency effects (Wallace and Wilson, 1969; Wallace, 1970). Some researchers contend that

> a major difficulty in reconciling the inconsistencies in the current literature is attributable to the fact that the same experimental design and procedure have seldom been repeated [Wallace and Wilson, 1969: 311].

Zeisel (1973) discusses an experiment to analyze the variance in damage awards in civil cases around the country. The research (to be reported in Kalven and Zeisel's forthcoming text on the civil jury) involved summaries of reports of five actual personal injury cases. In order to assess the different amounts of damages that the plaintiff in each case might receive, three insurance adjusters in large, medium and rural cities in the West, Midwest, South, and East gave their professional opinion on what a jury in their region would award. The results indicate a large variation around the country. Higher than average claims would be awarded in the western and eastern large cities, while lower claims would be awarded in the southern and midwestern rural areas. These results correlated highly with the average per capita income of the area.[9]

Some studies currently in progress are evaluating the product of deliberations. Zeisel (1973) mentions an investigation at the University of Chicago under a National Science Foundation grant studying the effects of peremptory challenges of jurors on jury verdicts. In this study two mock juries and one real jury observe cases in the Federal District Court for Northern Illinois. The real jury is made up of jurors who have undergone the usual voir dire challenges, the second jury (mock) is made up of jurors excused in voir dire by both sides; and the third jury (mock) had no challenges allowed. The problem here may be one of motivation. Zeisel and Diamond (1974) report that it might be wise to keep the juries from knowing which one is the real one because,

> despite all precautions, a real jury in a criminal case is less likely to convict than a mock jury of the same size sitting in the courtroom with the real jury. It would seem that the real jury has a more demanding concept of "proof beyond a reasonable doubt" [Zeisel and Diamond, 1974: 291, n. 47].

Here again we see the possibility of variables confounding the complex area of jury research.[10]

The above summary of product research leads to no unified theory of either the generalized area of small group research or of the specialized jury research. Basically, the literature is conflicting, replications are sparse, and much of the research is subject to confounding variables. Although the importance of jury deliberations may be contested, many of the studies focusing on product have also examined the process of group interaction, which is the subject of the next section of this chapter.

Research on Deliberation Process

Much of the recent research on the small group has centered on the factors which affect the interaction within a group. But process research as well as product research results must be viewed with care because different tasks have been used in each study, thereby making generalizability difficult. The following review of leadership, content, and participation research results will provide some insights into the process area.

The most numerous and varied studies on the small group have analyzed group leadership. A leader may be defined as the member who controls or directs a group. Leadership may occur within a group in two ways, either through assignment or emergence; and even when there is an assigned leader, various members may compete for control. Researchers have indicated that three basic styles of leadership may occur: autocratic, democratic, or laissez-faire (Lewin et al., 1939). While a strong dominant leader (autocrat) may cause low morale and hostility (Lewin et al., 1939), less time may be needed for solution and fewer errors may occur (Shaw, 1955). The democratic leader may encourage more original thought and group interaction (Lewin et al., 1939); while a laissez-faire leader may be like no leader at all, and other members of the group may take on the leadership role. Situational aspects, such as goals and individual members' needs and expectations, may determine type of leadership needed within a group (Cartwright and Zander, 1968). For instance, a group which is task-oriented may require a more task (goal)-oriented leader than a group which has a socioemotional (i.e., concern for personal feelings of members) orientation. Group size may also affect the leadership style. The larger the group, the more leadership skill is needed to coordinate the interaction (Hare, 1952). If there is no appointed leader, members with leadership potential may informally vie with each other until a leader emerges.

The concept of leadership within the jury deliberation process may be defined in two ways: the formal leadership of the foreman and the opinion leadership. Although these positions may be held by the same person, some research indicates that the foreman, the person selected by the other jurors to announce the verdict, may not be the most influential member of the group. Hawkins (1960) reports from observation of mock jury deliberations that the foreman participated a great deal at first by rereading the judge's instructions, and so on; but as the deliberation progressed, the foreman's participation more approximated the group's norm. Nevertheless, some foremen were very active throughout, while others tried to stay out of the discussion entirely (Hawkins, 1960: 26, 27). This observation might be compared with the general group literature dealing with the various styles of leadership (democratic, autocratic, laissez-faire) which possibly depend on the personality of the leader.[11]

Of great interest, also, is the method of foremen selection. Hawkins (1960) found that the first person to be nominated would be chosen either by acclamation or by absence of dissent, and that people seldom sought the position actively. On occasion, however, the person who began the discussion of who would be foreman was, in fact, selected. Criteria such as sex (see chapter 4 by Stephan for discussion of the effect of personal and demographic traits) and prior jury experience seemed to be a factor. People who sat at the ends of the table were very often chosen—three times as often as by chance occurrence (Hawkins, 1960: 22, 23).

Group size may not affect the amount of leadership demanded by the group (Kessler, 1973b), but further analysis of this issue would be of value in view of the small group research which suggests that group size may affect leadership. This question of what type of person controls or guides the jury is an area for more experimental study. If, in fact, deliberation may serve to change jurors' opinions in some cases, then the person who guides this change becomes the critical member for study.

In addition to leadership, the situational aspects of a group may affect the content of what is discussed during the interaction process. As groups increase in size, more ideas may be discussed until there is a point of diminishing returns (Hare, 1952). Not all of a group's time is spent discussing the assigned task, and studies have shown that socioemotional nontask-related issues take up some of a group's time. The amount of time spent on task versus socioemotional issues may depend both on group goals and on individual members' needs (Cartwright and Zander, 1968).

Lawyers usually try to anticipate and, therefore, gear their remarks to influence the issues to be discussed by the jury during deliberations. The first researchers actually to hear the jury (mock) deliberate were James-Simon (1957) and Strodtbeck et al., (1957). Since then researchers have attempted to study the content through audiotape, videotape, actual observations, and post-deliberation questionnaires. As a result of these studies, conflicting data exists on the competence of the jury to discuss the issues of the trial (see Erlander, 1970, for detailed discussion of this research). Judges' instructions, for instance, may cause confusion among the jurors. Forston (1970), observing videotaped mock deliberations, found that jurors have great trouble in understanding judges' instructions. O'Mara (1972), using postdeliberation questionnaires and real jurors, found jurors were influenced by the judge's demeanor and tried to return a verdict that might please him. The instructions "clarified their task and the law" and refreshed their memories. However, the judge's language also served to confuse the jurors if they did not understand it. Kessler (1973b) questioned student jurors and found boredom and confusion resulting from the instructions. In examining deliberations, Kessler found confusion over contributory negligence. For example, some student jurors were discussing "comparative negligence" instead. Broeder (1959) also found jurors constructing their own laws at times, regardless of the instructions. Simon (1967) analyzed the audiotaped mock deliberations and found that jurors carefully review all the evidence and rely on the record, although she also found (1959) that 50% of the jurors' time was spent discussing personal experiences. Kessler (1973b) noticed jurors spending some time in discussion of the irrelevant issues of plaintiff's and defendant's insurance (see also Kalven, 1964, for discussion of this) and the lawyers' advocacy skills. More study of what are the key issues discussed by jurors, and how fully jurors understand the law which they are expected to apply to the facts of the case, would be areas for further analysis through mock jury deliberation analysis and postdeliberation questionnaires of real jurors.

Group member participation also depends upon the situational aspects of the group and the various personality types involved. Small group research suggests that as group size increases, individual member participation decreases (Hare, 1952; Willems, 1964). Further, a person in the minority may be less likely to express his views when in a larger group as the number of unanimous majority members is greater (Asch, 1951; Gerard et al., 1968). However, a minority member is more likely to express his views if he has an ally (Asch, 1951), and a larger group might afford a greater probability of finding such an ally. The ability of the minority to hold its position may be directly related to the number in the minority (Hawkins, 1960: 159). Personal aspects such as perceived competence of self and of the majority may affect the conformity behavior of the minority member (Costanzo et al., 1968; Hollander, 1960).

When there is a deviant group member, such as a minority jury member, group research indicates that there will be more initial communication toward the deviate, especially if he greatly deviates from the group, or there seems to be a chance of changing his mind. If the group is unable to bring the deviate into the fold, he may be totally excluded from the group by decreasing the amount of communication toward him (Cartwright and Zander, 1968: 45). In mock juries observed by Kessler (1973a and 1973b), even though a jury might have been at a verdict (nonunanimous five-sixths needed in this study), in all cases the majority asked the minority members to express the reasons for deviating and attempted to bring them back into the majority camp. This aspect of minority or deviate participation thus may become important in nonunanimous verdicts, and critical when a unanimous verdict is required (see Zeisel, 1973, and Simon and Marshall, 1972, for discussion of unanimous verdicts).

Hawkins (1960) discussed various methods for gaining unanimity within the jury: voting, switching, informal announcements, and direct persuasion. Voting is a critical aspect of deliberations since the objective is to find consensus (Hawkins, 1960: 50). The group may all be in agreement initially and the vote may indicate this. Switching involves all members of one faction converting to the majority decision. Informal announcements may lead to the opinion change of uncertain members. Direct persuasion may be focused on a minority member as a means of getting him to switch his decision.

When juries divide into coalitions or splinter factions, where all jurors are openly aligned, there may be a high correlation between the number in the minority and the duration of the argument (Hawkins, 1960: 114). Once a movement of jurors began from one side of the debate to the other, that movement either continued or there was a stalemate, but never a regression (Hawkins, 1960: 158). If the finding previously discussed that most juries (about 90% according to Kalven, 1958) arrive at a verdict before deliberations begin, then the effect of the minority member in the other 10% is an important area for study. The power of the minority member or members to sway the majority may mean the winning or losing of the case (see Simon and Marshall, 1972; Kalven and Zeisel, 1966, for discussion of this point).

Zeisel (1971: 719) states that the Supreme Court misinterpreted *The*

American Jury (1966) in *Williams v. Florida* case (1970) when it quoted, "jurors in the minority on the first ballot are likely to be influenced by the proportional size of the majority aligned against them" (*Williams v. Florida,* 1970: 101, n. 49—citing Kalven and Zeisel, 1966, 462-463, 488-489). He emphasizes the importance of the probability of getting more minority jurors in a larger (twelve-member) jury. Zeisel states that the Asch (1951) research suggests the need for an ally to stand up for a minority view, and Zeisel suggests that there is a statistically greater chance for that ally to occur in the larger jury. This should be examined against the Asch (1951) and Gerard et al. (1968) conclusions that a lone minority member may be more likely to follow the majority opinion when group size increases.

Zeisel also suggests the problems of nonunanimous verdict in conjunction with his analysis of smaller juries. He contends that enacting a nonunanimous rule is another manner of reducing jury size,

> for a majority verdict requirement is far more effective in nullifying the potency of minority viewpoints than is outright reduction of a jury to a size equivalent to the majority that is allowed to agree on a verdict [Zeisel, 1971: 722].

The minority view will more easily stand, he states, in a unanimous jury of ten than a nonunanimous twelve-member jury where ten jurors must concur.

The size of the jury may also affect whether or not a minority-thinking member speaks at all. In a larger group, even though there may be a greater probability of getting more minority members, there may be a smaller percentage of minority participation as silent minority members may feel that others have already mentioned their ideas or feel that the number of majority members against them is too great (Kessler, 1973a and 1973b). The quantity and quality of a minority member's contributions may also depend on the forcefulness of his personality. Some people just naturally talk more in any group (see chapter 4 for further discussion of the effect of demographic and social traits that affect jury interaction).

Jury size and the requirement of unanimous or nonunanimous verdicts may affect the impact of minority members on the process of deliberations. Debate on these issues is currently going on both in the scientific literature (Zeisel, 1971; Kessler, 1973a and 1973b; Zeisel and Diamond, 1974) and in the Congress (Hearings on H.R. 8285).

The importance of persuasion within deliberations has been studied by Hawkins (1960). Deliberations may take place in unity or in factions, or through a combination of both types. A deliberation in unity leads to collective group opinion and a vote may not occur until the end. A jury divided into factions may vote quickly, and advocacy might arise to support the opposing views

(Hawkins, 1960: 106-107). Furthermore, Hawkins found a difference in the persuasive techniques that are required in arriving at a verdict in a civil action and in the awarding of damages. A verdict necessitates an "either/or" decision (i.e., plaintiff or defendant); and, therefore, jurors might use straight persuasion to gain other jurors' support for their side. A continuum may develop (i.e., $5,000; $10,000; $15,000) in deciding damages for the plaintiff, and bargaining and compromise may take place within the deliberations to arrive at an equitable settlement (Hawkins, 1960: 58-59).

Much of the process research discussed in this section is subject to criticism on many counts. First, many different tasks have been used in the small group and jury research, making generalizations difficult. In the jury area, for instance, some studies have examined civil cases (Kessler, 1973a and 1973b; Hawkins, 1960) while others have examined criminal cases (James-Simon, 1957). Since these are different tasks for a jury, generalizability to both types of juries is difficult. Further, many of the process studies have analyzed student jury deliberations (e.g., Kessler, 1973b) or mock real juries (e.g., Simon, 1967). Since it is illegal, no researchers have analyzed real juries deliberating. Thus, the realism of the analyzed deliberations may be in question. Further, the specific manner of evaluating deliberations is rather sketchy. No highly developed system of content analysis of the jury's verbal and nonverbal interaction yet exists; thus, many of the research conclusions rely on general observations. A more structured and reliable system must be developed.

DIRECTIONS FOR FURTHER JURY RESEARCH

As demonstrated by the above review, it is difficult to state a formalized theory of jury or even small group behavior (see Shaw, 1971: 360, for discussion of the problems of theory development in the small group area). There appears to be a paucity in the number of researchers who are willing to sustain and develop specific areas of research in order to unify the findings into a theoretical whole; the Chicago Project was an exception. The very nature of jury research, like all group research, requires the analysis of both group product and process. Questions of the effect of minority member participation, jury size, nonunanimous verdicts, judges' instructions, among others, must be more fully examined. However, members of the bench and bar are primarily concerned with results of deliberations and, therefore, the product studies would be of most interest to them.

If social psychology is defined as the study of how individuals behave in social situations, jury research must emphasize this dynamic process of individual behavior in the jury situation, in addition to the product, in order to gain a clearer picture of how juries operate. The area of sociolegal research has begun to enter the world of the jury and, hopefully, this century will see the development of a complete theory of jury deliberations.

NOTES

1. Although the actual deliberations cannot be recorded, jurors may be questioned after deliberations in order to find out what went on during the deliberations.

2. After the Kansas controversy, a federal law [18 USC § 1508] was enacted which prohibited the recording of, listening to, or observing of actual grand or petit jury deliberating or voting.

3. Productivity is an ambiguous term with several possible definitions. It may be the quality of the product or the quantity, judged by number of units produced or the speed of solving one problem or a combination of these aspects. The jury's product is specialized and may be defined as speed in reaching a verdict, ability to reach a verdict as opposed to being a hung jury, or finding of unanimous or nonunanimous verdicts. The quality of a verdict is rather difficult to define. In a criminal action, for instance, it might be difficult to assess the correctness of a guilty or nonguilty verdict. In a civil action the damages which might be awarded to the plaintiff might be a possible factor for evaluation of the jury product. Process in small group research usually means the manner in which group members interact. In jury research it specifically means the way jurors relate to each other in their attempt to reach a verdict.

4. However, when a judge writes an opinion in a trial without a jury or as a result of deciding an appeal, both the lawyers who tried or argued the case and the lawyers who look to the case as precedent are as concerned with the process of decision-making as with the decision itself. Because jury deliberations cannot be used as precedent, perhaps there is less legal interest in the process; but it could still be profitable to know, for instance, what issues were considered, what points were most persuasive, and what types of individuals were the most powerful persuaders, when trying a similar case. Research on mock jury deliberations could provide this insight into the decision-making process. This type of research is superior to postdeliberation questioning of jurors, since actual participants may be biased sources of information about the group process.

5. Furthermore, Holsti (1969) offers an excellent discussion of how content analysis is best accomplished in general research. His theories may be applied to the analysis of jury interaction.

6. In addition to verbal analyses, nonverbal evaluations are also possible. Some studies of group behavior have created systems to evaluate the nonverbal communication of group interaction in order to more fully understand group process (Mehrabian, 1969). No jury studies have yet applied this methodology, but future studies may develop such a system. Kessler is presently working on such a methodology.

7. There were two six-person hung juries (i.e., unable to decide by the five-sixths margin required in Michigan). An additional six-person jury settled publicly, while two jurors privately (on the postdeliberation questionnaire) were still for the plaintiff. There was one hung jury in the twelve-person condition: seven jurors in favor of the plaintiff and five for the defendant. This was the only jury in either condition with a majority of mamebers in favor of the plaintiff.

8. Strodtbeck, 1962, originally used this methodology to study civil juries.

9. Kulka and Kessler have also found this effect in running a replication of an earlier study (Kulka and Kessler, 1973). Student jurors in a large city (Chicago) tended to award higher damages in the same personal injury case than student jurors in a small midwestern town (Ann Arbor, Michigan). These studies, like many others, look solely at product rather

than process. In these cases juries were not used to evaluate the difference. However, the stimulus used in all cases was the same. It might be interesting to rerun such a study using mock juries from the jury pools around the country and evaluate the damages awarded and the major issues considered in each situation to see if factors other than income levels affect the awards.

10. Zeisel and Diamond (1974: 291) suggest the possibility of controlling this problem of mock-versus-real jury effect by simultaneously trying a series of real cases before six-member and twelve-member juries. The lawyers and court would know whether the six-member or twelve-member jury had been selected, but the juries would both feel it was their real responsibility.

11. A study of the effect of autocratic, democratic or laissez-faire foremen and their effect on the deliberation process would make an interesting study. Mock juries could deliberate on the same videotaped trial, and the leadership styles of the foremen and the resulting group process could be analyzed.

REFERENCES

AHERN, J. (1971) "Communication in juries: a study of decision-making in different sized groups." Presented to the Speech Communication Association Convention, San Francisco, December.

Ann Arbor News (1971) "Criminal trials put on videotape." (November 17): 5.

ASCH, S. E. (1951) "Effects of group pressure upon the modification and distortion of judgments," in H. Guetzkow (ed.), Groups, Leadership and Men. Pittsburgh: Carnegie Press.

AUGELLI, J. (1972) "Six-member juries in civil actions in the federal judicial system." Seton Hall Law Review 3 (Spring): 281-294.

BALES, R. F. (1970) Personality and Interpersonal Behavior. New York: Holt, Rinehart & Winston.

——— (1950) Interaction Process Analysis: A Method for the Study of Small Groups. Reading, Mass.: Addison-Wesley.

BEM, D. J., M. A. WALLACH, and N. KOGAN (1965) "Group decision-making under risk of aversive consequences." Journal of Personality and Social Psychology 1: 453-460.

BERMANT, G. and R. COPPOCK (1973) "Outcomes of six and twelve-member jury trials: an analysis of 128 civil cases in the state of Washington." Washington Law Review 48: 593-596.

BROEDER, D. W. (1959) "The University of Chicago jury project." Nebraska Law Review 38: 744-760.

CARTWRIGHT, D. and A. ZANDER [eds.] (1968) Group Dynamics: Research and Theory (third ed.). New York: Harper & Row.

Chicago Tribune (1974) "Use of videotape growing in courtroom." (July 18) 4A: 3.

Colgrove v. Battin (1973) 413 U.S. 149.

COSTANZO, P. R., H. T. REITAN, and M. E. SHAW (1968) "Conformity as a function of experimentally induced minority and majority competence." Psychonomic Science 10: 329-330.

Daily Herald-Telephone (1974) "Trial to be taped." (June 24).

ERLANDER, H. S. (1970) "Jury research in America: its past and future." Law and Society Review 4: 345-370.

FORSTON, R. F. (1972) "Research in jury structure and function." Presented to Speech Communication Association, Chicago, December.

——— (1970) "Judge's instructions: a quantitative analysis of jurors' listening comprehension." Today's Speech 18 (November): 34-38.

——— (1968) "The decision-making process in the American civil jury: a comparative methodological investigation." Ph.D. dissertation, University of Minnesota.

GERARD, H. B., R. A. WILHELMY, and E. S. CONOLLEY (1968) "Conformity and group size." Journal of Personality and Social Psychology 8: 79-82.

GORDON, R. (1968) "A study in forensic psychology: petit jury verdicts as a function of the number of jury members." Ph.D. dissertation, University of Oklahoma.

HARE, A. P. (1952) "Interaction and consensus in different sized groups." American Sociological Review 17: 261-267.

HAWKINS, C. (1960) "Interaction and coalition realignments in consensus-seeking groups: a study of experimental jury deliberation." Ph.D. dissertation, University of Chicago.

Hearings on H.R. 8285 (1974) Before the Subcommittee on Courts, Civil Liberties, and the Administration of Justice of the House Committee on the Judiciary, Ninety-second Congress, Second Session.

HOLLANDER, E. P. (1960) "Competence and conformity in the acceptance of influence." Journal of Abnormal and Social Psychology 61: 365-369.

HOLSTI, O. R. (1969) Content Analysis for the Social Sciences and Humanities. Reading, Mass.: Addison-Wesley.

HOVLAND, C. I., E. H. CAMPBELL, and T. BROCK (1957) "The effects of 'commitment' on opinion charge following communication," in C. I. Hovland et al. (eds.), The Order of Presentation in Persuasion. New Haven, Conn.: Yale University Press.

Institute of Judicial Administration, Inc. (1972) "Comparison of six- and twelve-member civil juries in New Jersey Superior and County Courts." (mimeo)

JAMES-SIMON, R. (1959) "Status and competence of jurors." American Journal of Sociology 69: 563-570.

——— (1957) "Jurors' reactions to definitions of legal insanity." Ph.D. dissertation, University of Chicago.

KALVEN, H., Jr. (1964) "The dignity of the civil jury." Virginia Law Review 50: 293-313.

——— (1958) "The jury, the law and the personal injury damage award." Ohio State Law Journal 19: 158-178.

——— and H. ZEISEL (1966) The American Jury. Boston: Little, Brown.

KESSLER, J. B. (1974) "Techniques of jury research." Presented to Central States Speech Association, Milwaukee, April.

——— (1973a) "An empirical study of six- and twelve-member jury decision-making processes." University of Michigan Journal of Law Reform 6: 712-734.

——— (1973b) "A content analytic comparison of the six- and twelve-member jury decision-making processes." Ph.D. dissertation, University of Michigan.

KULKA, R. and J. B. KESSLER (1973) "The influence of physical attractiveness on decisions of simulated jurors." Presented to the Speech Communication Association Convention, New York, November.

LANA, R. E. (1964) "Familiarity and the order of presentation of persuasive communications." Journal of Abnormal and Social Psychology 62: 314-320.

LAWSON, R. (1970) "Relative effectiveness of one-sided and two-sided communications in courtroom persuasion." Journal of General Psychology 82: 3-16.

——— (1969) "The law of primacy in the criminal courtroom." Journal of Social Psychology 77: 121-131.

LEWIN, K., R. LIPPITT, and R. K. WHITE (1939) "Patterns of aggressive behavior in experimentally created social climates." Journal of Social Psychology 10: 271-299.

LUND, F. H. (1925) "The psychology of belief. IV. The law of primacy in persuasion." Journal of Abnormal and Social Psychology 20: 183-191.

MEHRABIAN, A. (1969) "Some referents and measures of nonverbal behavior." Behavior Research Methods and Instructions 1: 203-209.

MILLER, G., D. BENDER, T. FLORENCE, and H. NICHOLSON (1974) "Real versus reel: what's the verdict?" Journal of Communications (Summer).

MILLS, L. R. (1973) "Six-member and twelve-member juries: an empirical study of trial results." University of Michigan Journal of Law Reform 6: 671-711.

New York Times (1971) "TV cameras used in Michigan court." (November 26): 5, 24.

——— and L. H. HOOK (1961) "The social dimensions of a twelve-man jury table." Sociometry 24: 397-415.

STRODTBECK, F., R. JAMES, and C. HAWKINS (1957) "Social status in jury deliberations." American Sociological Review 22 (December): 713-719.

TAYLOR, D. W. and W. L. FAUST (1952) "Twenty questions: efficiency in problem-solving as a function of size of group." Journal of Experimental Psychology 44: 360-368.

TEGER, A. I. and D. G. PRUITT (1967) "Components of group risk taking." Journal of Experimental Social Psychology 3: 189-205.

TRIPLETT, N. (1897) "The dynamogenic factors in pacemaking and competition." American Journal of Psychology 9: 507-533.

WALBERT, D. F. (1971) "The effect of jury size on the probability of conviction: an evaluation of Williams v. Florida." Case Western Reserve Law Review 22 (April): 529-554.

WALLACE, W. (1970) "Primacy and recency warnings and order effects on persuasive communications." Ph.D. dissertation, University of Alabama.

——— and W. WILSON (1969) "Reliable recency effects." Psychological Reports 25, 1: 311-317.

WELD, H. P. and E. R. DANZIG (1940) "A study of the way in which a verdict is reached by a jury." American Journal of Psychology 53 (October): 518-536.

WELD, H. P. and M. ROFF (1938) "A study of the formation of opinion based upon legal evidence." American Journal of Psychology 51: 609-628.

WIEHL, L. L. (1968) "The six-man jury." Gonzaga Law Review 4 (Fall): 35-44.

WILLEMS, E. P. (1964) "Review of research," in R. Barker and P. V. Gump (eds.) Big Schools, Small Schools. Stanford, Calif.: Stanford University Press.

Williams v. Florida (1970) 399 U.S. 78.

ZEISEL, H. (1973) "Reflections on experimental techniques in the law." Journal of Legal Studies 2: 107-124.

——— (1971) ". . . And then there were none: the diminution of the federal jury." University of Chicago Law Review 38 (Summer): 710-724.

——— and S. S. DIAMOND (1974) "Convincing empirical evidence on the six-member jury." University of Chicago Law Review 41: 281-295.

O'MARA, J. J. (1972) "The courts, standard jury charges—findings of pilot project." Pennsylvania Bar Journal 120 (January): 166-175.

PABST, W. R., Jr. (1973) "What do six-member juries really save?" Judicature 57, 1: 6-11.

——— (1972) "Statistical studies on the costs of six-man versus twelve-man juries." William and Mary Law Review 14: 326-336.

POWELL, D. M. (1971) "Reducing the size of juries." University of Michigan Journal of Law Reform 5 (Fall): 87-108.

ROSNOW, R. L. and E. J. ROBINSON (1967) Experiments in Persuasion. New York: Academic Press.

SHAW, M. (1932) "A comparison of individuals and small groups in rational solution of complex problems." American Journal of Psychology 44: 491-504.

SHAW, M. E. (1971) Group Dynamics: The Psychology of Small Group Behavior. New York: McGraw-Hill.

——— (1955) "A comparison of two types of leadership in various communication sets." Journal of abnormal and social psychology 50: 127-134.

SIMON, R. J. (1967) The Jury and the Defense of Insanity. Boston: Little, Brown.
——— (1963) "Mental patients as jurors." Human Organization 22: 276-281.
——— and L. MAHAN (1971) "Quantifying burdens of proof: a view from the bench, the jury and the classroom." Law and Society Review (February): 319-330.
SIMON, R. J. and P. MARSHALL (1972) "The jury system," pp. 211-233 in S. S. Nagel (ed.) The Rights of the Accused in Law and Action. Beverly Hills, Calif.: Sage Criminal Justice System Annuals, Vol. I.
SOUTH, E. B. (1927) "Some psychological aspects of committee work." Journal of Applied Psychology 11: 348-368, 437-464.
STEPHAN, C. (1975) "Selective characteristics of jurors and litigants: their influence on juries' verdicts," ch. 4 in R. J. Simon (ed.) The Jury System in America: A Critical Overview. Beverly Hills, Calif.: Sage Criminal Justice Systems Annuals, Vol. IV.
STONE, V. (1969) "A primary effect in decision making by jurors." Journal of Communications 19: 239-247.
STRODTBECK, F. (1962) "Social process, the law and jury functioning," in N. Evan (ed.) Law and Sociology.

4

SELECTIVE CHARACTERISTICS OF
JURORS AND LITIGANTS:
THEIR INFLUENCES ON JURIES' VERDICTS

C O O K I E   S T E P H A N

The function of the jury of peers is to render a verdict based on the sum total of evidence heard in the courtroom, exclusive of any diverse characteristics of the jurors or litigants. The author reviews experimental data from simulated juries and from actual jury trials in an attempt to determine which characteristics of litigants and jurors have an effect on the ultimate decision in a jury trial.

Sex, race, socioeconomic status, moral character, and physical attractiveness (or lack of same) are some of the characteristics examined in this study. Simulated juries illustrate the effects of these variables and also of attitudes toward capital punishment, authoritarianism, and the foreman's leadership ability.

It is concluded that two of the variables, race and sex, require further research as the available data is "contradictory and anecdotal." The socioeconomic variable, however, emerges most clearly from the experiments as a prejudicial problem. It is the author's contention that more documentation is needed and that it should be used as a means of sensitizing attorneys to potential jurors who are more likely or less likely to be biased toward their clients.

Chapter 4

SELECTIVE CHARACTERISTICS OF JURORS AND LITIGANTS: THEIR INFLUENCES ON JURIES' VERDICTS

COOKIE STEPHAN

The jury of peers is a legal institution designed to render verdicts based upon the evidence presented in the courtroom, exclusive of the personal and social characteristics of the litigants and exclusive of such characteristics on the part of jurors. Ideally the same verdict would be returned in a given case regardless of the individual litigants and the individual jurors involved. How closely does the actual approach the ideal? Clarence Darrow (as quoted in Sutherland and Cressey, 1966: 442) once stated:

> Jurymen seldom convict a person they like, or acquit one that they don't like. The main work of a trial lawyer is to make a jury like his client, or at least, to feel sympathy for him; facts regarding the crime are relatively unimportant.

While many observers of the legal profession surely would view Darrow's statement as extreme, the attention that has been paid to jury selection by the legal profession and the recent use of juror profiles composed by research groups for trials of wide public interest suggest that there is some validity to the belief

AUTHOR'S NOTE: *The author wishes to thank Sheldon Olson and Nancy Blaney for their comments on an earlier draft of this paper.*

that the personal characteristics of jurors are important determinants of the verdict rendered.

There is a considerable impressionistic literature on jury selection. Darrow (as quoted in Sutherland and Cressey, 1966: 442) had the following opinions:

> I try to get a jury with little education but with much human emotion. The Irish are always the best jurymen for the defense. I don't want a Scotchman, for he has too little human feelings; I don't want a Scandinavian, for he has too strong a respect for law as law. In general, I don't want a religious person, for he believes in sin and punishment. The defense should avoid rich men who have a high regard for the law, as they make and use it. The smug and ultra-respectable think they are the guardians of society, and they believe the law is for them.
>
> The man who is down on his luck, who has trouble, who is more or less a failure, is much kinder to the poor and unfortunate than are the rich and selfish.

The jury selection literature even contains suggestions as to the interpretation of such variables as kinesics:

> If the juror's feet are crossed, he is not accepting what you say. . . . The juror with poor posture is thinking off balance. . . . The man who is cracking his knuckles or wringing his hands is probably prosecution-minded and a capital punishment man [Katz, 1968].

There has been less written about the interaction between the characteristics of the litigants and those of jurors than about either set of variables. One subject, however, has received a fair amount of attention:

> Where women are parties in the case, most lawyers are loathe to retain woman jurors, since they are thought to be harder on their own sex. *Of course,* if the party is a young, attractive man, the more woman jurors, the better [Bloomstein, 1968-1969: 71; italics added].

There is some consistency in this belief that opposites attract in the courtroom, as well as outside:

> There is a general impression among lawyers that male jurors, out of gallantry, favor women litigants and so, when representing a woman, they seek an all-male jury which will overlook female deceit another woman would spot at once [McCart, 1964: 33].

On another aspect of litigant-juror interaction, McCart (1964: 33) writes: "There is an impression that a jury will favor a litigant of his own race or creed."

How much of this impressionistic writing is accurate? The purpose of this chapter is to review experimental data from simulated juries and from actual jury trials to determine which personal and social characteristics of litigants and jurors affect the outcome of jury trials. Major attention will be paid to experimental and trial data from criminal cases. Data published before 1950 will not be reviewed.

CHARACTERISTICS OF LITIGANTS
THAT AFFECT THE JURY'S VERDICT

Experimental Data

Six characteristics of litigants have been examined in simulated jury situations to determine whether they influenced the decisions rendered. In this section research investigating the following variables will be reported: litigants' sex, socioeconomic status, moral character, level of physical attractiveness, race, and attitudinal similarity to the simulated juror.

Several investigators (Stephan, 1974; Rose and Prell, 1965; Stephan and Tully, 1973) have found that college students acting as simulated jurors discriminate in favor of litigants of their own sex. Stephan's (1974) subjects were less likely to find a defendant of their own sex guilty of murder than they were to find a defendant of the opposite sex guilty. In the Rose and Prell (1965) study, students assigned punishments to men and women offenders convicted of thirteen selected crimes. They noted that female subjects assigned lighter sentences to women than to men. For some offenses, however, both men and women punished women defendants less severely. Overall, male and female defendants were sentenced to equivalent penitentiary terms, but men were assessed higher fines than women at each status level. In assessing fines, the subjects may have been taking into consideration men's greater earning abilities relative to women's. In the Stephan and Tully (1973) study, a personal damage simulation, males awarded the male plaintiff the smallest amount of money. The awards assessed by females fell between these extremes.

Rose and Prell (1965) also investigated the influence of the socioeconomic status of the defendant upon the decisions reached by the subjects. There was no evidence of differential sentencing for defendants of varying socioeconomic status. But higher-status defendants were assigned heavier fines than were lower-status defendants, probably because the former defendants were better able to pay such fines.

Several studies have been conducted to establish the effect of the moral character of the litigants upon the jury's verdict. Landy and Aronson (1969) reported two studies in which college students were asked to decide a negligent automobile homicide case. Combining the data from their two studies, the defendant was sentenced to a longer prison term when the victim was a person of good moral character than when the victim was of bad moral character. In the one study in which they varied the character of the defendant, defendants of good and neutral character were assigned shorter prison sentences than were defendants of bad character.

By contrast, in three studies in which college students also were employed as subjects, Foss (1973) found no differences in verdicts or recommended action attributable to the character of the victim. Foss (1973) also discovered no difference in verdicts or in sentences attributable to the character of the defendant in the one study in which he manipulated the defendant's character.

Hatton et al. (1971) exposed subjects to an automobile accident case with an antivictim bias, an antidriver bias, or no bias. The antivictim bias consisted of positive information about the character of the driver and the information that the victim had unsuccessfully sued for injury in the past, with questionable cause. The antidriver bias consisted of the information that the driver had a minor criminal record and a poor driving record and positive information about the victim's character. Although the questionnaire data showed that antivictim bias led to antivictim beliefs about the accident, and antidriver bias led to antidriver beliefs, there were no significant differences among conditions in percentages of guilty verdicts. Thus, the majority of these data suggests that the character of the litigants does not influence the decisions of simulated jurors.

But physical attractiveness of litigants does appear to influence the decision-making process. Stephan and Tully (1973) found that physically attractive plaintiffs in a personal injury suit involving a nondisfiguring injury had a higher recovery rate than unattractive plaintiffs and were awarded more money in damages than were physically unattractive plaintiffs. Kulka and Kessler (1973) varied the physical attractiveness of both plaintiff and defendant in an automobile negligence trial. College students in the attractive plaintiff-unattractive defendant condition found in favor of the plaintiff more often than college students in the unattractive plaintiff-attractive defendant condition. All subjects, regardless of initial verdict, were asked to award damages to the plaintiff. Subjects in the attractive plaintiff-unattractive defendant condition awarded more money than did subjects in the unattractive plaintiff-attractive defendant condition.

Efran (1974) found the defendant's attractiveness to be negatively correlated with a guilty verdict and with severe punishment. Sigall and Ostrove (1975) reported an interaction between physical attractiveness of the defendant and the relationship of physical attractiveness to the crime committed. When the offense was attraction-unrelated (burglary), the unattractive defendant was more severely punished than the attractive defendant. However, when the offense was attraction-related (swindle), the attractive defendant was more severely punished. The authors hypothesized that attractive individuals are viewed as "better" people, but that an attractive person who deliberately exploits this advantage is viewed with particular disfavor.

In the only simulation varying race, Kaplan and Simon (1972) ascertained that the race of the victim had no effect upon the verdict reached in a traffic fatality.

Griffitt and Jackson (1973) varied similarity of attitude between defendant and juror on four issues irrelevant to the criminal case in question. They found that the more dissimilar were the attitudes, the more guilty the defendant was judged to be and the longer the prison sentence he was assessed.

Data From Jury Trials

There have been many more studies in which actual trial data have been analyzed to determine the effect of characteristics of litigants than there have been jury simulations designated to investigate litigant characteristics. The analyses of these trial data include the following litigant variables: sex, socioeconomic status, moral character, family responsibilities, age, previous convictions, and race.

Sex. The data from actual jury trials regarding sex discrimination are inconclusive. In a study of first degree murder cases in California from 1958 to 1966 (Stanford Law Review, 1969), it was determined that there was no differential treatment of defendants in verdict nor in sentencing based upon sex. But in their investigation of jury trials in which the judge disagreed with the jury's verdict, Kalven and Zeisel (1966) concluded that a number of sex-linked variables—the defendant being a woman, an attractive woman, a mother, a war widow—created sympathy toward the defendant which led to disagreement between the judge and the jury such that the jury ruled more leniently than the judge felt was appropriate.

There are data concerning the question of sex discrimination that are not strictly relevant to this chapter, since they include the conviction records of defendants who did not have a jury trial as well as those who did. These data, too, are mixed. Green (1961) used records of over 1,400 convictions in Philadelphia courts from 1956-1957. He reported no sex bias that affected the defendant disposition, after differences between sexes in criminal behavior patterns were partialled out. Nagel's (1969) analysis of a portion of the Silverstein (1965) data ascertained that women convicted of assault and larceny were more likely to receive a suspended sentence or probation than were men.

Data collected by Jury Verdict Research, Inc. (1968: vol. 6) show that, while adult plaintiffs win an average of 73% of their personal injury cases, female adults win 69% of their cases, and male adults win 76% of their cases. Using data taken from the same source, Nagel and Weitzman (1971) found that men collected more money in damages for their own injuries than did women, and that men collected more money for vicarious injury to their wives than women collected for vicarious injury to their husbands. Interestingly, male genitals were valued in the courts about three times more than female genitals.

Socioeconomic status. Two of the three investigations of socioeconomic status utilizing trial data point to such a bias in the jury trial system. The Stanford study (1969) disclosed an association between blue-collar background and the death penalty and white-collar background and life imprisonment. Reed (1965) concluded that petit jurors in East Baton Rouge Parish were less likely to convict a defendant of high status than a defendant of low status. In contrast, Adler (1973) found no differences in verdict for defendants of varying socioeconomic status in a criminal court in Pennsylvania.

Data from criminal courts that include all convictions also suggests that there is socioeconomic discrimination in the court system. Green (1961) attributed the differential treatment he documented to economic bias. Silverstein's (1965) analysis of 11,258 criminal cases from 50 states determined that indigent defendants and defendants with only an elementary school education were disadvantaged in the court system. Nagel (1969), in analyzing the assault and larceny cases documented by Silverstein, found that 85% to 95% of the indigent defendants were convicted, in contrast to consistently lower percentages of nonindigent defendants. Nagel also determined that indigents were much less likely to receive probated sentences than nonindigents. A study of Detroit's Recorder Court (Saul R. Levin Memorial Foundation, 1959) concluded that, of those convicted of a felony who were able to make bail, 17% received prison sentences, while 68% of those who were convicted of a felony and who were unable to post bail received prison sentences.

Occupation of the litigants is another factor that influences jury decision-making. *Personal Injury Valuation Handbook* data show that, controlling for the type of suit and the seriousness of the injury, the recovery rate of professional people as personal injury plaintiffs is 25% below the average recovery rate. Professional people also are awarded 17% less money in damages than average. The higher paid the profession, the lower the recovery rate (Jury Verdict Research, Inc., 1965: vol. 5).

Moral character. A number of variables loosely related to the character of litigants has been shown to influence the outcome of jury decisions. A stable or otherwise good job history has been associated with fewer convictions of the defendant (Stanford Law Review, 1969; Kalven and Zeisel, 1966). Kalven and Zeisel (1966) determined that special circumstances—such as being a model prisoner, serving the government, exhibiting kindness to the victim, acting in self-defense, inability to repeat the crime, and a lengthy interval since last conviction—favorably predisposed the jury toward the defendant, as did a generally favorable courtroom appearance, repentance, and crying or collapsing in court.

Kalven and Zeisel (1966) further ascertained that immoral or vulgar behavior on the part of the defendant was associated with cross-over disagreements, where the judge would have ruled more leniently than the jury. They also found that impertinent and self-aggrandizing testimony negatively influenced the jury. In the Stanford study (1969), those defendants who actively resisted arrest and those who attempted an insanity defense were more likely to receive the death penalty than were other defendants. Defendants under the influence of alcohol at the time of the killing were less likely to receive the death penalty.

In civil suits, if the plaintiff was drinking at the time of the injury, his recovery rate was reduced by 45%. If the defendant was drinking at the time of the injury, the plaintiff's recovery rate was 27% above average, and his award was 4% above average (Jury Verdict Research, Inc., 1966: vol. 6).

Several studies have examined the life history and life patterns of litigants. In the Stanford study (1969), no significant differences in verdict were attributable to the defendant's military record, stability of family background, or record of psychiatric difficulties. Reed (1965) concluded that the defendant's religious preference, marital status, and church attendance were not significant variables in the jury decisions he studied.

Family responsibilities have been taken into consideration by some juries. The appearance of the wife or the family of the defendant in court has been shown to have made a favorable impression upon the jury, particularly if the wife were pregnant or the family were large (Kalven and Zeisel, 1966). Broeder (1956) found four personal injury cases out of sixteen in which damages seemed to have been increased because the plaintiff was a married man with a family to support. He determined that an aging laborer was given additional money in damages because he had no children to care for him, a widow was not awarded money for a nurse because she had daughters caring for her, and an attractive 22-year-old widow had damages reduced because it was felt she would remarry (although the award was increased to include compensation for the emotional loss of the husband-father).

Relationships among litigants. In personal injury cases, lawsuits within families average awards 1.25% higher than the average award. Compared to the overall recovery rate of 61%, the within-family recovery rates are as follows: if the defendant is a brother or sister, 58%; if the defendant is a child of the plaintiff, 61%; if the defendant is a parent or grandparent, 75%; and if the defendant is a cousin, aunt, or uncle, 91%.

Physical characteristics. Variables related to physical appearance also have been examined. Kalven and Zeisel (1966) noted that a physically handicapped defendant was viewed with sympathy by the jury. In the Stanford study (1969) the height of the defendant was determined to be an irrelevant characteristic in the murder trials studied.

The obese plaintiff loses 14% more personal injury cases than the nonobese plaintiff, due to the high proportion of occupier liability cases in which he becomes involved (Jury Verdict Research, Inc., 1966: vol. 6).

If the plaintiff dies after the injury from unrelated causes, the award is 10% higher than average. Oddly enough, if the defendant dies as a result of the accident, the plaintiff's recovery rate is increased by 40% and his award is increased by 15%. If the defendant's death was unrelated to the accident, the plaintiff's recovery rate is only 44%, as compared to the average of 61%.

Age. Age is another factor that could influence jury decisions. While Reed (1965) found no age bias in Louisiana civil or criminal cases, Kalven and Zeisel (1966) determined youth and old age to be two of the three most influential sympathy factors in the 1,063 cases they studied of disagreement in verdicts between judge and jury.

The 1964-1965 *Personal Injury Valuation Handbook* data showed the following pattern of age discrimination in personal injury cases: children under twelve win only 59% of their cases, as compared to 61% for the total population of plaintiffs. Teenagers, thirteen to fifteen, are similarly disadvantaged in verdict, winning only 51% of their cases. When the decision favors these teenagers, however, their awards are 6% above average. Male teenagers sixteen to nineteen win less than the average number of cases, while female teenagers in this age range win more than the average number of cases. The awards of both sexes aged sixteen to nineteen average 3% above the national mean. Aged plaintiffs also are handicapped, winning only 51% of their cases.

The 1966 *Personal Injury Valuation Handbook* data dealt with personal injury recovery rates in other age categories. Adult male plaintiffs in their thirties and forties are favored in judgments more than adult women or adult men in the other age categories. Plaintiffs suing a teenaged defendant are awarded damages 6% below the average. Those suing aged defendants have a slightly higher than average recovery rate, but receive awards 1% below the average.

Prior criminal record. Prior conviction of the defendant has been shown to influence jury decisions significantly. The Stanford study (1969) disclosed that the defendants convicted of first degree murder with prior criminal records were more likely to receive the death penalty than the defendants convicted of first degree murder who had no such records (59% versus 19%, respectively). Green's

(1961) data on 1,437 criminal convictions were consistent with this finding: 13% of the convicted felons with no prior conviction were sentenced to the penitentiary, while 35% of the convicted felons with prior conviction were sentenced to the penitentiary.

The recovery rate in a personal injury suit for a plaintiff with a criminal record is no different from that of the plaintiff without a criminal record. Neither is there a differential rate of monetary award for these plaintiffs. But the plaintiff who sues a defendant with a criminal record wins 31% more cases than the average, and is awarded 6% more money in damages (Jury Verdict Research, Inc., 1967: vol. 7).

Race. There is little trial data directly relevant to the question of whether there is racial discrimination in the jury trial system. Kalven and Zeisel (1966) determined that Blacks had a negative sympathy index. But they noted a tendency for juries to demand less strict standards of conduct when the defendant and the victim both were Black. In Broeder's (1965c) study of jurors from 23 trials, he concluded that racial prejudice was present in four of the seven criminal cases in which the defendant was Black. In one case, the acquittal of the defendant seemed to be influenced by extreme racial bigotry on the part of two of the jurors, which led the remaining jurors to disassociate themselves from them. In the other three cases, all convictions, Broeder found a good deal of racial prejudice on the part of the jurors. Importantly, he felt all three defendants would have been convicted regardless of color. In the Stanford study (1969) it was ascertained that Anglos, Mexican-Americans, and Blacks received equal treatment by jurors. Whites who killed Blacks fared no better than Blacks who killed whites.

Members of minority groups win slightly fewer of their personal injury cases (57% to 61%), and on the average they are awarded damages 15% lower than are other plaintiffs (Jury Verdict Research, Inc., 1966: vol. 6).

Records of many convictions from criminal courts also are available. Silverstein's (1965) data suggested that Black defendants were less likely to have a jury trial and were punished more severely in the courts than were whites. Gerard and Terry (1970) examined data collected in Missouri in 1962 for the ABA and reported that a higher proportion of Blacks than whites were found guilty. Ten out of every thirteen Blacks, but only two out of every six whites, were convicted. For every crime but rape and homicide—where everyone convicted was sent to prison—and burglary—where equal proportions of Blacks and whites were sent to prison—a higher proportion of Blacks than whites received penitentiary sentences. Seventy-five percent of the convicted Blacks received prison sentences, compared to 61% of the convicted whites. The proportion of those granted probation was almost twice as high for whites as for

Blacks (37% and 19%, respectively). Vines and Jacob (1963) determined that Blacks received harsher treatment in the courts than whites in 70% of the categories they examined. Discrepancies between the percentages of Black and white defendants sentenced to a year or more in prison increased from 2.8% in 1954 to 13.5% in 1960. Warren (1970), in a study of misdemeanor cases in Detroit, found that Blacks were less likely than whites to receive probation and a fine rather than a more severe penalty. Chiricos and Waldo (1971) reported that Blacks in the state of Florida were found guilty more often than whites and were placed on probation less often for committing felonies.

Not all of the available criminal court studies show differential treatment favoring white defendants. Bensing and Shroeder's (1960) study of homicides found no evidence of racial discrimination. Green (1961) determined the verdicts in Philadelphia courts were free of racial bias. In a smaller study of burglary and robbery convictions from these courts, Green (1964) concluded that there was no support for the hypothesis that punishment was differentiated according to the race of the offender relative to the race of the victim. Further, he could amass no evidence for the charge of racial discrimination in sentencing. Bullock (1961) surveyed 3,644 Black and white inmates in a Texas state prison who had been committed for burglary, rape, and murder. He showed that Black prisoners were committed for shorter sentences than whites for the crime of murder and were committed for longer sentences than whites for the crime of burglary. Blacks were assessed shorter sentences than whites for rape. However, rape across racial lines was punished more severely than within-race rape.

Summary of Findings: Litigant Characteristics

The trial data and the experimental data do not yield any overall conclusions concerning the presence of sex discrimination. The experimental evidence suggested that there is discrimination in favor of same-sex defendants. Some of the trial data suggests that there is no sex discrimination in the criminal jury trial system, while other of the trial data suggests that women are advantaged in criminal jury trials. There is evidence from other aspects of the criminal court system supporting this latter finding. In one study it was shown that women accused of assault or larceny were jailed, released on bail, acquitted, and had their cases dismissed more often than men accused of such felonies. But women were less likely to have a lawyer or a jury trial (Nagel and Weitzman, 1971). *Personal Injury Valuation Handbook* data documented discrimination against women in personal injury trials.

The single experimental study including socioeconomic status of the defendant as an independent variable found no differential treatment in sentencing. However, higher-status subjects were assessed heavier fines. The bulk of the trial data demonstrates socioeconomic discrimination in the criminal jury trial. The evidence from criminal courts including data both from jury trials and guilty pleas also suggested that there is socioeconomic discrimination favoring the higher-status defendants in the criminal court system. In personal injury cases, the plaintiff's occupation and amount of money earned have been considered by juries in deciding some cases.

Evidence from studies of other types of criminal court records is consonant with these data. Silverstein (1965) determined that court-assigned counsel, relative to paid counsel, was less experienced in criminal law and more likely to advise the client to plead guilty. Further, court-assigned counsel is not reimbursed for investigation and preparation expenses, making a defense comparable to paid counsel unlikely. Arrangements for court-assigned counsel typically come too late, usually at arraignment (Allison, 1964). In a study of 3,000 felony convictions (Saul R. Levine Memorial Foundation, 1959), 28% of those who had private counsel received prison sentences, while 57% of those who had court-appointed counsel received prison sentences. Bing and Rosenfeld (1970) determined that 52% of the Black defendants who sought trial *de novo* in the lower criminal courts of metropolitan Boston were defendants committed for failure to make bail; in similar circumstances only 29% of the white defendants were committed.

The trial data and the experimental data suggested different conclusions about the influence of moral character upon jury decisions. Experimental data were mixed, but favored the conclusion that the moral character of the litigants does not differentially influence jury decisions. Trial data suggested that moral character is an important determinant of jury decisions. Evidence of good character that positively influenced some trial juries included repentance, good work records, and various mitigating circumstances surrounding the crime. Negative influences upon the jury in criminal cases included such factors as immoral or vulgar behavior, making a poor impression while testifying, resisting arrest, and prior conviction. In civil suits defendants having a criminal record and drinking on the part of either litigant negatively predisposed the jury to the litigant involved.

How can these differing conclusions concerning the influence of moral character be reconciled? One obvious difference between the data collected from simulations and from real jury trials lies in the composition of the jury. Most experimental studies make use of easily available college students as subjects. It is reasonable to presume that college students are less conservative in their judgments about moral character than are actual jury members, and are less biased toward a defendant as a result of such evidence.

It also could be hypothesized that information concerning character can be presented more effectively in the courtroom than in the paper-and-pencil measures employed in the experimental studies cited, making such data harder to discount in rendering verdicts in a courtroom setting. Similarly, during the course of the courtroom proceedings, information concerning the character of the litigants might come to be seen as relevant to other evidence presented. This association between characteristics of the litigants and the crime committed is much less likely in a simulation, given the abbreviated information typically presented.

A final difference between data-collection situations that might have led to the difference in findings concerns the number of decision-makers. The experimental studies cited employed individual subjects as decision-makers, while almost all of the trial data were based on twelve-member jury decisions. An individual's opinions may be changed during the course of deliberation with other jury members, a situation that is impossible for the solitary simulated juror.

Military record, family stability, marital status, psychiatric history, and religious attitudes and behaviors are factors that juries did not consider important in rendering verdicts in the studies conducted. Juries did seem to be influenced by family obligations, both in criminal trials and in the awarding of damages in personal injury cases. Attitudinal similarity between juror and litigants was associated with leniency while prior conviction significantly biased the jury against the litigant.

The experimental evidence suggested that physical attractiveness is an asset to a litigant, except when the jury has reason to believe that attractiveness facilitated commitment of the crime. Trial data implied that physical handicaps may predispose the jury to the defendant. Similarly, extreme youth and old age may also play upon the sympathies of the criminal jury. In contrast, youth and old age work to the disadvantage of most personal injury plaintiffs.

The data from jury trials concerning racial discrimination is meager and contradictory. The only empirical study showed no racial discrimination in first degree murder cases in the state of California. But the majority of data that involve convictions from all criminal courts supports the hypothesis that minorities are disadvantaged in the criminal court system. Just as the poor may be subject to less discrimination in the jury trial system than in the criminal court system as a whole, so may Blacks and other minorities be subject to less discrimination if they opt for a jury trial than if they do not.

There is evidence to suggest that Blacks are disadvantaged in other aspects of the criminal court system. Silverstein (1965) reported that Blacks are not as likely as whites to be released on bail. Warren (1970) determined that, in Recorder's Court of Detroit, cases involving Black defendants generally were heard in less time than cases involving whites. Further, Blacks were less likely to have been apprised of the charge, the right to testify, or the right to call and cross-examine witnesses. The President's Commission on Law Enforcement (1967) cited examples of blatant racial practices that continue to exist in rural southern courts and acknowledged discriminatory practices by northern court employees and white jurors. Broeder (1965c) noted that, in the case he studied, Black witnesses were called only in cases where there were Black defendants; Crockett (1971) has alleged that the word of white social workers, policemen, and so on, typically outweighs the sworn testimony of Black witnesses.

CHARACTERISTICS OF JURORS
THAT AFFECT THE JURY'S VERDICT

Experimental Data

This section reviews simulated jury studies in which the characteristics of the jurors were varied. The variables that have been investigated are sex, socio-economic status, various demographic variables, attitudes toward capital punishment, authoritarianism, and the foreman's leadership style.

Several studies have been conducted in which the sex of the simulated jurors was an important determinant of the decisions reached. Simon (1967) employed actual jurors as subjects. They listened to a recorded simulation either of a house-breaking trial or of an incest trial in which the defendant pleaded not guilty by reason of insanity. She found women to be more sympathetic toward the defendant in the house-breaking case than were men. However, housewives were more punitive than men and other females in considering the incest case. Brown (1973) conducted two studies in which college students individually stated their opinions about six criminal cases and then made a final group decision after discussion in like-sex groups of three to four members. Female subjects became more harsh in their judgments after discussion, while male subjects showed a tendency to shift toward lenience.

Strodtbeck and his colleagues (Strodtbeck et al., 1957; Strodtbeck and Mann, 1956) reported that men participated more during mock jury deliberation than did women. James-Simon (1959) also found greater participation on the part of males. However, in a larger study including both house-breaking and incest cases (Simon, 1967), she concluded that there was no difference in participation rates between male and female jurors. In the Strodtbeck et al. (1957) study, jurors from regular jury pools deliberated in two mock civil trials. The authors determined that men were elected to the position of foreman more frequently than would be expected by chance, and that the most active jurors shifted their predeliberation positions less frequently than did the less active jurors.

Socioeconomic status has been shown to relate to simulated jurors' decisions in several ways. Rose and Prell (1955) concluded that lower-status subjects, particularly women, were less egalitarian in assessing fines than were higher-status subjects. There was a nonsignificant reversal for sentencing: higher-status subjects assessed longer sentences overall than did lower-status subjects. Similarly, Simon's (1967) high-income jurors and jurors with a college education were less likely to acquit a defendant on grounds of insanity in both the incest and the house-breaking case than were lower-income and less-educated jurors. Thus, higher-status jurors may be more punitive than low-status jurors.

Strodtbeck et al. (1957) found that the simulated juror-elected foreman was a business proprietor more often than would be expected by chance. Simon (1967) noted that the foreman was more likely to be of high status, but saw no evidence that higher-status members' opinions were more influential in reaching decisions than were the opinions of lower-status members. Similarly, in the 1959 James-Simon study, jurors with higher education participated in the discussion more than jurors with less education, but seemed to have no more influence on other jurors than did the lesser educated jurors. Bevan et al. (1958) conducted two studies in which the foreman, actually a confederate of the experimenter, argued strongly for a high settlement in a civil suit. In one of these studies, panels of subjects showed a greater increase in damages when the foreman was of lower prestige than when he was of higher prestige. In the second study, the prestige of the foreman did not influence the compensatory damages awarded by the mock juries.

Other demographic factors of jurors have been investigated. Jurors' age and religious preference were found not to affect decisions of real jurors listening to a recorded house-breaking or incest case (Simon, 1967). Place of residence was found to be an influential variable in the decisions of simulated jurors. The results of the Rose and Prell (1955) study showed that subjects from small towns and rural areas were more likely than other subjects to make class distinctions in assessing fines. These subjects also assessed higher fines and longer prison sentences than did other subjects.

Several studies have suggested that subjects who favor capital punishment are conviction-prone relative to subjects who do not favor capital punishment (Jurow, 1971; Wilson, 1964; Bronson, 1970; Goldberg, 1970). Goldberg (1970) determined that college students who had no scruples against the death penalty assessed more severe sentences and acquitted less on grounds of insanity in sixteen cases in which the death penalty could have been given than did subjects who opposed capital punishment. Jurow (1971) reported that the more the industrial workers in his study favored capital punishment, the more likely they were to be politically conservative and punitive in assigning penalties upon conviction. Bronson (1970) interviewed 700 prospective jurors in Colorado. He found that the more strongly these respondents favored capital punishment, the more likely they were to vote for conviction. Surprisingly, jurors' attitudes toward the mentally ill, toward various forms of sexual expression, and the jurors' knowledge of and attitudes about psychiatric interpretations of motivations and behavior did not influence their decisions regarding an incest case (or a house-breaking case) in which the defendants pleaded insanity (Simon, 1967).

The personality variable of authoritarianism has received considerable empirical attention. Boehm (1968) asked college students individually to reach a verdict in a manslaughter case. She concluded that authoritarian subjects are relatively acquittal-prone. Mitchell and Byrne (1973) conducted a study in which college students were asked to render individual determinations of guilt and assessments of punishment in a case involving theft of an examination from a college departmental office. These authors found an interaction between authoritarianism and similarity of the defendant to the subject. When the defendant was similar to the subject, authoritarians were less certain of his guilt than were subjects low on authoritarianism. When the defendant was dissimilar to the subjects, authoritarians recommended more severe punishment than did nonauthoritarians. Jurow (1971) ascertained that the more his subjects favored capital punishment, the more likely they were to be authoritarians. Hatton et al. (1971), in a civil suit based upon a driver-pedestrian accident, found no significant differences in sentencing or in questionnaire data attributable to subjects' dogmatism scores.

Bevan et al. (1958) reported some evidence suggesting that the nature of the foreman's leadership influenced jury decisions in a simulation of a civil suit. In one of their two studies, simulated jurors awarded higher damages (in accordance with the wishes of the confederate-foreman) when the foreman led autocratically than when he led democratically. In the other study, there was no differential award based upon type of leadership of the foreman.

Data From Jury Trials

This section reviews studies that have utilized actual trial data in order to examine the influence of juror characteristics. The variables that have been investigated are sex, socioeconomic status, occupational variables, previous experience as a juror, various life history characteristics, race, and political affiliation.

Sex. Civil suits are the source of all of the data in which the sex of the juror has been studied. The data are contradictory. Nagel and Weitzman (1971), using data from Jury Verdict Research, Inc., reported that in personal injury cases predominantly male juries awarded higher damages to male plaintiffs than did predominantly female juries; and that predominantly female juries awarded higher damages to female plaintiffs than did predominantly male juries. But other data from the same source have shown that jurors found in favor of plaintiffs of the opposite sex more than they did plaintiffs of their own sex. In addition, plaintiffs win approximately the same percentage of cases, whether the jury is composed predominantly of men or of women (Jury Verdict Research, Inc., 1966: vol. 7). Snyder (1971) determined that all-male juries awarded more money in damages than did juries composed of both males and females, and that they were more likely to decide in favor of a "superior status litigant"—that is, a man, a Caucasian, an adult, or a business (rather than an individual).

Socioeconomic status. Socioeconomic status has been shown to be an important variable in the rendering of verdicts. In a study of defendents and juries from one hundred criminal trials, juries who found the defendant guilty had a higher mean prestige rating than did juries who found the defendant not guilty (Adler, 1973). In over 80% of the cases, there was a greater discrepancy between the defendant who was found guilty and his jury than between the defendant who was found not guilty and his jury. Reed (1965) determined that the socioeconomic status of civil jurors in Baton Rouge was unrelated to their decisions, but that higher-status petit jurors were more likely to find the defendant guilty than were lower-status petit jurors.

The occupations of civil jurors have been found to have a significant impact upon their verdicts and the damages they award. For example, professional people decide in favor of the plaintiff 9% more than the national average for favorable decisions to the plaintiff, and they assess awards 6% higher than the national average for compensatory damages (Jury Verdict Research, Inc., 1968-1969: vol. 8). Hermann (1970) noted that retirement was inversely related to generosity, that housewives were not very favorable jurors from the point of view of the plaintiff either in assessing liability or damages, and that jurors who favored the plaintiff on liability usually voted for smaller than average awards. Also the occupational background of the juror and of the plaintiff interact significantly in the determination of verdicts. Most jurors favor plaintiffs of their own occupational group. For example, professional people favor other professionals most and executives least (Jury Verdict Research, Inc., 1968-1969: vol. 8).

Broeder (1965d) reported that occupational expertise affected the decision rendered in eight out of sixteen civil cases from which he interviewed jurors, and in none of the seven criminal cases investigated. Similarly, in four of the seven criminal cases, the jurors' occupations biased their points of view concerning the evidence.

Prior service on juries. Several studies have examined the influence of prior service as jurors on decisions rendered. Reed (1965) showed that the petit jurors he studied who had previous experience as jurors found the defendant guilty more often than the petit jurors without previous jury experience. Broeder (1965a) determined that jurors who had served in similar cases tended to use the verdict reached in the prior case as a standard by which to judge the current case. Previous service led to various individual reactions, but overall tended to give jurors confidence in their abilities as jurors.

Place of birth, ethnicity, and race. Several different life history characteristics have been examined. Reed (1965) ascertained that age, size of the firm with which the juror was associated, birthplace, and years of residency in Baton Rouge were variables not associated with differential jury decisions of civil jurors in Baton Rouge. But petit jurors with Anglo-Saxon birthplaces rendered more guilty verdicts than did petit jurors with French birthplaces. In a survey of jurors from New Mexico, Grisham and Lawless (1973) found that those jurors from the most densely populated county in the state were less likely than jurors from less populous areas to have served on criminal juries rendering guilty verdicts.

Broeder (1959) concluded that jurors of German and British descent were more likely to favor the government in criminal cases, while jurors of Slavic and Italian descent were more likely to favor the defense. In civil suits, he found that awards in eastern courts were 40% to 50% higher than if the court was located in the rural Midwest or the South. Kalven and Zeisel (1966) reported that criminal juries along the two seacoasts were more generous than juries from the Midwest and the South. They noted also that the larger the community from which the jury came, the larger the award granted.

In two studies (Broeder, 1959; Simon, 1967) it was established that Blacks were more likely to favor acquittal than were whites.

Political affiliation. Hermann (1970) found that registered Democrats were more favorable to the personal injury plaintiff than were registered Republicans. Democrats assessed damages 8% higher than the national average, while Republicans assessed damages 2% lower than the average. A juror not registered with either party was least favorable to the plaintiff, especially to minor plaintiffs.

Summary of Findings: Juror Characteristics

The experimental data in which the sex of the juror served as an independent variable established few consistent differences between the decisions of male and female jurors. The bulk of the data suggested that men are more active in jury deliberations than women and thus may be more influential in determining verdicts. All of the actual trial data relating to sex were based upon civil suits. Jurors favored plaintiffs of their own sex in verdicts, but consistently awarded higher damages to men than to women.

The experimental data suggested that higher-status jurors are harsher in reaching decisions and in assessing fines and are less likely to be differentially influenced by the socioeconomic status of the defendant than are lower-status jurors. Higher-status jurors appeared to be more active, but no more effective, than lower-status jurors. The majority of the trial data was consistent with the experimental data in showing that socioeconomic status is positively correlated with guilty verdicts and with relatively lengthy sentences.

There is a good deal of data pertaining to jury selection which strongly suggests that socioeconomic discrimination is promoted by the selection procedure for jury duty. For example, Robinson (1950) determined that potential jurors of lower occupational levels or lower economic status were systematically excluded from jury duty in the Los Angeles Criminal Courts from 1935 to 1947. Kuhn (1968) found that jury lists were based upon economic sources and that education, economic hardship, and "intelligence, judgment, and character" were preemptory challenges used to exclude jurors on the basis of race. Mills (1962) compared grand and petit jurors with the eligible labor force (as taken from census data) in the district of Maryland. He discovered overrepresentation mostly in professional, managerial, and sales occupations and underrepresentation primarily among craftsmen, operatives, service workers, and laborers. Of the ten categories examined, nine were statistically different from chance deviation.

Data from personal injury cases demonstrated that the juror's occupation has a definite influence upon the verdict reached and upon the award assessed. These data also indicated that the occupation of the plaintiff interacts in the rendering of verdicts and in the determination of awards. Occupational bias appeared in other ways as well. Occupational expertise was shown to affect decisions in civil suits, while jurors' occupational bias affected decisions in criminal cases.

Several studies employing actual trial data found that place of residency and national origin were influential variables in determining the verdict rendered in criminal cases. In civil suits, large awards are associated with eastern courts, and in criminal suits, with courts on both coasts. The larger the community from which the jury came, the larger the award. These data are consistent with experimental evidence which suggested that jurors from cities were more lenient in verdicts and in sentencing than jurors from small towns and rural areas.

Using trial data it was argued that in civil suits Democrats are most favorable to the plaintiff, while jurors not registered with either major political party are least favorable to the plaintiff.

Experimental data suggested that subjects who favor capital punishment and authoritarian subjects are more severe in rendering verdicts and in sentencing than are subjects opposed to capital punishment and nonauthoritarian subjects.

There is trial data showing that Blacks are more likely to favor acquittal in criminal cases than are whites.

While there is little data from jury trials documenting racial prejudice on the part of jurors, jury selection procedures argue for the belief in such a phenomenon. There are considerable data demonstrating the lack of representation of minority citizens on jury panels. For example, Lindquist (1967) cited an empirical study of southern federal courts in which it was determined that the percentage of Black representation on juries in these courts was generally much lower than the percentage of Blacks of jury service age in such districts. Finkelstein (1966) examined two cases where Blacks were convicted and where the courts ruled there was no evidence of racial discrimination. In one case, a total of seventeen Blacks had served on twelve grand juries. Finkelstein calculated the chance of this proportion being consistent with random selection at one in one thousand. In the second case there was a claim of discrimination in grand jury venires, since venires with five or fewer Blacks appeared in thirty consecutive cases. The probability of such a result appearing by chance was shown to be one in less than one hundred million. Crockett (1971) noted that Black jurors especially tended to be eliminated from service when there was a Black litigant involved. Broeder (1965c) reported that those Black jurors who were selected to serve in the cases he investigated were ignored by the other jurors. Of course, discrimination against potential jurors of low socioeconomic status often is discrimination against minority jurors as well.

CONCLUSIONS

A great number of variables have been shown to have influenced the jury verdict. However, with few exceptions, there are too little data employing these variables to draw firm conclusions about their effects. Much more data need to be collected, both from laboratory experimentation and from actual criminal trials, to strengthen the tentative conclusions that can be made at present. But at the present time, replication is needed more than additional studies pointing to yet more social or personal characteristics that may affect the outcome of jury trials.

Two variables especially need continued study: race and sex. There is very little research dealing with racial discrimination in the criminal court system, and some of it is less experimental than anecdotal. Data pertaining to characteristics of both litigants and jurors are needed. The small amount of data about the sex of litigants is contradictory, and information concerning jurors is lacking. The importance, pervasiveness, and interest in such a variable hardly can be exaggerated.

Socioeconomic status is the variable that most clearly shows the presence of discrimination in the criminal jury system. There are experimental and trial data which show the effect of such discrimination both on the part of particular types of jurors and toward particular types of litigants. The documentation of such bias hopefully will sensitize attorneys to the kinds of jurors who are more and less likely to show bias toward their clients. Perhaps the information concerning socioeconomic discrimination against certain types of litigants can be disseminated directly to jurors in an attempt to discourage such discrimination.

The data that have been gathered about these and other characteristics of jurors and litigants might be more useful to the reader if they could be subsumed under a smaller number of variables which incorporate the majority of the findings. A combination of the concepts of the social similarity of the litigant to the juror and of the anticipated social consequence of the loss to society of the services of the litigant might be a possible starting point for synthesis. The similarity hypothesis seems consistent with the findings that higher-status jurors are more punitive, that occupational biases, physical appearance, political affiliation, and similarity of attitudes between jurors and litigants affect jurors' decisions, and that there may be discrimination based on sex and race in the jury system. The loss-of-services hypothesis can include the findings that jurors favor higher-status litigants and litigants without prior convictions, and that jurors may favor white Anglo litigants and those of good character. If future research could be guided by an exploration of these or other small groupings of variables, some order might be brought to this broad and poorly integrated area of study.

The impact on jury verdicts of the social and personal characteristics of counsel, judges, and witnesses was not reviewed because there are practically no data on those topics. But the large number of variables that has been shown to influence jury decisions from the point of view of juror and litigant characteristics suggests that such data are worthy of collection.

Both of the types of data that have been examined, the experimental and the trial, have drawbacks. The experimental data are subject to the charge of unreality. Only replication of findings and consistency with trial data can refute or support such a criticism. But there are difficulties with the actual trial data as well. In using actual trial data to investigate a single independent variable, one cannot know how many factors might be varying together. For this reason, the use of partial correlation to control for the presence of extraneous variables is most important. In most of the studies that have been done of actual jury trials, simple correlational techniques have been used. The obvious cost of this practice is that the relationships reported could be spurious, and the actual relationship may be under the control of entirely different variables.

The collection of both experimental and trial data toward the goal of uncovering biases in the criminal trial system seems a worthy and rewarding undertaking. The results of such research have obvious critical implications for our criminal justice system. In the next decade, much important information should be uncovered. Careful experimentation, use of sophisticated statistical techniques, and patient replication should continue to produce a wealth of interesting and useful findings.

REFERENCES

ADLER, F. (1973) "Socioeconomic factors influencing jury verdicts." New York University Review of Law and Social Change 3: 1-10.

ALLISON, J. L. (1964) "Poverty and the administration of justice in the criminal courts." Journal of Criminal Law, Criminology, and Police Science 55: 241-245.

BENSING, R. and O. SCHROEDER (1960) Homicide in an Urban Community. Springfield, Ill.: Charles C. Thomas.

BEVAN, W., R. S. ALBERT, P. R. LOISEAUX, P. N. MAYFIELD, and G. WRIGHT (1958) "Jury behavior as a function of the prestige of the foreman and the nature of his leadership." Journal of Public Law 7: 419-449.

BING, S. and S. ROSENFELD (1970) "A report by the lawyer's committee for civil rights under law, to the governor's committee on law enforcement, and administration of justice and the quality of justice in the lower criminal courts of metropolitan Boston." Unpublished manuscript cited in D. A. Bell, Jr. (1973) "Racism in American courts: cause for Black disruption or despair?" California Law Review 61: 165-203.

BLOOMSTEIN, M. J. (1968) Verdict: The Jury System. New York: Dodd, Mead.

BOEHM, V. B. (1968) "Mr. Prejudice, Miss Sympathy, and the authoritarian personality: an application of psychological measuring techniques to the problem of jury bias." Wisconsin Law Review: 734-747.

BROEDER, D. W. (1965a) "Previous jury trial service as affecting juror behavior." Insurance Law Journal: 138-143.

——— (1965b) "Plaintiff's family status as affecting juror behavior: some tentative insights." Journal of Public Law 14: 131-143.

——— (1965c) "The Negro in court." Duke Law Review (Winter): 17-31.

——— (1965d) "Occupational expertise and bias as affecting juror behavior: a preliminary look." New York University Law Review 40: 1079-1100.

——— (1959) "The University of Chicago jury project." Nebraska Law Review 38: 744-760.

BRONSON, E. J. (1970) "On the conviction processes and representativeness of the death-qualified jury: an empirical study of Colorado veniremen." Colorado Law Review 42 (May): 1-32.

BROWN, F. K. (1973) "Choice shifts in simulated juries." Presented at the annual meeting of the American Sociological Association, New York.

BULLOCK, R. (1961) "Significance of the racial factor in the length of prison sentences." Journal of Criminal Law 52: 411-415.

CHIRICOS, T. and G. WALDO (1971) "Inequality in the imposition of a criminal label." Unpublished study prepared for the Correctional and Criminological Research Center, Florida State University, cited in D. A. Bell, Jr. (1973) "Racism in American courts: cause for Black disruption or despair?" California Law Review 61: 165-203.

CROCKETT, G. W. Jr. (1971) "Racism in the courts." Journal of Public Law 20: 384-389.

EFRAN, M. G. (1974) "The effect of physical appearance on the judgment of guilt, interpersonal attraction, and severity of recommended punishment in a simulated jury task." Journal of Research in Personality 8: 45-54.

FINKELSTEIN, M. O. (1966) "The application of statistical decision theory to the jury discrimination cases." Harvard Law Review 80 (December): 338-376.

FOSS, R. D. (1973) "Group dynamics in the simulated jury trial: misleading conclusions through naivete." Presented at the annual meeting of the Western Psychological Association, Annaheim, California.

GERARD, J. B. and T. R. TERRY, Jr. (1970) "Discrimination against Negroes in the administration of criminal law in Missouri." Washington State University Law Quarterly: 415-437.

GOLDBERG, F. (1970) "Toward expansion of Witherspoon: capital scruples, jury bias, and use of psychological data to raise presumptions in the law." Harvard Civil Rights Liberties Law Review 5: 53-69.

GREEN, E. (1964) "Inter- and intra-racial crime relative to sentencing." Journal of Criminal Law, Criminology, and Police Science 55: 348-358.

——— (1961) Judicial Attitudes in Sentencing. London: Macmillan.

GRIFFITT, W. and T. JACKSON (1973) "Simulated jury decisions: the influence of jury-defendant attitude similarity-dissimilarity." Social Behavior and Personality 1: 1-7.

GRISHAM, T. L. and S. F. LAWLESS (1973) "Jurors judge justice: a survey of criminal jurors." New Mexico Law Review 3: 352-363.

HATTON, D. E., J. R. SNORTUM, and S. OSCAMP (1971) "The effects of biasing information and dogmatism upon witness testimony." Psychonomic Science 23: 425-427.

HERMANN, P. J. (1970) "Occupations of jurors as an influence on their verdict." Forum 5: 150-155.

JAMES-SIMON, R. M. (1959) "Status and competence in jury deliberations." American Journal of Sociology 64: 563-570.

JUROW, G. L. (1971) "New data on the effect of a 'death qualified' jury on the guilt determination process." Harvard Law Review 84: 567-611.

Jury Verdict Research, Incorporated (1964-1969) Personal Injury Valuation Handbook (vols. 5-8).

KALVEN, H. Jr. and H. ZEISEL (1966) The American Jury. Boston: Little, Brown.

KAPLAN, K. J. and R. J. SIMON (1972) "Latitude and severity of sentencing options, race of the victim, and decisions of simulated jurors: some issues arising from the 'Algiers Motel' trial." Law and Society Review 7: 87-98.

KATZ, L. S. (1968-1969) "The twelve man jury." Trial 5 (December-January): 39-40, 42.

KUHN, R. S. (1968) "Jury discrimination: the next phase." Southern California Law Review 41: 235-328.

KULKA, R. A. and J. B. KESSLER (1973) "Is justice really blind? The influence of physical attractiveness on decisions of simulated jurors." Presented at the national meetings of the Speech Communication Association, New York, November.

LANDY, D. and E. ARONSON (1969) "The influence of the character of the criminal and his victim on the decisions of simulated jurors." Journal of Experimental Social Psychology 5: 141-152.

LINDQUIST, C. A. (1967) "An analysis of juror selection procedure in the United States district courts." Temple Law Quarterly 41: 32-50.

McCART, S. W. (1964) Trial by Jury. New York: Chilton.

MILLS, E. S. (1962) "A statistical study of occupations of jurors in a United States district court." Maryland Law Review 22: 205-214.

MITCHELL, H. E. and D. BYRNE (1973) "The defendant's dilemma: effect of jurors' attitudes and authoritarianism on judicial decisions." Journal of Personality and Social Psychology 25: 123-129.

NAGEL, S. S. (1969) The Legal Process from a Behavioral Perspective. Homewood, Ill.: Dorsey.

——— and L. J. WEITZMAN (1971) "Women as litigants." Hastings Law Journal 23: 171-198.

President's Commission on Law Enforcement and Administration of Justice (1967) The Challenge of Crime in a Free Society: A Report. Washington, D.C.: Government Printing Office.

REED, J. P. (1965) "Jury deliberations, voting, and verdict trends." Southwestern Social Science Quarterly 65: 361-374.

ROBINSON, W. S. (1950) "Bias, probability, and trial by jury." American Sociological Review 15: 73-78.

ROSE, A. M. and A. E. PRELL (1955) "Does the punishment fit the crime? A study in social valuation." American Journal of Sociology 61: 247-259.

Saul R. Levin Memorial Foundation, Incorporated (1959) "Report of study of recorder's court over twenty-month period, November 1, 1957 through June 30, 1959." Unpublished manuscript cited in M. E. Hindelang (1969) "Equality under the law." Journal of Criminal Law, Criminology, and Police Science 60: 306-313.

SIGALL, H. and N. OSTROVE (1975) "Beautiful but dangerous: effect of offender attractiveness and nature of the crime on juridic judgment." Journal of Personality and Social Psychology (in press).

SILVERSTEIN, L. (1965) Defense of the Poor in Criminal Cases in American State Courts. Chicago: American Bar Foundation.

SIMON, R. J. (1967) The Jury and the Defense of Insanity. Boston: Little, Brown.

SNYDER, E. C. (1971) "Sex role differential and juror decisions." Sociology and Social Research 55: 442-448.

Stanford Law Review (1969) "A study of the California penalty jury in first-degree-murder cases." Stanford Law Review 21: 1296-1497.

STRODTBECK, F. L. and R. D. MANN (1956) "Sex role differentiation in jury deliberations." Sociometry 19: 3-11.

STRODTBECK, F. L., R. M. JAMES, and C. HAWKINS (1957) "Social status in jury deliberations." American Sociological Review 22: 713-719.

STEPHAN, C. (1974) "Sex prejudice in jury simulation." Journal of Psychology 88: 305-312.

——— and J. C. TULLY (1973) "The influence of physical attractiveness of a plaintiff on the decisions of simulated jurors." Paper read at the meetings of the North Central Sociological Association, Cincinnati.

SUTHERLAND, E. H. and D. R. CRESSEY (1966) Principles of Criminology (seventh ed.). New York: Lippincott.

VINES, N. and M. JACOBS (1963) "Studies in judicial politics," pp. 77-98 in Tulane Studies in Political Science, vol. 8.

WARREN, D. (1970) "Justice in the Recorder's Court of Detroit." Unpublished study cited in D. A. Bell, Jr. (1970) "Racism in American courts: cause for Black disruption or despair?" California Law Review 61: 165-203.

WILSON, W. (1964) "Belief in capital punishment and jury performances." Unpublished manuscript, University of Texas, cited in G. L. Jurow (1971) "New data on the effect of a 'death qualified' jury on the guilt determination process." Harvard Law Review 84: 567-611.

5

THE IMPACT OF PRETRIAL PUBLICITY ON JURORS' VERDICTS

ALICE M. PADAWER-SINGER and
ALLEN H. BARTON

An experiment was conducted under realistic conditions to determine the extent to which jurors are prejudiced by exposure to specific media information, the characteristics of media-susceptible and influenced jurors, and possible remedies for counteracting prejudice in the minds of jurors.

In carefully anonymous experiments run in courts in two different counties of New York, the authors discovered that case-specific publicity is not the only factor which may prejudice a jury. Events on a national or international scale may have an equally biasing effect, predisposing a jury to either a "hard nosed" approach in favor of stringent anti-crime legislation or, conversely, engendering sympathy for specific defendants under certain circumstances. In either case, the publicity apparently affects the jury's ability to absorb and objectively analyze clear-cut data. Concomitantly, the experiments showed "prejudiced" jurors (exposed to case-specific publicity) more likely to convict on the basis of the same set of evidence which would not necessarily predispose conviction by "nonprejudiced" jurors (not exposed to case-specific publicity).

Although the authors do not conclude that unfavorable publicity will either prejudice all juries or damage all defendants, they found that more jurors "exposed" to unfavorable publicity find the defendant guilty than do jurors who are not so exposed. The authors strongly advocate the careful and thorough use of voir dire to minimize pretrial bias.

Chapter 5

THE IMPACT OF PRETRIAL PUBLICITY
ON JURORS' VERDICTS

ALICE M. PADAWER-SINGER and
ALLEN H. BARTON

The impact of pretrial publicity on jurors' verdicts is an issue arising from the "effects of news reporting, whether in print or by broadcast media upon the fairness of the trial" (Meyer, 1970: 287). A conflict has emerged between two constitutional guarantees: the rights of defendants to a fair trial and the freedom of the press. This conflict results in what Judge Bernard S. Meyer (1970) has described as "one of the vexing problems for a judge handling a criminal trial."

THE FREE PRESS—FAIR TRIAL PROBLEM

Pretrial publicity has led to reversal of verdicts on appeal,[1] to motions for mistrial, for change of venue, and for dismissal on the grounds that a fair trial is not possible in the context of sensational publicity.[2] Consequently, pretrial publicity may unduly lengthen the time necessary to perform voir dire examinations, causing long delays and heavy expenses; in turn, protracted selection of jurors leads to additional news media coverage. The contentions of defense lawyers that defendants cannot receive a fair trial may adversely affect public trust in the administration of justice.

For example, in the Charles Manson murder case in Los Angeles, one of the defense lawyers told newsmen that "the case has been prejudiced through pretrial publicity to the point of not allowing a fair trial." Three times the lawyers asked that the trial be called off, and three times Superior Court Judge Charles H. Older denied the motions. Coprosecutor Vincent Bugliosi commented that this would be one of the "biggest cases in history regarding prejudicial publicity."[3] In the case of Angela Davis, a defense lawyer declared that extensive trial publicity had "made it impossible for her to receive a fair trial anywhere in the country."[4]

Cases receiving publicity represent a variety of crimes. Sensational cases, as may be seen in some of the quotations above, are reported not only throughout the country but throughout the world.[5] Contentions that defendants may not receive a fair trial reach an ever-increasing audience.

In summary, the issue of trial publicity leads to protracted selection of jurors, to various motions which in turn create more delays, to greater costs, to mistrials with additional burdens in the already congested court calendars, and possibly to public loss of confidence and alienation from the legal system. In addition to the public's fear of possible miscarriages of justice, the issue of Free Press—Fair Trial has resulted in added cost of time and money through delays in court arising from motions and hearings.

The public is mainly aware of the sensational trials covered by the news media and hardly aware of the trials which do not receive publicity and in which the issue of Free Press—Fair Trial is absent. Subsequent public loss of confidence may increase the alienation of large segments of our population and the disregard of laws.

PREVIOUS STUDIES OF FREE PRESS—FAIR TRIAL

Previously the problem of Free Press—Fair Trial has been discussed in descriptions of highly publicized trials and in expressed opinions of the press, the bar, and the judiciary about the effects of news media publicity on the public, on the procedure in court, on jury behavior and verdicts.[6] Most simulation experiments have been done with paper-and-pencil description of cases, or with sound tapes of highly simplified "cases"; individuals or groups of individuals acting as jurors are asked to render a verdict. Mock jurors are either college students (e.g., Kline and Jess, 1966) or come from a list of registered voters of upper middle-class background who volunteered to take part in these experiments (e.g., Simon, 1966). The settings of these paper-and-pencil trials (e.g., Tans and Chaffee, 1966) and of recordings of simulated trials (as in Simon, 1966) have varied from experiment to experiment, except for one common similarity: no experiment on Free Press—Fair Trial has yet been held in the authentic setting of the courtroom. Again the underlying assumption of previous studies is that of high correspondence between simulation and the real situation. Yet, unless utmost realism is achieved not only in the setting of jury studies, but in the choice of juror population, in the trials presented and in the deliberation process, the results will not add persuasive data to the debate on Free Press—Fair Trial. Lawyers and journalists will question the relevance of these studies to real juries in court.

Studies of Free Press—Fair Trial have great potential for influencing policy over and above theoretical value and interest. If these studies are to receive wide recognition from all interests involved—from judges, lawyers, journalists, and behavioral scientists—they must satisfy the criteria of realism and scientific control. The situation must be authentic (courtroom setting); the population must be that of the usual jury population; the courtroom procedure ought to be followed wherever possible; the materials in the study (such as the trials and newspaper clippings) must correspond to real trials and newspapers; and a rigorous research design must be followed.

THE FREE PRESS—FAIR TRIAL PROJECT

The Free Press—Fair Trial Project[7] has conducted experimental research in the field under realistic conditions with the following purposes in mind:

(a) to determine whether and to what extent prejudicial effects occur when jurors are exposed to specific types of information in the news media;

(b) to determine the characteristics of jurors who are susceptible to the influence of particular types of information; and

(c) to determine possible means of effectively counteracting prejudices.

This is the first interdisciplinary, experimental study of Free Press—Fair Trial carried out in the field, with a population of jurors in an actual courtroom setting and with the active assistance of the judiciary, the bar, and the news media. It demonstrates the feasibility of realistic jury experiments. In this study, jurors were called from the regular jury pools, asked to participate in the study, and each jury was then given either "prejudicial" or "nonprejudicial" newspaper clippings referring to the defendant to read. Each jury listened to a tape of a trial in a courtroom, then retired to a jury room for deliberations. The jury reached a verdict (or pronounced itself deadlocked) and indicated its final vote. Jurors then answered a long questionnaire. Ten experimental juries were run in the Supreme Court of the State of New York, Mineola, Nassau County, and 23 in the Supreme Court of the State of New York, Brooklyn, Kings County.[8]

Materials for the Experiments

The choice of a trial. In persistent attempts at faithful reproduction of the "real world," a search for films of a real trial had been instituted. Unfortunately, the effort to find a filmed trial suitable to our experiments proved fruitless. An inquiry was made into the possibility of filming a real trial in the few states which allow cameras to be introduced in court. Since the cost of such films is high and since these films—because of their uniqueness at that time [9]—would have constituted historical and social documents of the administration of justice in our times, consent to use these films for experimental and educational purposes (in libraries of schools of law and journalism, as didactic aids in training law students) was sought and obtained. However, the available funds precluded the filming of a trial; we decided then to run the experiments with audiotapes based on a real trial. This step took quite some time because a suitable trial had to present the following features:

(1) The prosecution had based its case mainly on weak circumstantial evidence;

(2) The defendant had not taken the stand.

These two main requirements were set up in order to study the effects of revealing the criminal background of the defendant and an alleged retracted confession on jury verdicts.

Prejudices can best be demonstrated in a trial in which the prosecution's case is not too strong, rather than a case in which the evidence points overwhelmingly to the guilt of the defendant. The second requirement insured that the defendant would not be cross-examined as to his background and as to a confession. These two requirements then allowed the introduction of information pertaining to the criminal background of the defendant and alleged retracted confession in newspaper clippings.

After a careful search, a trial transcript which met our criteria was located and edited by two lawyers, a writer, and the experimenter. [10] A three-hour audiotape based on the edited transcript was produced.

Audiotapes. The audiotapes were the vehicle through which the trial was presented to the jury. This was a difficult concession made to the reality of meager funds, and a step away from the realism inherent in a film of an actual or of a staged trial. The audiotapes represent the collaboration of about thirty student volunteers from various colleges and high schools who met to read the transcript and to be recorded under the direction and coordination of the writer, an attorney, a newsman, and two college students. [11] The tapes were divided into three parts, allowing the jurors to take two breaks: one between the first two parts containing opening statements, examinations, and cross-examinations of witnesses for the prosecution and for the defense; and one break before the third part which contained the lawyers' summations and the judge's charge to the jury.

Description of the murder case on audiotapes. A prominent woman in Washington, D.C., was found shot to death in a park. A man was found in the area and arrested. He was identified by someone who had seen him from over 100 feet away as the man who bent over the victim a short time after the witness had heard the victim's cries. The gun was never found. The prosecution claimed that all official exits were closed only minutes after the murder had been committed. The defense established the existence of other unofficial, unmarked exits. The defendant did not take the stand. Lawyers presented their summations and the judge charged the jury.

Government exhibits. The two Government exhibits which were reproduced in the experiment consisted of (1) a picture of the scene of the murder with the locations indicating where the defendant's clothes and the victim's body were found, and (2) a map of the area. [12]

Newspaper clippings. Newspaper clippings were produced after an examination of the original publicity. Two presumably "prejudicial" elements were added: (1) as to the criminal background of the defendant, and (2) as to his alleged retracted confession. Neither of these pieces of information would be admissible in the trial since the defendant did not take the stand. Two sets of newspaper clippings were written: (1) the "prejudicial" set was composed of one newspaper clipping reporting the criminal background of the defendant, one clipping covering the alleged retracted confession, one "neutral" clipping dealing with facts which were admissible in court; (2) the "neutral" set contained three clippings similar to the prejudicial set, but omitted the "prejudicial" information. To keep the length of the articles identical in the two sets, additional presumably "neutral" filler material was included in the "neutral" set. The journalist who prepared the newspaper clippings, a lawyer, and the experimenter (social psychologist) judged this material as essentially faithful to the case and "neutral." [13]

The style of the news clippings was purposely left very dry; no sensationalism was allowed. What was investigated was the effect of cognitive information only, and not an added effect due to sensationalism. (This does not preclude the likelihood that cognitive information induces affective emotional reactions in jurors.)

Experimental Procedures: First Phase

This part of the study was conducted in the Supreme Court of the State of New York in Mineola, Nassau County. Jurors were selected at random from the court's jury pool, and impaneled without voir dire examinations. They were asked to participate in a jury experiment in which they would hear and decide a recorded reenactment of a case, with full knowledge that their decision would not influence the fate of any actual parties, but as a means of helping to improve the working of the courts by providing knowledge about the jury system through jurors' suggestions and direct participation in our study.

Exposure variable. Juries selected to be "exposed" were then given newspaper clippings to read which contained material reporting on the defendant's prior criminal record and his retracted confession for the crime now charged. Juries selected as "control" or "not exposed" juries read "neutral" press clippings omitting the presumably prejudicial information. Both sets of juries then listened to the audiotape of the trial, including the judge's instructions.

Data collected. The juries retired and deliberated for up to six hours, the maximum time available in the particular court situation. The deliberations were tape-recorded with their knowledge and consent. The jury reached a verdict, or found itself deadlocked, and returned to the courtroom to announce its outcome. This group outcome—a unanimous verdict, or the result of the final vote in the case of hung juries—was the first datum.

The jurors then answered a detailed questionnaire covering: how they would now individually decide the case; jurors' general demographic characteristics; previous personal experience with criminals and as jurors; perceived difficulty of decision; recall of facts favorable and unfavorable to the defendant; change of opinion during the deliberations; perceived group pressure; what their verdict would have been in case the motive for the crime had been rape, robbery, or mental illness; jurors' satisfaction or dissatisfaction with judge's instructions, whether the judge seemed to be pro- or antidefendant. The questionnaire also contained attitude statements on the role of the jurors; on the credibility of newspapers, TV, radio and magazines; on the treatment of criminals and defendants; on the rate of crime and the causes for crime; and finally, whether the tape recorder interfered with the free flow of discussion.

Each jury then took part in a free-wheeling group discussion with the experimenter, covering their reactions to the case, the study, the questionnaire, and anything they wanted to bring up spontaneously. The experimenter asked a few questions as to the jurors' wish to see a film of the trial and their knowledge about the rights of a defendant not to take the stand.

Anonymity was stressed throughout the study by assigning numbers to jurors, and requiring them only to write their numbers in the questionnaires, not their names. They were reminded that it was impossible to recognize one voice among twelve voices, especially since the experimenter had not met the jurors previously, and that anonymity was therefore preserved in the recorded deliberations.

Results: First Phase

Verdicts and alignment of jurors. There were five juries in each experimental condition. Each experiment was run in a maximum of two days' time. Most experiments resulted in hung juries because of the time constraint: four to six hours of deliberations constituted the maximum time available, and this time was fully utilized by most juries. In Table 1 we report the individual voters of jurors for hung juries and the verdicts which were reached in the other juries.

Inspection of Table 1 reveals that the alignment of individuals in the juries in the "prejudicial" condition differs markedly from that of the juries in the "nonprejudicial" condition. In the "prejudiced" juries, 47 out of 60 jurors (78%) decided the defendant was guilty; 22% decided he was not guilty. In the "nonprejudiced" juries, 33 out of 60 (55%) decided the defendant was guilty; and 45% decided he was not guilty. Only in a "nonprejudiced" jury had a unanimous verdict of "not guilty" been reached.

The votes of individual jurors at the final vote or verdict stage are not of course independent decisions, but are the result of a group process which tends toward, although it does not always reach, a group consensus. It is, therefore, not possible to apply significance tests to the difference in the individual juror postdeliberation votes. The percentage figures are reported only as a means of characterizing the two sets of juries as decision-making groups since, under the circumstance, within the short available time, most juries did not reach a group verdict.

In the unprejudiced juries, the ratio of 45% to 55% seems to indicate that the trial was well-chosen inasmuch as the prosecution did not have an overwhelmingly strong case. Only a little more than half of these jurors felt that the defendant was shown to be guilty beyond a reasonable doubt.

Table 1. FINAL VERDICTS* AND VOTES OF MINEOLA JURIES

	"Exposed" or "Prejudiced" Juries		Control or "Unprejudiced" Juries	
	Not Guilty	Guilty	Not Guilty	Guilty
	0	12	12	0
	2	10	8	4
	1	11	4	8
	5	7	3	9
	5	7	0	12
Jurors (n)	13	47	27	33
Percentage	22	78	45	55
Verdicts	0	1	1	1
Hung juries	4		3	

*Verdicts = 12 unanimous votes

Table 2. FIRST BALLOT AND FINAL VERDICT

Guilty votes on first ballot (n)	0	1-5	6	7-11	12
Final Verdict (%)					
Not guilty	100	91	50	5	–
Hung	–	7	–	9	–
Guilty	–	2	50	86	100
Total (%)	100	100	100	100	100
Number of cases	26	41	10	105	43

SOURCE: Kalven and Zeisel, 1966: 488

Data from 225 actual jury trials of criminal cases were compiled by the Jury Project of the University of Chicago, through interviews with jurors on completion of their term of service. Kalven and Zeisel (1966) conclude from these data (reproduced in Table 2 here) that "with very few exceptions the first ballot decides the outcome of the verdict." Furthermore, hung juries are rather rare, approximating 5% in two samples studied by Kalven and Zeisel. Therefore we may project that we would have ended up with guilty verdicts from all five exposed juries, but only three of the control juries, had more time been available for deliberations (see Table 3).

The number of cases under each condition is too small to provide either statistical significance or intuitive confidence in this result, but it is in the expected direction and it appears fairly large. It at least urges the researcher on to conduct further experiments to provide more adequate tests.

Experimental Procedures: Second Phase

The second phase of the 23 jury experiments was conducted in the Kings County Supreme Court, Brooklyn, New York. The experimental procedures were the same as in the first phase, with three exceptions:

(1) *Selection variable:* In addition to the exposed versus control treatment, a second experimental variation was imposed within both exposure groups: random selection from the general pool of jurors without voir dire examinations (as in Mineola) versus selection through customary voir dire examinations conducted by lawyers for the defense and the prosecution. Various lawyers from

Table 3. JURIES WITH GUILTY VERDICTS OR FINAL VOTES
       WITH MAJORITY FOR GUILTY (Mineola juries)

Exposed Juries	*Control Juries*	*Percentage Difference*
100%	60%	+40%
(5)	(5)	

Table 4. FOUR-WAY TREATMENT OF BROOKLYN JURIES

	Exposed	Not Exposed	
Voir dire	5	5 + 3*	13
No voir dire	5	5	10
	10	13	23

*Three additional jury experiments were conducted because of the observed tension due to the events at Kent State University and the nationwide closings of universities in May 1970.

the Legal Aid Society [14] and the District Attorney's office [15] volunteered to play these roles, while another lawyer acted as a judge and ruled on objections during jury selection. The purpose of this variation was to see whether selection through voir dire examinations—compared to selection of jurors from the general pool without voir dire examinations—reduced the possible prejudicial effect of the newspaper clippings on the "exposed" juries. The result was the four-way treatment described by Table 4.

(2) *Predeliberation ballot:* All juries in the second phase were asked, after hearing the trial, to fill out a secret ballot for the experimenter indicating their opinion as to whether the defendant was guilty or not guilty. They then proceeded to the deliberation.

(3) *Deliberation time:* Somewhat more time was available in the Brooklyn court, so that the jurors were more often able to reach a verdict.

Experimental sequence. A crucial problem in running a large series of jury experiments in one court is the possibility of contaminating jurors intended to be "unprejudiced" through contact with others who have gone through the "prejudicial" treatment, since they all return to the same jury room. A decision was therefore made to run the experiments in blocks of one treatment-combination at a time. The specific sequence of treatments was also influenced by the availability of volunteer lawyers to carry out voir dire examinations.

Ideally the treatments should be rotated in such a way that each one is spread over the entire fieldwork period—for example, by running sequences in which each of the four treatments is given in turn, followed by another set of all four treatments, and so on. This provides protection against the effects of outside events which might influence the behavior being studied. Unfortunately, this could not be done. During the fieldwork period in 1970, there was indeed a dramatic outside event—the U.S. invasion of Cambodia and Laos, with the resulting nationwide student demonstrations and the shooting of students on the campuses of Kent State University and Jackson State College. It is possible that at least one set of juries, representing a particular combination of exposure and selection variables, may have been influenced by this. We do not have hard data to show that this happened, but this was the impression of the field workers, based on conversations with these experimental jurors. Therefore an additional set of three juries was run with this combination, in an attempt to smooth out any temporary "backlash" effects due to generalized hostility against "trouble-makers."

Results: Second Phase

This paper reports only the result of the exposure to the press clippings. The analysis of the effectiveness of voir dire examination in controlling prejudice is complex: it depends on detailed comparisons of all four treatments, with five cases in each of three treatments and eight cases in the fourth treatment. Partially discussed in a previous article,[16] it will be reported in greater detail at a later date. The impact of the press clippings, on the other hand, should be fairly clear in an overall comparison of the ten "exposed" and the thirteen "not exposed" juries.

The results in terms of verdicts follow the lines of the hypothesis that the information contained in the "prejudicial" clippings does influence juries to bring in more guilty verdicts—6 out of 10, compared with 2 out of 13. Altogether, 69% of the "exposed" jurors ended up voting for guilty, compared with only 35% of the "nonexposed" jurors. Again we must emphasize that the

Table 5. FINAL VERDICTS AND VOTES OF BROOKLYN JURORS

	"Exposed"		"Not Exposed"		
	Not Guilty	Guilty	Not Guilty	Guilty	Undecided
	0	12	12	0	
	0	12	12	0	
	0	12	12	0	
	12	0	9	3	
	12	0	5	4	3
	12	0	0	12	
	0	12	1	11	
	0	12	5	4	2
	0	12	0	12	
	1	11	12	0	
			10	2	
			5	7	
			12	0	
Jurors (n)	37	83	86	55	5
Percentage	31	69	62	35	3
Verdicts	3	6	5	2	
Hung juries	1		6		

Table 6. JURIES WITH GUILTY VERDICTS OR FINAL VOTES
WITH MAJORITY FOR GUILTY (Brooklyn juries)

Exposed Juries	Control Juries	Percentage Difference
70%	31%	+39%
(10)	(13)	

individual juror votes are not actually independent, but are subject to group effects which render significance tests inapplicable at the individual level. Looking at the jury as a unit of analysis, the results of the Brooklyn experiment are summarized in Tables 5 and 6.

Again making the assumption that the majorities would win in most cases if enough time for deliberation were available, there would be 39% more guilty verdicts among the exposed juries. The difference between exposed and unexposed Brooklyn juries is virtually identical with that found in the first ten experiments in Mineola. (The rate of convictions by our Brooklyn juries is lower by 30% under each condition than the rate of our Mineola juries. Whether this is due to differences in backgrounds and attitudes of suburban versus city residents will be explored using the questionnaire materials.)

If we combine all of the Mineola and Brooklyn experiments to compare the exposed and control juries, we obtain a result which suggests that the prejudicial materials used in our experiments result in doubling the rate of guilty verdicts which might be expected (see Table 7).

This result is statistically significant (by the chi-square test) at the .05 level, meaning that there is less than one chance in twenty of its being due to mere chance fluctuations in the outcomes.

CONCLUSION AND DISCUSSION

Only part of our data has been presented; this part of the study was intended to test one of the legal system's devices for controlling prejudice. These data suggest that one solution perhaps lies in thorough voir dire examinations in which lawyers can stress the importance of examining the evidence and rejecting

Table 7. JURIES WITH GUILTY VERDICTS OR FINAL VOTES
WITH MAJORITY FOR GUILTY (Combined juries)

Exposed Juries	Control Juries	Percentage Difference
80%	39%	+41%
(15)	(18)	

prejudicial information which is not part of the trial. (Additional data to be reported in later publications will deal with the effects of lawyer's voir dire examinations—jury questioning and selection by lawyers—as compared with random selection of jurors from the jury pool without any screening.) Clear, short, simple judges' charges to that effect would also impress upon jurors that only the facts admitted in the trial should be considered.

In recent years, many defendants have been exposed to massive unfavorable publicity and still been found not guilty by juries. This leads one to speculate that different kinds of unfavorable publicity may have different outcomes, whether because of the political or nonpolitical nature of the cases or the national-versus-local type of publicity, among many other factors, and that methods of screening and instructing jurors to avoid prejudice do exist.

Specific news media publicity is not the only factor which prejudices jurors against or predisposes them to be favorable toward defendants in various cases. Factors such as national and international events may, on one hand, engender an atmosphere of hostility—which presumably is displaced onto defendants in the case of jurors, or which gives rise to sentiments in favor of stringent legislation, such as advocating the death penalty as a deterrent to crime (with disregard for the importance of collecting and analyzing empirically clearcut data). On the other hand, national and international factors may also engender sympathy for specific defendants—for example, when crimes have been committed in the name of freedom, in the name of civil rights, and so on.

The experimental procedures which have been developed in this study can reliably produce "prejudiced" juries, in the sense of juries more likely to convict on a given set of evidence than juries not exposed to prejudicial information. This gives us a baseline from which to measure the effectiveness of various remedies. The main problems with such experiments are the time they take on the part of jurors, court personnel, and experimenters; the required efforts from a system already overburdened; and the money necessary to run these experiments and to analyze the data. But if, through such experiments, reliable methods for reducing prejudicial effects of pretrial news coverage without interfering with the freedom of the press can be found, these experiments will be worth the time and money.

The results of the Free Press—Fair Trial experiments show a definite impact of newspaper stories which contain information as to the defendant's previous criminal record and an alleged retracted confession. The experiments cannot be generalized to mean that any kind of unfavorable publicity is equally damaging, but they clearly show that there is a serious problem at least insofar as these kinds of information are concerned. Future reporting of data on voir dire examinations in our experiments and discussion of the implications of our findings will suggest the importance of screening and instructing jurors.

NOTES

1. See, for example, *Tuscaloosa News,* May 17, 1972, p. 16:

The Alabama Court of Criminal Appeals has overturned the second-degree murder conviction of a Tuscaloosa County man in a 1967 slaying.

The court Tuesday sent the case of Robert Lee Hunter back to the Tuscaloosa Circuit Court, citing the inclusion of prejudicial matter in the record during testimony.

2. In *New Jersey v. Louis Van Duyne,* certiorari was denied by the U.S. Supreme Court on April 26, 1965:

The defendant was convicted of first degree murder upon a jury trial in Passaic County Court, New Jersey. One of the defendant's contentions was that a mistrial should have been granted because of articles appearing in local papers while the jury was being drawn, which stated matters pertaining to the defendant's arrest record and to a statement made to the police upon arrest, such matters not having been proved at the trial.

On appeal by the defendant, the conviction was affirmed by the Supreme Court of New Jersey, which, in an opinion by Francis J., held, inter alia, that the newspaper articles had not, of themselves, prevented a fair trial or prejudiced the jurors against the defendant.

In the opinion of the U.S. Supreme Court concerning *Samuel H. Sheppard v. E. L. Maxwell,* argued February 28, 1966 and decided June 6, 1966:

Habeas corpus proceeding by prisoner seeking release from custody. The United States District Court for the Southern District of Ohio, held conviction void, and an appeal was taken. The Court of Appeals, Sixth Circuit, reversed, and certiorari was granted. The United States Supreme Court, Mr. Justice Clark, held that failure of state trial judge in murder prosecution to protect defendant from inherently prejudicial publicity which saturated community and to control disruptive influences in courtroom deprived defendant of fair trial consistent with due process. . . . Reversed and remanded with instructions. . . . Mr. Justice Black dissented.

3. Associated Press report from Los Angeles, August 6, 1970, which appeared in the *International Herald Tribune* (Paris), August 7, 1970.

4. Quoted in an article by Philip Hager in the *New York Post,* January 12, 1971. Since that time, Angela Davis has been tried and acquitted.

5. See note 3 above. The Watergate inquiry constitutes another example of worldwide coverage.

6. See Friendly and Goldfarb (1968), Klapper and Glock (1949), and Siebert (1970).

7. The project has been conducted at Columbia University as an interdisciplinary study: full use of the resources of the Law School, the School of Journalism and the Bureau of Applied Social Research has been made by the principla and coinvestigators: Dr. Alice M. Padawer-Singer, experimental social psychologist, Director of Free Press—Fair Trial Project, and Professor Allen H. Barton, sociologist, Director of the Bureau of Applied Social Research, in cooperation with Professor Maurice Rosenberg of the School of Law and Professor W. Phillips Davison of the Graduate School of Journalism.

Grants have been received from sources concerned with research on law as well as from sources concerned with research on the news media and in psychology; grants from the

Columbia Broadcasting System, the New York Times, the National Science Foundation, and the Russell Sage Foundation were added to the initial grants from Walter E. Meyer Research Institute of Law and the Lawrence E. Wien Foundation.

8. The senior author wishes to express her gratitude to Judges Frank Gulotta and Bernard S. Meyer for welcoming the first ten experiments in the Supreme Court, Mineola, Nassau County, New York: and to Judges Arthur Hirsch and Miles McDonald for welcoming this study in the Supreme Court, Brooklyn, Kings County, New York.

9. In 1969, no feasibility study of videotaping as a means of recording trials had yet been undertaken. Since then, however, various states have been experimenting with videotaping as records of trials.

10. Respectively: Mr. Ronald Goldfarb of Washington, D.C.; Mr. Lewis Singer of New York City; Mr. Kenneth Alvord, now a reporter with the National Broadcasting Company; Mr. Milton Viorst; and Dr. Alice M. Padawer-Singer.

11. Respectively: Mr. Lewis Singer; Mr. Ken Alvord; Mr. Andrew N. Singer, studying presently at New York University Law School; and Ms. Rickie Singer, studying presently at Brooklyn Law School. These individuals helped direct and coordinate the production of the tapes, as well as reading the major parts in the audiotape.

12. The senior author is very grateful to Mr. A. Hantman, District Attorney in Washington, D.C., for his cooperation and help in this study.

13. The senior author wishes to thank Mr. Lewis Singer, attorney, who has donated legal advice and consultation throughout the study, and Mr. Ken Alvord, NBC newsman, New York.

14. We wish to thank Mr. Caesar Cirigliano of the Legal Aid Society and the Legal Aid lawyers for supporting our study and performing voir dire examinations.

15. We wish to thank Mr. Eugene Gold, Kings County District Attorney, and the assistant district attorneys for supporting our study and performing voir dire examinations.

16. The importance of voir dire examinations has been discussed in Padawer, Singer, and Singer (1974).

Errata in the article should be corrected as follows: on page 39 (in the paragraph following the caption "Voir dire tends to reduce the effects of prejudicial information"), the first two lines should be crossed out and replaced by: "These results indicate that . . ."

Page 390 should be corrected to read: "2. Jurors selected without voir dire display large shifts of opinion during deliberations: when exposed to prejudicial information 14.8% shift towards guilty, and when not exposed 35% shift towards not guilty."

REFERENCES

FRIENDLY, A. and R. GOLDFARB (1968) Crime and Publicity. New York: Alfred A. Knopf and Random House.

KALVEN, H., Jr., and H. ZEISEL (1966) The American Jury. Boston: Little, Brown.

KLAPPER, J. T. and C. Y. GLOCK (1949) "Trial by newspaper." Scientific American 180: 16-21.

KLINE, F. G. and P. H. JESS (1966) "Prejudicial publicity: its effects on law school mock juries." Journalism Quarterly 43: 113-116.

MEYER, B. S. (1969) "The trial judge's guide to news reporting and fair trial." Journal of Criminal Law, Criminology, and Police Science 60, 3.

PADAWER, A. M., A. SINGER, and R. SINGER (1974) "Voir dire by two lawyers: one essential safeguard." Judicature 57, 9.

SIEBERT, F. S. (1970) "Trial judges' opinions and prejudicial publicity," pp. 1-35 in C. R. Bush (ed.) Free Press and Fair Trial. Athens: University of Georgia Press.

SIMON, R. J. (1966) "Murder, juries and the press." Transaction 3 (May-June): 40-42.

TANS, M. D. and S. H. CHAFFEE (1966) "Pretrial publicity and juror prejudice." Journalism Quarterly 43: 647-654.

Part III

PERSPECTIVES ON THE FUNCTION
AND VALUE OF THE JURY
IN AMERICA

6

FROM THE BENCH

CHARLES W. JOINER

The jury is an integral part of the justice system, providing a means of problem-solving that is far superior to any other system. Here, the jury is discussed in terms of its deliberative and verdict-reaching functions/roles. The author contends that this decision-making process tends to "expose and eliminate erroneous impressions of facts, erroneous views of the . . . law . . . and to expose . . . and isolate . . . and control individual biases. . . ." Further, it is asserted that the foregoing is true due to jury size, cultural and social composition of jury membership, and the fact that more than a majority of the jury members must agree before the verdict can be reached.

The author questions the traditional insistence on unanimous verdicts, asserting that ten of twelve votes could be a fair basis for a good verdict. Too often a deviant member of a jury can destroy a satisfactory verdict when unanimity is required, with the deviance due to any number of reasons, e.g., deep-seated prejudices, incomprehension of the evidence or a law, or simply an irrational personality. Conversely, Judge Joiner foresees problems with the suggested five- or six-member jury: it would constitute too small a group to facilitate productive communication among the jurors.

The qualifications of today's jury members are examined in light of the impact of various modern stimuli—i.e., media and, specifically, television—as well as the increased mobility of individual jurors. All of these factors are critical in reducing provincialism and heightening juror awareness.

Chapter 6

FROM THE BENCH

CHARLES W. JOINER

I am a strong believer in the jury system. This conviction is bottomed on the various avenues of exposure I have had with jury trials. I have tried jury cases as a lawyer. I have taught procedure, trial, and appellate practice, and have been the chairman and principal draftsman of the revised Michigan Procedural Rules. I have also been a member of the Advisory Committees on Civil Procedure and Evidence of the Judicial Conference of the United States; and in 1962, prior to becoming a Judge, I wrote a small essay (Joiner, 1962) on the civil jury.

The thrust of my opinions expressed in 1962 was that the jury was an important part in the process of administering justice, that it provided a method of deciding many problems superior to any other system and that much of the criticism of the jury was not valid.

As a judge, I have presided over jury trials about two-thirds of my time in court. These trials, on the criminal side, involve a broad variety of federal crimes, including serious narcotics violations, bank robberies, frauds against the government, civil rights violations, interstate gambling conspiracy, and forgery. On the civil side, a whole range of problems have been presented to juries in my court, including personal injury matters, contract violations, copyright matters, antitrust cases and civil rights.

In my jury trials, I have made a special effort to communicate with the jury and to make certain they feel they are a part of the system of administering justice.

I make an effort to inform them of what is happening at every stage of the trial and to answer any questions they may have about the procedure. I instruct them in advance of the voir dire about their place in the trial and again, in advance of the opening statement, about the trial, the lawyers' duties, the jurors' duties, and sometimes—in complicated cases in which the issues are difficult but defined—I give them instructions on the law of the issues they will have to decide. I tell them about the function of all of the actors in the courtroom drama, about the reasons for excusing individual jurors, as well as the reasons for the sidebar conference. I give them notepaper and pencils for their discretionary use, and I give them a written copy of the charge when they retire. In other words, I try to let them know of their importance and the fact that I believe they can only do their task if they understand the whole process. When I release them for lunch or in the evening, I try to make certain there are no unanswered procedural questions about their activities, their duties, or about the occurrences of the day. These steps, of course, are taken by many judges, but I believe they are essential to making the system work.

With this background, the reader is in a better position to judge the value of the opinions expressed below.

DELIBERATION: THE PRINCIPAL VALUE OF THE JURY

Sitting as a trial judge has reinforced my view that the greatest value of the jury is its ability to decide cases correctly. I have generally, but not always, agreed with the jury verdict at the time it was rendered. But in each instance, except one, on reflection and on deeper analysis, I have decided the jury was correct. My reflection involved an effort to expose myself to my biases and attempt to counteract them in my mind. I have concluded that the process of deliberation did this for my jury and their decision was correct.

A trial judge feels isolated when involved in his decision-making process. The kinds of group therapy and learning that takes place in jury deliberation are missing. He cannot talk with others. He may be uncomfortable, exposing tentative or incomplete thought processes to the lawyers. His clerk can help, but the relationship between the two makes it difficult for full value to be obtained from this exchange. As a result, he is alone as he decides.

The members of the jury, on the other hand, must agree, or at least a large majority of their number must agree. They are told to discuss and they do. This means if they are reasonably intelligent, are properly instructed and are given the basic facts, the competing views will be weighed and balanced. The irrelevancies that creep into decision-making will be exposed and rejected. Any one of their number may become a teacher, and at times different jurors will teach. They call to the attention of other jurors items of evidence that have been forgotten or processes of decision-making that have not been thought of by the others. Although all of the jurors are exposed to the same evidence, argument, and instructions, persons with different backgrounds will see and hear differently. When the jury is deliberating, they are teaching each other. They teach about the facts, the rationale of the case, and even the law. This helps prevent error in the final decision. The result is more likely to be sound and correct.

Deliberation of the jury, similar to the deliberation of other small group decision-makers reported in numerous studies (see reference section), tends to expose and eliminate erroneous impressions of facts, erroneous views of the applicable law, and to expose and isolate and control individual biases that get in the way of hearing or seeing things correctly. This seems to be true for three reasons: (1) the size of the jury; (2) the cultural and social composition of the jury, and (3) the requirement that substantially more than a majority of the members of the jury must agree upon the ultimate decision.

The traditional size of the jury, of course, is twelve. In some courts fewer jurors may be used, but is a decision to use fewer jurors wise? In my judgment there is no magic in the number twelve. Instead, the magic number is the number that will permit and require full discussion of the facts and the application of those facts to the law in their deliberation. During such discussion misconceptions of fact and law and individual biases will be exposed. I know twelve will do this. I have seen it happen many times. I know twelve jurors are sufficiently few so all members of the jury can participate in the discussion. I know twelve are sufficiently many requiring, in most cases, the substantial discussion that is essential before a decision is reached.

I do not know that six will do this job, although in my state we have used six-person verdicts for some time. In 1962, I suggested states should consider the use of the six-person verdict. I do not feel strongly that this should be done at this time, although I think six would be a sufficient number to insure serious deliberation when a unanimous verdict is required. If, however, a six-person jury were coupled with a less than unanimous verdict, I doubt that the kind of deliberation essential to good decision-making by the group would be produced. Thus, an important consideration in reducing the size of the jury is the question of using less than a unanimous verdict.

The unanimous verdict requirement forces the jury to deliberate before a verdict can be reached. It guarantees the values that come from deliberation. The problem in requiring a unanimous verdict is that the jury may contain an irrational person or two. The larger the number of jurors, the more likely this will be true. Irrationality can occur from an inability of a juror to comprehend the evidence or the law, from a deeply held bias or prejudice, or from some deep-seated character defect. Such a person, of course, will destroy the possibility of a good verdict if unanimity is required. It is for this reason that ten of twelve jurors should be able to return a verdict. Agreement by ten should produce the kind of discussion and deliberation essential. Being able to eliminate two members of the jury from the final vote should permit the rest of the jury to fully control the irrationality of individuals who, for whatever cause, were not enlightened and controlled by argument and discussion. A verdict of ten of twelve could be used to deal with jurors whose biases or other irrational conduct cannot be brought into line.

Although I believe a verdict by ten of twelve will be as good or better than a unanimous verdict, I foresee problems with a verdict by only five of six jurors. I am afraid the number of those who must agree are too few to require the kind of give-and-take in the jury room to insure a correct result. A unanimous verdict requirement for a six-person jury would probably provide the argument and teaching required; eight of nine could do likewise. The preservation of the deliberative process must be paramount in any decision as to the number of jurors and the number required for a verdict. I would opt strongly for a jury of sufficient size so that the irrational juror could be eliminated and yet retain the process of deliberation. If unanimity were not required, I do not see how this could be done with fewer than nine jurors with an eight-person verdict. It is far more important to deal with the errant juror in a way that permits the other members of the jury to continue their rational approach, than to provide a system that may save a few minutes or a few dollars by having fewer jurors. Saving time and expense would be achieved by fewer persons, but it must not impinge on the decisional process. A system which provides sufficient number of jurors to assure deliberation and also provides a method by which the other members of the jury can isolate the single irrational juror would improve the process.

JUROR QUALITY

Our jurors come from voter lists drawn broadly from our district. I have been favorably impressed with the quality of the persons I have seen on the juries. They are far superior to the jurors I saw in practice in Iowa. They appear to be a reasonable cross-section of a significant portion of our society. Many have not gone to college. A few have not completed high school. Some are young; some are old. Many have raised families. In most instances, all jurors have achieved in their own way and are performing responsible tasks in our society.

On the whole, the juries I have selected appear to include men and women I would enjoy arguing with about the decision of a case, and persons who are interested in doing the right thing. The jurors seem to be the same sort of men and women who are involved in community government, who are teaching our children in our schools or our Sunday schools, who are raising their own children as our neighbors, who are repairing our phones, our television sets, our automobiles, who are driving the trucks, typing the letters, selling us merchandise in our stores, and doing all of the other thousands of tasks that make society operate. In doing these tasks, all of them in their own way have developed some system of making decisions, of listening and seeing and screening and evaluating. In many instances, these are highly sophisticated systems. In others, they are relatively simple. But when you put a number of these different systems of evaluation and screening together and tell them to reach a result, according to certain rules and standards given to them, generally a good result is reached. It is important, of course, to make certain the judge and the lawyers relate to the experience of the jurors. When they do, the aggregate decision is likely to be better than that of a single person.

Lawyers are rightly proud of their ability to absorb facts and law and to draw conclusions based upon a rational process. Others, too, develop traits for doing this. As a result, the composite of a deliberative verdict of a group of persons drawn from a large cross-section brings insight to this process and achieves better results than that of a single lawyer or judge, even though no single juror could match the judge in deciding the matter. In this respect, my experience as a judge has reinforced the views I expressed in 1962 and accords with the studies done on small group decision-making by psychologists (see references below).

One other incidental fact that indicates the high quality of the jurors' ability, and reinforces my feeling of confidence in the jury, is the kind and quality of persons they select as forepersons. Their selection of a foreperson without exception indicates a serious intention to do their best. Both men, women, ethnic majorities and minorities have been selected. There does not seem to be a pattern of either selecting or rejecting the most highly educated person among the group for foreperson. Whether such a person is selected, the foreperson as a rule is likely to be the one who has had substantial experience of some kind relevant to important decision-making.

I have noted that jurors today appear to be more highly qualified than they were thirty years ago. This seems to be the result of three factors:

(1) *The key number system* of drawing jurors from the voter lists provides a method of gathering a fair cross-section of all the voters in the area on the jury panel. This results in fewer old and unemployed persons on our jury panels and brings to these same panels the vigorous young or middle-aged persons. If these

persons are to become a part of a single jury, of course, the court must have a sound program requiring all qualified persons drawn to serve at a time least inconvenient to them in light of their job and other commitments. A program that does not excuse persons from jury service, but simply postpones jury service to a time when service causes the least problems to the prospective juror, provides a panel of high-quality jurors. Juries need men and women who are successes in business or labor, who are thoughtful employees, diligent in their work, as well as all other representatives of the rank and file. Juries need persons who are vigorous, creative, and who have their life in front of them, as well as those who have the broad experience of many years of living. The key number system is producing this result better than the alternative systems in use thirty or forty years ago. The key number system brings into jury service a fair cross-section of all races and ethnic groups. I find on juries that Black persons, persons of distinct European origin, and persons having ethnic backgrounds in the Near East appear in numbers that seem to be in proportion to the reported population of these groups in this area.

(2) *The increased mobility of people* through the use of the automobile and the airplane have given more persons of all economic status a background they did not have thirty or forty years ago. People are less provincial; they have traveled and have seen how others live. All of this has an impact on their ability to make decisions and to deal with ideas and facts that may be strange to them.

(3) *Finally, television* has increased the knowledge of almost all of us beyond what we realize. Men and women today have far greater knowledge about the world and about how it operates than they did thirty years ago, largely because of the experience of seeing so much on television. We have damned television, and rightly so, for a good deal of what appears on it. There is also much that is good, and it has given to people who watch knowledge and insights into people, events, and processes that could never have been achieved prior to its introduction to the American scene. I have yet to see a jury of twelve that did not have a significant number of persons on it who had a wide perspective, sensitive methods of absorbing and screening information, and a well-tuned ability to make decisions.

ABILITY TO FOLLOW LAW

Generally, my experience with juries following the law has been good. I take careful pains to help them in this respect. One of the mistakes many persons make, including some judges and lawyers, is to become too refined in their view of the law and to expect ordinary behavior to reflect this refinement. The law should be as simple as possible, and the behavior of persons should be judged by relatively broad, understandable statements of legal principle. I think this is all that can be expected of the normal person in our society. As activity becomes more specialized and refined, of course, the legal doctrines surrounding that activity may become more specialized and refined as well; but, in general, too much detail and too many qualifications, too many exceptions, cannot be absorbed by the rank and file of our citizens in their decision-making behavior. It is not fruitful to attempt to apply overly refined doctrine to activity and persons not capable of conforming their lives to such detailed statements. Thus, in instructing juries on the law in general, my standard approach is to paint with a relatively broad brush.

After some general instructions given in every case, I try to tell the jury in one instruction what must be proved in order for the plaintiff to recover or in order for the government to convict. Usually this amounts to only two to five points. These are listed on a sheet of paper, and I tell the jury that, if they have been proved by the appropriate standard of proof, the verdict must be for the plaintiff or guilty. If any one of them has not been proved by the appropriate standard, the verdict will be for the defendant or not guilty. I then take up each of the itemized points to be proved and explain the words used and give standards to be applied in broad terms to help the jury deal with each of the various items. Finally, I end with the duties of the jury as to unanimity and the verdict forms. The whole charge is read to the jury so they get an overall picture, and then given to them to take with them to the jury room. I know, as a general rule, they turn to the page that defines what must be proved and go through this item by item in light of the explanation in the following pages. The evidence as to each of these items is discussed in connection with the statement of the law. I have checked with jurors and find that they spend their time on the one or two issues of significance. They look at the language of the law and apply the evidence to the language. As I have said before, I think the verdicts are sound.

In some cases, it is doubtful as to whether it is wise to have a jury because of the complicated nature of the legal doctrine involved. My doubt does not stem so much from the inability of the jury to follow the law, but from the fact the law cannot always be accurately stated so that any reasonable person could understand it in the short time available to prepare instructions. Indeed, judges have difficulty in these cases stating the law correctly for other judges. Judges are sometimes reversed in their statements of the law in cases of this kind. Juries can be expected to respond effectively if the judge can assist and identify the problems in simple terms and avoid introducing into the instructions complicated matters that may not be controlling or involved in the case. This takes effort and skill on the part of the judge and the lawyers, as well as some willingness not to be fearful of the consequences.

The instructions, among other things, must be reasonably accurate. If they are to be helpful and if a fair result is to be achieved, they must be arranged so that the jury is given direct issues to consider. These can be lined up alternatively or consecutively in the rational process of deliberation with instructions as to their effect. I have yet to see a case that could not be reduced to these issues and the jury instructed so their deliberations could take up each of these issues one by one and arrive at a just verdict. I am sure there are cases so complicated so as to make fair jury decisions improbable, just as there are cases so complicated a decision by a judge is likely to be reversed. The more complicated the law, the more difficult is the judging. In summary, with the help of a judge and lawyers who are willing to set out the issues for decision, and to define and explain their meaning, and who will send such instructions to the jury room for the jurors' assistance, the jury is capable of following the law.

JURY ESPRIT

Jurors come to jury service with mixed feelings. A few resent being required to participate in the judicial process. The majority, however, are excited and interested at being asked to perform this public duty. On the whole, jurors seem to be affirmative when they first come to court. This mood or attitude can be materially affected by the first contact the juror has with the system. Is the space where the jurors are asked to assemble adequate? Are there sufficient chairs for them to sit in? Are the chairs comfortable? Is someone there to answer questions and to explain what is happening? Are they given adequate orientation on the meaning of jury service? All of these small matters and many others materially affect the jurors' attitude.

Our court has been criticized by jurors and in the press on some of these matters. Space and accommodations were not adequate, and jurors were at times left in the jury assembly area for extended periods of time without explanation of the reasons for the delay. Clearly the spirit among the jurors sagged as a result of a failure to devote the time, effort, money, and space to be courteous in a common way to people who were requested to help out in an environment quite removed from the normal daily surroundings of their private lives. I suggest that not only should we have adequate space and chairs, but there must be a sufficient number of telephones available for the jurors. Television sets, books, magazines, card tables and cards, typewriters and desks, should also be available so jurors, when they are waiting to be called, could continue to do some of the same things they do in their ordinary life.

Generally, jurors are interested in doing the right thing. They want to understand the rules by which they are playing. For this reason, it is important for a judge to pay special attention to them in any extended trial. They want to know at the beginning what the case is all about. The attorneys' opening statements help in this regard, although a good judge will also assist in their orientation. They are entitled to know at that time the rules that are going to govern the case insofar as they can be stated for their benefit. Sometimes the rules are clear. When this is so, they are entitled to know against what legal rules the testimony of witnesses is to be judged. Their interest is better maintained if the judge provides, at an early stage of the trial, as much of a description of the issues and applicable law as possible.

Jurors are human beings who are brought into a strange environment, trusting those in charge of that environment to tell them how they can help. This puts a heavy burden on the judges and lawyers, and oftentimes loss of attention and confusion on the part of the jury come directly from the failure of judges and lawyers to respond to this need effectively. I let jurors take notes. I give them paper and pencil. A few do so in detail. A few do so for things they think are important. At least 50% do not. I do this mainly to make the jurors comfortable. A significant number of jurors have come from an environment which in at least a part of their lives includes note-taking as a part of the learning process. Listening as a juror is a learning procedure. Denying them the right to take notes would make them uncomfortable and would make them feel they were in a more alien environment than they are. I think whatever value notes may have in a jury room (and I cannot help but think they are valuable), the permission to take notes improves the spirit of the jury during the trial process. We have surveyed a number of juries in our court and a significant number of jurors have commented that they should be permitted to take notes.

Jurors become bored. They twist and turn, look at the ceiling, at their shoes; but so do judges. I have noticed when I am attentive and listening carefully, not bored, the jury is likewise. They are not listening because I am, but because we both, independently, are interested in what is going on between the witness and the lawyers. On occasion when I become bored, because it seems to me that the proceedings are not very relevant or important or material, I find that members of the jury are acting in the same way. I find their attention span is on the whole as good as mine, but not any better. We have a rule in my court, explained to the jury at the beginning of the trial, that whenever there is a pause in the trial—e.g., a lawyer conferring with a lawyer, a lawyer marking an exhibit, or a sidebar conference—the jurors are to stand up, stretch, exercise in place, or bend to get the blood back in their head and away from the larger part of their lower body. I tell them it is important to have the blood available to their brain so they can pay attention. After I have led them in these calisthenics once or twice, I find they act on their own. This increases their attentiveness.

Long trials are problems for the jury, as well as for the judge. My experience involves two trials of eight weeks each. In each instance the jury was attentive and bored, depending on the nature and relative importance of the evidence. Time-consuming identification of documentary evidence can better be done outside the presence of the jury, with a simple statement to the jury describing its admission, and allowing its value and effect to be explained to the jury in argument. When the length of a trial is extended beyond the time allotted to the normal jury service, jurors' lives are disrupted and their esprit is depressed. Special attention must be paid to the importance of the jurors' part in such cases. Lawyers should give special attention to this matter. Lawyers who prolong cases that do not involve important issues, great sums of money, or serious personal liberty run the risk of destroying jury esprit. The juror begins to ask himself "Why am I asked to spend more than my allotted time on such a case?" If a case is likely to last beyond the normal term of a juror (in my court, it is twenty days), serious consideration should be given to waiving a jury unless it is a case the jury will believe to be of major importance.

The spirit of individual jurors is affected by the kind of case tried. I have not had it reported to me that jurors feared reprisals from the government if they returned a not guilty verdict; but I have seen statements on questionnaires returned from jurors that in certain kinds of cases—mainly serious narcotics cases—they feared reprisals if they voted for conviction. The fear was that their names and addresses were available to the persons of whom they were afraid. I have no indication that this fear affected their vote, but it does emphasize that attention should be given to the confidentiality of jurors' addresses as an esprit-developing device.

In summary, I believe jurors come for service properly motivated. They want to do what is right according to the standards set by the court. If this spirit fails or decreases, it is because the courts do not handle the jurors correctly by providing adequate facilities and accommodations, adequate detailed instructions explaining jury service and how to act, and adequate attention to the common civilities appropriately due to an outside person who is invited to come and help solve problems. When courts have good facilities, accommodations, court personnel including lawyers and judges, and remember that people thrust into strange situations feel uncomfortable until they know the rules and constantly pay attention to help the jurors understand, the spirit of wanting to do what is right will not lessen.

CONCLUSION

I do not suggest that all is perfect with the jury system. It takes a lot of work on the part of the judge and lawyers to make the system work; but when both try, I believe good results are reached. On the other hand, when lawyers are not prepared or when they are unequal in ability, the judge carries an especially heavy obligation to help the jury and to keep it from becoming confused. When the judge does not work at helping the jury, the system does not work well.

A jury trial is an easier trial for judges. It is easier to instruct on the law than it is to decide the facts and write Findings of Fact and Conclusions of Law. I also find I can try a greater number of jury cases than nonjury cases because, as a judge, I need more time to deliberate with myself and to prepare Findings of Fact and Conclusions of Law than it takes to pick a jury. Furthermore, I can start a second jury case when the first jury is deliberating. I do not believe the proof phase of a jury case is significantly longer than in a nonjury case largely because most of the problems have been eliminated by careful pretrial consideration of trial matters.

There are cases in which juries go wrong, just as there are cases in which a judge errs. The method for correcting the error in either case today commonly calls for a reconsideration of the evidence by a judge or jury. In this area alone, nonjury trials are superior to jury trials for less time will normally be taken in the reexamination by the judge than in a retrial by a jury.

In summary, my conclusions about the jury expressed in 1962 have been reinforced by my sitting as a trial judge:

(1) I believe the decisions by juries properly instructed and taught are better than decisions by a single judge.

(2) The principal reason for this is that the process of deliberation is a process through which the biases of individual jurors are exposed and isolated or controlled, and it is an ideal teaching procedure continuing throughout the decisional process.

(3) Juries are better today than they were thirty years ago, largely as a result of the effort to make them represent a reasonably fair cross-section of the voting community, and as a result of the impact that television and easier transportation have had on their knowledge and experience.

(4) Judges, lawyers, and court staff have a heavy burden to make the system work. All of them must make jurors feel at home in the strange environment of the courthouse by making certain the jurors understand everything they are asked to do.

(5) Lawyers must not ask jurors to do more than they are capable of doing; in particular, jury trials of an extended case—unless it has major issues or matters of great moment or involves substantial personal

liberty—should be avoided, because individual jurors have difficulty understanding why their lives should be disrupted for such substantial periods of time on matters that do not seem to be important to them.

REFERENCES

ASCH (1952) Social Psychology. Englewood Cliffs, N.J.: Prentice-Hall.

BARNLUND, (1959) "A comparative study of individual, majority, and group judgment," Journal of Abnormal Psychology 58: 55-61.

DASHIELL (1935) "Experimental studies of the influence of social situations on the behavior of individual human adults," pp. 1097-1158 in Murchison (ed.), Handbook of Social Psychology. New York: Russell.

DEUTSCH (1951) "Task structure and group process." American Psychologist 6: 324-325.

FESTINGER, SCHACHTER, and BACK (1950) Social Pressures in Informal Groups. Palo Alto, Calif.: Stanford University Press.

GRACE (1951) "Effects of different degrees of knowledge about an audience on the content of communication." Journal of Social Psychology 34: 111-124.

GURNEE (1937) "A comparison of collective and individual judgments of facts." Journal of Experimental Psychology 21: 106-112.

JENNESS (1932) "The role of discussion in changing opinion regarding a matter of fact." Journal of Abnormal Social Psychology 27: 279-296.

JOINER (1962) Civil Justice and the Jury. Englewood Cliffs, N.J.: Prentice-Hall.

KELLEY and THIBAUT (1954) "Experimental studies of group problem solving and process," in Lindzey (ed.), Handbook of Social Psychology. Reading, Mass.: Addison-Wesley.

SHAW (1932) "A comparison of individuals and small groups in the rational solution of complex problems." Journal of American Psychology 44: 491-504.

SHERIF (1935) "A study of some social factors in perception." Archives of Psychology 187.

TAYLOR and FAUST (1952) "Twenty questions: efficiency in problem solving as a function of size of group." Journal of Experimental Psychology 44: 360-368.

THORNDIKE (1938) "The effect of discussion upon the correctness of group decisions when the factor of majority influence is allowed for." Journal of Social Psychology 9: 343-362.

TIMMONS (1939) "Decisions and attitudes as outcomes of the discussion of a social problem." Contributions to Education 777. New York: Columbia University Teachers College, Bureau of Publications.

WATSON (1928) "Do groups think more efficiently than individuals?" Journal of Abnormal Psychology 23: 328-336.

7

FROM AMERICAN LITERATURE

EMILY STIPES WATTS

A major theme in American literature is that of the "hero" as an individual—a creator of his personal history—who is made to confront a hostile world: the solitary hero and the "alien tribe."

In this chapter, the jury is discussed in its "alien tribe" role in literature. It is the "other"—"those people up in the hills"—with its impartiality compromised by a myriad of factors including racial and regional prejudices, ignorance, and even monumental blundering by God.

The author examines literature dealing with this repetitive theme and illustrates through examples a profound mistrust of the jury system in works ranging from James Fennimore Cooper's *The Pioneers* (1823) to James Dickey's four adventurers in *Deliverance* (1970).

If one assumes that Art is indeed a reflection of Life, the symbolic literary jury appears to reflect crucial misgivings about the jury system in America.

Chapter 7

FROM AMERICAN LITERATURE

EMILY STIPES WATTS

"We ought to do some hard decision-making before we let ourselves in for standing trial up in these hills. We don't know who this [murdered] man is, but we know that he lived up here. . . . I can almost guarantee you that he's got relatives all over the place."

James Dickey, *Deliverance* (1970)

From the time that America's archetypal woodsman, Natty Bumppo, was convicted by a jury for resisting an "officer of justice" in James Fennimore Cooper's *The Pioneers* (1823), characters in serious American fiction, poetry, and drama have often had to face prejudiced, ignorant, merciless, or otherwise wrong-headed juries. As the men in Dickey's *Deliverance* realized, it is risky to face a jury "in these hills"—at least in the context of that limited number of works by American authors who choose to depict a jury. After "some hard decision-making," Dickey's four men decide to hide the body and thus avoid a trial and exposure to a prejudiced jury. In *Deliverance,* the first novel by Dickey, who is a prominent contemporary poet, the four men quickly bury the body and flee (and thus risk almost certain conviction if their crime were discovered) rather than confess voluntarily and suffer what they believe is the foreordained decision of a prejudiced jury, even though the murder is justified.

Family and local prejudices are not the only factors which compromise the impartiality of a jury in American literature. Racial prejudice is the reason that a black man is found guilty and sentenced to death on only circumstantial evidence for allegedly raping a white woman in Harper Lee's *To Kill a Mockingbird* (1960). Lee is, in fact, one of only a handful of American writers to make an effort to depict the personalities and backgrounds of the jurymen. Lee does not describe the jury simply as "the jury" or "the twelve jurors."

The jury in *To Kill a Mockingbird* is white, all-male, of respectable but poor families from the surrounding countryside, or "from out in the woods." The townspeople who would, it is implied, have granted an acquittal do not serve on juries because as merchants they fear losing business and also because "Serving on a jury forces a man to make up his mind and declare himself about something." The respectable, rural men, however, are unfortunately governed by racial prejudice and local custom: "The one place where a man ought to get a square deal is in a courtroom, be he any color of the rainbow, but people have a way of carrying their resentments right into a jury box." Only one juror holds out for acquittal for any length of time, and he is a member of the Cunningham family: "the Cunninghams hadn't taken anything from or off anybody since they migrated to the New World." In short, the black defendant had little chance of acquittal in the small southern community.

The most careful depiction of individual jurors—as well as of their prejudices and limitations as jurors—is in Theodore Dreiser's *The Financier* (1912). The financier, Frank Cowperwood, has been brought to trial for investments illegally made with money of the city of Philadelphia, with the complicity of the city treasurer. Cowperwood, a young man, has been successful in legitimate investment and financing and is a respectable member of the city's financial community. Such "illegal" use of city monies had been a common practice (and continued even after Cowperwood and the city treasurer are convicted). On the other hand, it is clear that the case would never have come to trial had the local political leaders not wanted Cowperwood shamed, for Cowperwood's mistress is the daughter of the boss of the city's Republican machine.

Nevertheless, as the trial approaches, Cowperwood's lawyer assures him that the trial will be "fair" because

> In the first place, a jury could not easily be suborned by any one. In the next place, most judges were honest, in spite of their political cleavage, and would go no further than party bias would lead them in their rulings and opinions, which was, in the main, not so far.

The jury is not in fact "suborned" and the trial is "fair," but Cowperwood and his lawyer do not take into account the individual prejudices and personalities of the jurymen.

Chapters LII through LVI center not so much on the myriad aspects of any trial as upon the jury selection and the jury's deliberations. Dreiser carefully notes the profession and some particular personal belief or bias for each of the twelve jurymen; and, by his authorial omniscience, he polls each juror's opinion as the trial proceeds and then charts the jury's course to the eventual unanimous vote of guilty.

In the most strict sense, Cowperwood is guilty as charged, but enough contingencies are presented in evidence at least to cast doubt on his guilt. In fact, in the first actual vote of the jury, there are seven guilty and five not guilty votes. Eventually, only one juror voting for acquittal remains. Cowperwood is finally convicted and sent to jail when this last juror, Joseph Tisdale, "a retired glue manufacturer," reasons thus to himself: "About midnight he yielded, and then only because he wondered why he was fighting so hard for Cowperwood, who was nothing to him, and why he should thus inconvenience himself when he was so very tired."

On appeal to the State Supreme Court, the verdict is upheld by a vote of three to two, with the three judges voting in the majority described as "most amenable to the political feeling of the time and the wishes of the bosses." After only thirteen months in jail, however, Cowperwood is pardoned by the governor for two reasons: first, the political boss who has opposed him dies and, second, "a large petition signed by all important financiers and brokers had been sent to the governor pointing out that Cowperwood's trial and conviction had been most unfair."

The "unfairness" of the trial against which the businessmen are protesting and which the governor, by means of the pardon, condones is in large part the ignorance of the jury in matters of high finance and investment. Before the Supreme Court, Cowperwood's lawyer had argued that

> The jury, an ordinary body of men not trained in finance, were not capable mentally . . . of dealing with such a subtle problem. They could not possibly be made to understand the ramifications of finance. . . . Such a case . . . should not be tried by a jury at all. It ought to be submitted to a committee of financial experts. . . .

Thus, Cowperwood is pardoned, and the decision of the jury is to a large extent circumvented. The reader understands why Dreiser was so careful to delineate the respectable, but financially limited, backgrounds of each juror.[1]

Ignorance is also the cause of mistrust of the jury in Mark Twain's *Pudd'nhead Wilson* (1894). It is, however, a nonspecified ignorance, a quality of people in general, an aspect of Twain's misanthropy:

> Wilson had regarded the case of the twins [who have been indicted by a grand jury for murder] as desperate—in fact, about hopeless. For he argued that if a confederate was not found, an enlightened Missouri jury would hang them, sure; if a confederate was found, that would not improve the matter, but simply furnish one more person for the sheriff to hang. Nothing could save the twins but the discovery of a person who did the murder on his sole personal account. . . .

Wilson, by careful detective work and the then new methods of fingerprint identification, discovers the actual killer during courtroom dramatics of which Perry Mason would have been proud.

Twain's use of the jury in this late nineteenth-century novel foreshadows the use of the jury in much of popular twentieth-century detective and mystery fiction. In this genre, the jury itself becomes only the audience for the lawyer's on-the-spot investigative procedures. The jury is dismissed when the criminal suddenly confesses, as in *Pudd'nhead Wilson;* or, because of conclusive evidence revealed in the trial, the decision of the jury is predictable. In this second type of trial, the jury has often been manipulated by the lawyers or the witnesses. In William Faulkner's *Sanctuary* (1931), the jury's decision is not even recorded in the novel because the lie of one witness, Temple Drake, is sufficient to prejudice the jury's decision, and Faulkner ends the courtroom scenes with Temple's testimony (which the defendant, his lawyer, and the reader know is perjured). In this kind of trial, the jury is really unnecessary, except as it represents society's judgment as to the "facts." And the "facts" are of course not the "truth."

Thus, in this kind of novel, the jury becomes only an audience and its function as impartial truth-finder is minimized, either because the true criminal is discovered during the trial or because evidence is manipulated or testimony perjured. I should also note the many instances in which crimes are never brought to trial, but are solved by a detective or policeman. In fact, the first "detective" story, Edgar Allan Poe's "The Purloined Letter" (1845), has just this kind of plot and led, on one hand, to detectives like the English Sherlock Holmes and, on the other hand, to such "detective-heroes" of popular fiction as Mickey Spillane's Mike Hammer. In this kind of narrative, a jury is also unnecessary, as the hero-detective becomes both judge and jury.[2]

If the jury's impartiality is not compromised by local, family, racial, or political prejudices, by ignorance, or by the manipulations of lawyers and witnesses, there is always bribery or other forms of jury tampering. James Fennimore Cooper's *The Ways of the Hour* (1850) provided a veritable handbook for any of his contemporaries who might have wished to tamper with a jury by out-of-court means, or—as Cooper defines it—by "irregular proceedings out of doors." Lawyers for both the state and the defendant practice the art of "pillowing" or "horseshedding": lawyer's agents are hired to spread rumors throughout the general community both before and during the trial. Such rumors either directly or indirectly reach the ears of jurors who are, of course, members of the community before the trial and who, after they become jurors, enjoy social intercourse with nonjurors at the "horsesheds," which they have been allowed to visit during court recesses for the very practical purpose of checking on the feed and care of their horses. So significant is the work of these agents that jury selection often depends on just which agents have "gained the ear" of the prospective jurors. According to Cooper, the work of these paid agents is supplemented and even complemented by the journalists whose method of news gathering "threatens to set at defiance all laws, principles, and facts."

The jurors themselves are damned by Cooper with faint praise:

> As for the jurors they were just what that ancient institution might be supposed to be, in a country where so many of the body of the people are liable to be summoned. An unusually large proportion of these men, when all the circumstances are considered, were perhaps as fit to be thus employed as could be obtained from the body of the community of any country on earth; but a very serious number were altogether unsuited to perform the delicate duties of their station. Fortunately, the ignorant are very apt to be influenced by the more intelligent . . .; and by this exercise of a very natural power less injustice is committed than might otherwise occur.

For Cooper, the jury represents mob or majority rule and thus he rejects the jury system per se, perhaps even to the extent of favoring anarchy.[3] Needless to say, the jury in *The Ways of the Hour* wrongfully votes guilty. However, within only moments after the verdict is announced, the convicted defendant herself takes charge of the still-crowded courtroom and proves her own innocence, much to the embarrassment of the judge, the jury, and the state's attorney, not to mention the chagrin of her own lawyer.

Jury tampering is not so subtle in John Barth's *The Sot-Weed Factor* (1960), a novel quite generally based on the life of Ebenezer Cook (1620-c. 1732), whose harsh satiric poem, "The Sot-Weed Factor," concerns colonial Maryland and her tobacco ("sot-weed") merchants. Although the action of Barth's novel occurs in "the last years of the seventeenth century," the events are clearly intended also to reflect situations and conditions in contemporary society (as is generally true with "historical" novels by contemporary American writers of serious fiction, such as Bernard Malamud's *The Fixer* and William Styron's *The Confessions of Nat Turner*). Barth himself characterizes his novel as "a moral allegory cloaked in terms of colonial history."

At the rough pioneer court of Dorchester County, Maryland, spectators openly bet as to the outcome of the trials, with jury members making wagers only among themselves. The spectators cheer or jeer as legal arguments are made for or against their betting positions. In one civil case, the judge's charge to the jury is " 'What say ye, jurymen? . . . Is the defendant guilty, or will ye let the scoundrel go?' " In this case, surprisingly enough, for whatever reason (a desire to render a fair verdict is not suggested), the jury finds not guilty. However, the judge, who is obviously in collusion with plaintiff, overrules the jury (indeed, the judge charges the jury with contempt of court), and reverses the decision. In the next case, the judge dismisses the jury before it can even render a decision. So much for the effectiveness of the jury system in this "moral allegory." As the protagonist reflects, "In such a court as this . . . nothing was disallowed but Justice; only an honest verdict would be surprising."

Barth's novel suggests (and, in fact, incorporates elements of) two other types of literature in which a jury is depicted: the "historical" work based on actual materials from history and the essentially symbolic, expressionistic, allegorical, mythical, or metaphorical work of art. Thus far, my discussion has centered upon American novels which are generally traditional in form, with a "realistic" but fictive situation and narrative. American writers have chosen this form most often for depiction of a jury and for examination of the jury system undoubtedly because the traditional novel offers a more suitable structure for the kind of expansion of context of character necessary for presentation of a courtroom situation. However, in imaginative literature based on historical events and in literature with a more abstract or conceptual structure and intention, we can also find important depictions of a jury or significant statements concerning the jury system.

Perhaps most striking in literature based on actual historical events is the decision of certain authors to omit any mention of a jury, even when a jury trial is part of recorded history. For example, Stephen Vincent Benét passes quickly over the trial (omitting any mention of the jury) in his long poem, *John Brown's Body* (1927):

>   Questions creaking
> Uselessly back and forth.
>   No one can say
> That the trial was not fair. The trial was fair,
> Painfully fair by every rule of law,
> And that it made not the slightest difference.
> The law's our yardstick, and it measures well
> Or well enough when there are yards to measure.
> Measure a wave with it, measure a fire,
> Cut up sorrow in inches, weigh content.
> You can weigh John Brown's body well enough,
> But how and in what balance weigh John Brown?

Benét implies that man's legal systems cannot adequately measure a "martyr" such as Brown. Why does Benét omit the jury? Benét understands that the jury must decide the facts, but only within the framework of the law. When the law is inadequate, as from Benét's point of view it was in Brown's case, the function of the jury is restricted and minimized. Thus, Benét implies, the jury functioned adequately in Brown's trial ("The trial was fair"), but its role in Brown's case was simply irrelevant.

In *The Crucible: A Play in Four Acts* (1952), Arthur Miller allows the judges to take full blame for the tragedy of the Salem witch trials, which is the concern of his play. As the play is acted, there is no hint that a jury actually rendered verdicts of guilty in the oyer and terminer court of Judges Hathorne, Sewall, and others. Only in a postscript, "Echoes Down the Corridor," is there a mention of the jury and then only to note that in 1712 the surviving jury members "wrote a statement praying for forgiveness of all who had suffered"—indeed, a historical fact.

Artistically, Miller quite possibly had to omit the jury for reasons of dramatic economy. His intention was to center upon the conflict between the individual citizen and the government. Thus the major characters are persecuted citizens, ministers, and the judges. Moreover, Miller wrote this play during the time of the McCarthy "witch-hunts," and scholars are quick to point out the relationships between the two.[4] The parallel between the Puritan oyer and terminer court and the McCarthy Committee is made more obvious by the omission of the jury.

Finally, Miller might also have omitted the jury because he believed that the decisions of the Salem jury were predicated by the kinds of evidence admitted by the judges during the trials. Miller had certainly studied the historical facts carefully and admits that his play "is not history in the sense in which the word is used by the academic historian." As he studied the Salem trials, he would surely have learned that the convictions were based largely on "spectral evidence," admitted by the Salem judges. Indeed, what evidence is given for witchcraft in *The Crucible* could all be classified as "spectral." Thus once the judges decided to admit spectral evidence, the jury's decision would be predictable. Here is not a distrust of the jury, but rather a recognition of the insignificance of the jury in these trials.

Other writers who have based their works on historical facts do consider the jury as an integral part of the event. Theodore Dreiser based *An American Tragedy* (1925) on the case of Chester E. Gillette, who drowned a girl in 1906 and was executed in 1908. Dreiser does maintain general historical accuracy, but imaginatively recreates characters, motivations, and scenes. Clyde Griffiths, Dreiser's protagonist, has actually planned to kill Roberta, his pregnant "working-class" girlfriend. A poor relative of a wealthy manufacturing family, Clyde had finally been accepted by the "upper-class" young people and was no longer interested in Roberta. When various attempts to abort the fetus fail, Roberta demands that Clyde marry her, but the upwardly mobile Clyde plans to murder her. However, as the reader knows, Roberta's death is really an accident, but the circumstantial evidence is so complete that Clyde is convicted of murder and electrocuted.

As in Dreiser's earlier *The Financier,* the legal process is inextricably intertwined with politics. In *An American Tragedy,* the district attorney sees his chance for political advancement in this spectacular murder case, and even arranges for a special session of the court so that he might win a conviction before the upcoming elections. For the same reason, he argues against a change of venue plea by Clyde's lawyers. The trial thus takes place in the primarily rural county, where the murder/accident occurred, under the direction of a district attorney whose personal political ambitions provide somewhat less than honest motivation for his courtroom conduct, his legal strategies, and his statements to the press. The local citizens are convinced of Clyde's guilt: a lynch mob gathers unsuccessfully before the trial, Clyde is booed and hissed in court, and Clyde must be carefully protected during the walks between jail and the courtroom. Finally, it should be pointed out that, to a large extent, Clyde's own lawyers fabricate the crucial portion of his testimony.

Five days are needed to select the jury whom Dreiser describes:

> And such men—odd and grizzled, or tan and wrinkled, farmers and county storekeepers, with here and there a Ford agent, a keeper of an inn at Tom Dixon's Lake, a salesman in Hamburger's dry good store at Bridgeburg, and a peripatetic insurance agent residing in Purday just north of Grass Lake. And with but one exception, all religious, if not moral, and all convinced of Clyde's guilt before they sat down, but still because of their almost unanimous conception of themselves as fair and open-minded men, and because they were so interested to sit as jurors in this exciting case, convinced that they could pass fairly and impartially on the facts presented to them.

At a crucial point in the trial, Dreiser tells his readers that the jurors do not really believe Clyde's testimony; and thus it is no surprise that the jury votes guilty:

> Yet out of the whole twelve but one man—Samuel Upham, a druggist —(politically opposed to Mason [the state's attorney] and taken with the personality of Jephson [one of Clyde's lawyers])—sympathizing with Belknap and Jephson. And so pretending that he had doubts as to the completeness of Mason's proof until at last after five ballots were taken he was threatened with exposure and the public rage and obloquy which was sure to follow in case the jury was hung. "We'll fix you. You won't get by with this without the public knowing exactly where you stand." Whereupon, having a satisfactory drug business in North Mansfield, he at once decided that it was best to pocket this opposition to Mason and agree.

When the jury announces the verdict, Clyde sees the men as "a blackish-brown group of wooden toys with creamish-brown or old ivory faces and hands." The response of the district attorney is that he will soon be a judge. The crowd cheers. The case is upheld upon appeal, and the governor refuses to grant clemency. Clyde is executed for a crime he planned, but did not in fact commit.

The jury, however, is really no worse than the judge, the attorneys, the crowd, or even Clyde Griffiths. At this point in his career, Dreiser viewed all life as hopeless and meaningless. As H. L. Mencken has noted, "in *An American Tragedy* [Dreiser] was still content to think of the agonies of mankind as essentially irremediable, and to lay them . . . to the blind blundering of the God responsible for complexes, suppressions, hormones, and vain dreams." [5] As prejudiced and wrong as the jury's verdict is, Dreiser implies that such was to be expected.

Robert Penn Warren's *World Enough and Time* (1950) is not quite so pessimistic, nor is Warren so critical of the jury. In fact, the jury rightly convicts a man who is guilty of a crime—a rare event in serious American literature. Like Dreiser, however, Warren understands the entire legal process to be intertwined with politics. *World Enough and Time* is based on the early nineteenth-century life and trial of Jereboam Beauchamp of Kentucky, and at least through the trial generally maintains the accuracy of what historical facts have survived. Beauchamp, whom Warren renames Beaumont, was convicted of murdering a prominent Kentucky political leader during a time of statewide economic and political turmoil. Beaumont's motivation for the murder, however, was wholly personal.

The narrator of the story is a mid-twentieth-century historian, with a philosophic-meditative tendency, perhaps Warren himself. On the first page, he tells the reader that his reason for reviewing Beaumont's "drama" is the need to find "Truth." As he examines old newspaper clippings and Beaumont's journal, he asserts that

we have what is left, the lies and half-lies and the truths and half-truths. We do not know that we have the Truth. But we must have it. Puzzling over what is left, we are like the scientist fumbling with a tooth and thigh bone to reconstruct for a museum some great, stupid beast extinct with the ice age.

World Enough and Time is thus a "meditation on history," to borrow the phrase later used by William Styron to describe *The Confessions of Nat Turner.*

Rather than plead guilty with provocation to the crime, Beaumont pleads innocent throughout the trial. Although he fools his own lawyers, he cannot fool the jury. In this trial, however, the jury primarily plays the role of audience, as lawyers manipulate evidence and witnesses lie. Although two days are used to select the jury, the reader is told nothing specifically about any juror. Occasionally, the jurymen inspect a piece of evidence, and once they are described as "shuffling and snickering." It takes the jury only one hour and thirty-six minutes to decide guilty, and the reader is not allowed to see inside the jury room. For me, at least, such a quick verdict of guilty is somewhat surprising since so many lies are told by witnesses for both sides that the evidence is contradictory.

Guilty, however, the jury foreman announces, a judgment which is based on the wrong reasons, but which is in fact a correct verdict. For, as Beaumont reflects during the trial, *"Ah, that is the thing to fear,* he thought, *not the lie the world tells as a lie, but the lie the world holds as its truth"* [Warren's emphasis]. Warren is here dramatizing a theme pervasive in Faulkner's *Sanctuary,* and in others of Faulkner's novels, that what actually happens is ultimately not important. What is important is what seems to have happened, how the event exists in the minds of people, or what "the world holds as its truth." In *World Enough and Time* (and in *Sanctuary*), the jury's judgment represents the world's or community's opinion, or the world's sense of the truth.

However, the verdict of Beaumont's jury seems to be predestined or foreordained. Very early in the novel, Warren prepares the reader for the verdict as he tells of another jury:

> When the Jury was hung, and the hour grown late when men go home to bed, a juror proposed that they should settle the question by a game of Old Sledge, for, as he said, "We don't know a goldurned thing about this fellow, nohow." So the cards were fetched and the game commenced between the two champions of the opposed factions of the jury. On the stroke of midnight the score was seven to seven, when the hanging champion threw the jack and won the game. So the gallows was built and on it was nailed the Jack of Spades. When the man was brought forth on the appointed day and stood on his own coffin on the cart, he cursed them all soundly for the injustice that he, being a good man at the cards, had not been allowed to turn even one to save his neck.

At least in the context of this novel, this story represents the "blindness of man's fate," not so much in the Calvinistic or Classical sense, but rather a fate which is the result of historical forces—a theme also found in Malamud's *The Fixer,* a novel which ends as the protagonist is going to court. Thus, the jury in *World Enough and Time* is not necessarily evil, corrupt, ignorant, or prejudiced, nor is it necessarily symbolic of mob or majority rule. It is rather simply a part of those historical forces in which a man is swept up and from which he can only partially extricate himself by making his life a "drama" (as Beaumont did).

Like Barth's *The Sot-Weed Factor,* Warren's *World Enough and Time* at least approaches allegory or, as Warren labeled his book, "romance." In such works, the "real" becomes mixed with the unreal or abstraction or myth. In certain other works which depict a jury, the characters and events are clearly meant to be interpreted and understood in ways other than "real." Thus, for example, in Cooper's *The Pioneers,* when that noble and independent woodsman, Natty Bumppo, is convicted by a jury for resisting an "officer of justice," the confrontation is not so much "legal" as it is symbolic. Even without Cooper's later, more explicit explanations of his opinion of the jury (as in *The Ways of the Hour*), the reader understands the significance of Natty's retreat to the woods, his preference for personal freedom as opposed to the hypocritical restrictions of society (as represented by the jury). Natty is, in fact, the first of many "heroes" in both serious and popular American literature to depart for the West, toward the setting sun, accompanied only by his gun and his dogs.

Natty is tried by a "grand jury" in upstate New York in the late eighteenth century, shortly after the War of Independence. Natty has been living in a hut on the outskirts of the pioneer village of Templeton (modeled upon Cooper's own boyhood home, Cooperstown, New York). When the villagers believe that Natty is hiding illegally gained wealth in his hut, a search warrant is obtained by the sheriff. Natty, who is, of course, innocent of any such action, resists the entrance of the sheriff into his hut to the extreme of pointing his gun at the officer and, finally, of burning down his own hut. Clearly, Natty has disobeyed the law, and Cooper is careful to let Judge Temple explain why strict adherence to the law is necessary, especially on the outskirts of civilization: "the sanctity of the laws must be respected. . . . Society cannot exist without wholesome restraints. Those restraints cannot be inflicted, without security and respect to the persons of those who administer them."

The jury itself is depicted only as a "jury," and its decision is made on the spot, with a brief consultation. According to law, the jury really has no choice, and it fulfills its function apparently without prejudice or tampering. Nevertheless, Natty has some sympathizers such as the Judge's daughter, her fiancé, and Ben Pump, a member of the community. Together these three help Natty escape jail. As he gathers his dogs to head for the western woods, Natty tells his friends,

> our ways doesn't agree: I love the woods, and ye relish the face of man; I eat when hungry and drink when a-dry, and ye keep stated hours and rules; nay, nay, you even over-feed the dogs, lad, from pure kindness; and hounds should be gaunty to run well. The meanest of God's creaters be made for some use, and I'm form'd for the wilderness.

The world of civilization, symbolized by the court, jury, and jail, from which Natty is fleeing, too severely limits the independent and free spirit of the anarchical Natty.

The Pioneers is the first of the five Leather-Stocking Tales, and, as the novels progress, Natty more completely assumes a mythological stature. In later novels, he will face evil Indians and harsh wilderness conditions, but these he can ultimately subdue or overcome. It is only the court, the laws, the judge, and the jury of Templeton from which he must flee.

Natty Bumppo, the independent, inherently innocent man, in conflict with society, reappears throughout American literature in many different forms. In one manifestation, he is, for example, Mr. Zero in Elmer L. Rice's *The Adding Machine: A Play in Seven Acts* (1923). Mr. Zero has worked for twenty-five years adding receipts in a department store. On the day of his twenty-fifth anniversary of employment, Mr. Zero hopes for a raise; however, his boss, who does not even know Mr. Zero's name or the length of his employment, fires Mr. Zero, who is to be replaced by an adding machine. Mr. Zero kills the boss with the "bill-file."

Mr. Zero pleads guilty at his trial, during which a judge is present, but has no part. Because there are no lawyers, Mr. Zero himself pleads his case before the jury, which is composed of "Messrs. One, Two, Three, Four, Five and Six and their respective wives" (the only instance of women jurors I can find in serious American literature). Mr. Zero tells his story and concludes with "I'm just a regular guy like anybody else. Like you birds, now." At this point, the jurors "relax, looking indignantly at each other and whispering." As Mr. Zero continues ("Suppose you was me, now. Maybe you'd 'a' done the same thing"), the jurors shout "GUILTY!" and march smartly out of the courtroom "in a double column."

On one level, Mr. Zero's story represents the plight of the worker in a quickly mechanizing society. On another level, Mr. Zero can be understood as the individual citizen who finally rebels against the established customs and practices of his society and society's heartless indifference to the individual. The jury which condemns Mr. Zero represents the complacent citizens who are willing to conform to society's practices and thus reinforce the limitation and ultimate destruction of individuality. Mr. Zero, who, as the audience is told, is "stupid," rebels only as he knows how—by murder. He does not escape to the woods, as Natty could. He is, however, allowed to spend part of his afterlife in a pastoral Eden.

Neil McRae, in George S. Kaufman and Marc Connelly's *Beggar on Horseback* (1924), is a promising but impoverished composer who must choose marriage either to a wealthy woman (whose money would give him the time needed to create his masterpiece, but who might also corrupt him) or to an artistically sensitive and sympathetic poor woman. It is a common theme in the literature of the 1920s and 1930s, best known perhaps in Ernest Hemingway's "The Snows of Kilimanjaro." The trial in *Beggar on Horseback* occurs as a portion of Neil's surrealistic dream, which forms the conclusion of the play.

During the dream, Neil marries the wealthy girl, but finally is driven to killing his wife, her parents, and her brother. The courtroom is symbolized as a play with a "Ticket Taker" calling out "Oyez!" and the jurors remarking how "good" the judge had been in other trials. The jurors predict that "this will be the best trial he's ever done." There is no jury selection; jurors simply appear and take their seats. They elect their foreman in a brief parody of national political conventions, with speeches, bands, and flags.

The Judge is Neil's wealthy father-in-law, whom Neil has just murdered in the last scene. The prosecuting attorney is Neil's brother-in-law, another of his victims. One of the witnesses for the prosecution is his mother-in-law, another victim. Just as the jury is trying to decide whether or not Neil's "looks are all right," Neil's wife (actually, his fourth murder victim in the dream) enters the courtroom and announces that she wishes to go dancing at "a big new place opening that night." The jurors, who are all "dancing teachers," want to go with her, but the judge allows only the foreman to accompany her. After more foolishness, Neil is allowed to demonstrate one of his musical compositions, which is accused of being "Rotten! . . . No Good! . . . Highbrow!"

Needless to say, the eleven remaining jurors vote guilty, and Neil is sent to "the Cady Consolidated Art Factory," with this closing statement from the judge: "This thing of using the imagination has got to stop. We're going to make you work in the right way. You see, your talents belong to us now, and we're going to use every bit of them. We're going to make you the most wonderful [commercial] song writer that ever lived." When Neil awakens from his dream, it is no surprise that he chooses to marry Cynthia, the poor, but sympathetic, girl.

Kaufman and Connelly are not the first American writers to symbolize the polarization of the artist and society by the adversary situation in a courtroom;[6] however, *Beggar on Horseback* demonstrates clearly just how the jury is used to represent the artistic taste of the philistine American public (at least in the view of Kaufman and Connelly). It is a public who prefers the kind of music, art, and literature produced in "the Cady Consolidated Art Factory." Neil is another kind of Natty, the individual of integrity who must confront the restrictions of the conforming majority. As the play ends, Neil plans to retreat to a cottage in the country, where he might keep a cow, much as Natty fled to the woods. However, Neil will take Cynthia along (in place of Natty's dogs).

The only jury I have found in this type of "nonrealistic" literature to vote an acquittal is a jury composed of dead sinners in Stephen Vincent Benét's short story, "The Devil and Daniel Webster" (1937). Ironically, the jury's decision therein would have to be considered legally questionable. Jabez Stone has become a wealthy farmer and state senator in New Hampshire, because he has mortgaged his soul to the Devil. When, after ten years, the mortgage falls due, Stone asks Daniel Webster to fight the case "in court."

After Webster attempts to break the contract in a conference with the Devil (who serves as his own legal advocate), Webster demands a trial for Stone, with the only restriction being that the trial be held before "an American judge and an American jury." The Devil then produces Judge Hathorne, "a jurist of experience," and such jurymen as "Simon Girty, the renegade;" "Teach the pirate;" King Phillip; and Morton of Merry Mount. Although Stone faints, the trial continues, with Webster losing every point and Judge Hathorne denying his every objection. In his summation, however, Webster wins the jury's vote of acquittal by a speech in which he discusses "the simple things that everybody's known and felt," the history of the United States, and the sense of humanity commonly shared by all men, even the damned. As one of the jurors, Walter Butler "the loyalist," admits, "Perhaps 'tis not in strict accordance with the evidence . . . but even the damned may salute the eloquence of Mr. Webster."

Benét tends to extoll the American common man (as in *John Brown's Body*). In "The Devil and Daniel Webster," even those men who are eternally damned are able to assert their sense of goodness to vote the acquittal of Jabez Stone. The evidence, however, is certainly sufficient for a conviction; but, with Daniel Webster's help, the damned form a jury which ignores the "law" and renders a "merciful" verdict.

Of special interest is Ayn Rand's play, *Night of January 16th* (written in 1933 and having a successful run on Broadway in 1935). Rand, who based the character of the dead man roughly on the Swedish "Match King" Ivar Kreuger (who committed suicide in 1932), states that her play is "not to be taken *literally;* [its events] dramatize certain fundamental psychological characteristics, deliberately isolated and emphasized in order to convey a single abstraction: the character's attitude toward life."[7] Despite Rand's symbolic intentions, the play reads well on a realistic level, with the dead man's mistress on trial for his murder. Rand has intentionally and carefully contrived balanced evidence. The jury is composed of twelve male or female volunteers from the audience who sit on the stage during the performance and whose vote is announced, with the final lines of the play depending on the jury's decision.

As Rand further explains, the events of her play "feature the confrontation of two opposite ways of facing existence: passionate self-assertiveness, self-confidence, ambition, audacity, independence—versus conventionality, servility, envy, hatred, power-lust" (p. 2). Rand associates her play with that long tradition in American literature reaching back to Natty Bumppo, when she observes, "for the purpose of dramatizing the conflict of independence versus conformity, a criminal—a social outcast—can be an eloquent symbol" (p. 2). Rand herself believes the correct verdict in *Night of January 16th* to be not guilty; in the only tally kept of the decisions of the audience-jurors, the vote was three to two in favor of acquittal during the six-month run of the play on Broadway.

The novels, poems, and plays I have discussed represent nearly all of the works by writers of serious American literature to depict jury trials. Several of our acknowledged major writers are included in the group—Cooper, Twain, Dreiser, and Faulkner. Others, however, are missing: Hawthorne, Melville, James, Hemingway, and all of the major poets. (It is, of course, difficult to find agreement concerning the quality of contemporary writers.) Perhaps most strikingly absent from the group are black writers. A six-man coroner's jury is depicted in Richard Wright's *Native Son* (1940), but Bigger is guilty of the crime and has signed a confession, so that the jury's decision is pro forma. The subsequent criminal proceeding is a bench trial, with Bigger's lawyer pleading only for mercy. Wright's authorial intention is to plead the black man's predicament and situation, and, as a result, the trial is an exchange between Bigger's attorney and the racially prejudiced state's attorney. In other works by black writers, for example, Jean Toomer's *Cane* (1923), a black man is lynched without benefit of a trial.

Thus, comparatively few plays, novels, or poems by serious writers of American literature concern or depict a jury. The technical difficulties of characterizing a jury must certainly be a major reason for this circumstance, especially in the work of our major poets, who have tended to specialize in the shorter verse forms. It is clear, moreover, that more twentieth-century than nineteenth-century writers have chosen to render artistically the jury and courtroom.[8] The modern writer does not necessarily depict the jury realistically, but rather as it stands as a symbol or metaphor for the organized forces of society (or history) against which the protagonist must struggle.

In this sense, the State v. Natty Bumppo (in Templeton, New York, in the late eighteenth century) must stand as a landmark case. A major theme (if not the major theme) of our literature is that the American "hero" is an "individual going forth toward experience, the inventor of his own character and creator of his personal history; the self-moving individual who is made to confront that 'other'—the world or society . . . the solitary hero and the alien tribe."[9] The American writer has tended to look upon the American people as conformists who would rob the individual of himself; or, as Henry David Thoreau observed in *Civil Disobedience* (1849), "The American has dwindled into an Odd Fellow." Against the "Odd Fellow" has stood Ralph Waldo Emerson's "plain old Adam, the simple genuine self against the whole world."

The jury in American literature has generally represented this "alien tribe" or group of "Odd Fellows," with the accused "plain old Adam, the simple genuine self." The "alien tribe" of jurors is, at least according to authors of American literature, unable to perform its function as impartial truth-finder for a variety of reasons, as we have seen. In Stanley Elkin's *A Bad Man* (1967), the most recent work by a respected contemporary novelist to depict a jury, the jury has become a kangaroo court of Feldman's fellow prisoners in a state correctional institution. Even in this situation, the "bad man" Feldman can finally affirm his individuality and his innocence as he is beaten to death by his fellow prisoners, who have become representatives of the "institution."

Such a dichotomy of the solitary hero and the alien tribe is not only an artistic symbol to represent what is for our writers a crucial problem in America; the dichotomy also presupposes a profound mistrust of the jury system on the part of the American writer. In the works I have discussed, the impartiality of jurors has been compromised by personal, racial, regional, family, or political prejudices, by weakness of will or by ignorance, by the manipulation of judges, lawyers, or witnesses, by jury tampering, even by fatalistic forces of history or by the blundering of a God. When the jury has rendered a correct or merciful decision, the judgment is based on the wrong reasons (*World Enough and Time* and "The Devil and Daniel Webster"). The American writers have not offered an alternative system, except perhaps for James Fennimore Cooper who sends Natty to the comparative safety of the western wilderness. For Natty in the late eighteenth century, it was dangerous to stand trial "in the hills" of Templeton, much as it undoubtedly would have been for the four men in Dickey's *Deliverance* to stand trial "in the hills" of Georgia in the 1970s.

NOTES

1. It should be noted that *The Financier* demonstrates how difficult it is to depict the individual jurymen with any thoroughness and just why such characterizations are rare in literature. To introduce a jury—twelve new characters—into a novel or play or poem, to depict these characters as individuals, and to incorporate them into only a small segment of the narrative is a nearly impossible task with the written word (but not, of course, in that more visual medium, cinema). Even as careful as Dreiser is in *The Financier* to characterize each juror, the reader is still somewhat confused and perplexed by the necessarily hasty generalizations. Technically, therefore, a full characterization of each juror is a task both difficult and, in fact, often of questionable value in the context of the novel, play, or poem.

2. The jury is also "unnecessary" and thus hardly mentioned in works dealing with cases of obvious or admitted guilt (generally of minor or supporting characters) as, for example, in Willa Cather's *O Pioneers!* (1931).

3. At least as one critic understands Cooper. See Kay Seymour House, *Cooper's Americans* (Ohio State University Press, 1965), p. 169.

4. See, for example, Richard Watts, Jr., Introduction, *The Crucible: A Play in Four Acts* (New York: Random House, 1959), pp. ix-x.

5. Introduction, *An American Tragedy* (Cleveland and New York: World Publishing Co., 1948), p. 12.

6. As far as I can tell, the first work in American literature to depict symbolically an artist (or "artistic principle") brought before a jury occurs in Frances Sargent Osgood's 84-line poem, "A Flight of Fancy," written sometime in the 1840s. The members of the jury who vote guilty are not specified, but the witnesses are "maidens of uncertain age,/With a critic, a publisher, lawyer, and sage." Nearly forgotten now, Osgood was a popular poet in her own day, a friend of Edgar Allan Poe and William Cullen Bryant.

7. Introduction, *Night of January 16th* (New York: New American Library, 1968), p. 1.

8. For a time in the nineteenth century (about 1860-1900), a number of minor southern writers of "local color" fiction depicted the courtroom and jury. For authors such as Joel Chandler Harris and Mary Noailles Murfree, the courtroom was a place of entertainment for the local residents, and most trials were farces, with ludicrous situations. The jury's role is limited in such stories, although prejudice against both blacks and "mountaineers" is evident. See Merrill Maguire Skaggs, *The Folk of Southern Fiction* (Athens, Georgia: University of Georgia Press, 1972), pp. 91-99.

9. R.W.B. Lewis, *The American Adam: Innocence, Tragedy and Tradition in the Nineteenth Century* (Chicago and London: University of Chicago Press, 1955), p. 111. Despite the title, Lewis extends his study to include works by major writers of the twentieth century. For a tracing of this same concept of the American "hero" in our poetry, see Roy Harvey Pearce, *The Continuity of American Poetry* (Princeton, New Jersey: Princeton University Press, 1961).

8

FROM THE BAR

PHILIP H. CORBOY

The characteristics and function of the party adversary system are delineated, and arguments for "trial by expert" are refuted.

The judge's role is examined as the arbitrator in a judicial process which has, at its base, a clash of interacting parties (prosecution and defense)—both attempting to best serve their clients' interests.

Controversial facets of the jury system are examined, including plea bargaining, the length of time jurors spend impaneled, and the general ability of jurors to follow the instructions of the Court. The author concedes that criticism of the latter topic is difficult to examine thoroughly—researchers are generally unable to interrogate jurors after the fact.

Finally, in his suggestions for reform of the jury system, the author discusses the need for a vehicle for public information and education, one which would enable the layman to better understand judicial procedure and which ultimately would result in improved jury performance.

Chapter 8

FROM THE BAR

PHILIP H. CORBOY

In the mainstream of jury research, more academic controversy seems directed to when juries were first employed—i.e., was it Athens (590 B.C.), Gaul (900 A.D.) or during the reign of Henry II (1164);[1] why their number is fixed at twelve or whatever;[2] or how many (in the space age) should be enough in civil and criminal cases for a legal due process verdict?[3] The more interesting question is *why*—conceding that juries took a few hundred years to evolve at all—does the jury system today appear static, unchanged in essentials, and largely the same in character and function as the eighteenth-century common law jury?[4]

Evolution of the petit jury, in any event, is not difficult to trace.[5] In its first stage, friends, neighbors, or oath-helpers (sometimes called compurgators) were both witnesses and judges. Later, the requirement of unanimity and the problems associated with calling knights and oath-helpers who were not always totally informed led to the practice of calling "outsiders" or witnesses.

Eventually, the jury came to know nothing much before trial, to hear all at trial, and to thereafter find the facts. The size of the jury, how grand or how little, and the status of witnesses, whether called by a party or sponsored by the jury, remain mired or obscured in the history of early English procedure which, after the Norman conquest in 1066, became a mix of English, Celtic, and French colonial.[6] It is clear, at least, that by the late Henry's time in the twelfth century (1164), a grand or changing jury, the forerunner of today's probable cause grand jury, became separated and distinct from a second smaller or petit fact jury which decided judgment in guilt or innocence terms with or without the benefit of a chief steward or judge.[7]

Today, fact-finding in judicial tribunals is divided into three various stages. There is the fact-gathering stage (pretrial procedure), the presentment phase (trial under evidence rules), and the judgmental stage (where the jury retires to deliberate and decide).

CHARACTERISTICS OF THE PARTY ADVERSARY TRIAL

The twentieth-century concept of trial by party adversary was framed in large measure from a very early mode, method, procedure, or ordeal called "trial by battle." This model is marked by the clash of parties who do their own investigation, sponsor their witnesses, examine and cross-examine witnesses through their counsel, work with a jury and a judge who is there to insure good sportsmanship and fair play.

A competing second basic system of fact-finding, yesterday and tomorrow, is the trial by inquest, coming from the Latin word "inquisito," to inquire.[8] The hallmark of inquest justice is that investigator and finder are *combined* in one person or body. Under adversary justice, parties do the seeking and present the evidence; in inquest justice, fact-finder investigates as well as decides the truth.

There remain profound differences in practice and procedure between the trial by adversary system and trial by inquest.[9] It does naught, however, in researching jury history, to concentrate on whether the jury developed more from England's many inquest-oriented courts[10] or more from common law adversary rules. There were juries under both systems. There always was collegiality or lay participation in momentous criminal or civil causes, for no one wants long to decide important matters alone.[11] To return, however, to why our petit jury (once rules of evidence, an order of proof, and a judge became settled) remained constant in structure and development, the key lies not so much in the system the jury serviced, but instead on their *eventual* function not merely to resolve credibility or determine what witnesses are believable, but in addition, and as part thereof, to find and decide what is original truth.

The function of an oath proceeding today remains foremost to discover truth in a real existential, ontological, and objective reality sense of that word. This is so, whether the procedure model used be in style or mode one of sport, battle, due process, crime control, a family vision, or strictly third-world.[12]

Thus, the function of an oath proceeding is to find truth. This seems like a trite observation; it does help, however, explain why juries act the way they do. Too often, perhaps because of liberal *pretrial* disclosure, discovery, and exchange of information in criminal and civil cases, people tend to think of "fact" and "the truth" as known (or at least knowable) and certain prior to trial. On the contrary, nothing is certain until a case has been dismissed, settled, or tried before a fact-finder—typically, the petit jury.

The jury trial is, of course, a serious play; but for the jurors, it is a first performance. The court enactment must be live, which is behind the restriction on hearsay or gossip that is unsworn or unaccounted for in court.

The jury, in order to perform its finder's role, requires certain rules and procedure for itself and others. If reality is to emerge only *under oath in court,* it is necessary that the jurors be insulated from out-of-court extraneous influences which, if allowed, could result in nonevidentiary input or possible prejudgment.

It is this concept that accounts for voir dire procedure in order to make sure that the jury is impartial and free from bias. Also, jury privacy is needed to insure that any verdict returned will be (1) based only on the evidence presented and (2) after group deliberation in isolation from even the judge.

A fact-finder should hear all the evidence which accounts for the need for formal presentation, examination, and cross-examination. The data should be presented in an orderly manner, which explains the need for counsel,[13] the order of proof,[14] and the summary before (opening) and after (closing) presentations.

If reality is to "appear" in court before the jury, witnesses ought not to be generally led, coached, or misled. Witnesses should state facts, not conclusions or opinions, unless, of course, the jury is to forego their function to conclude or decide what those facts are.

Rules of legal relevancy are needed and must be deemed something more than mere logical probability.[15] Oft-times data is excluded based on consideration of time, confusion, or a litigant's purse. This is nothing less, as Mr. Justice Holmes put it, than "a concession to the shortness of life."[16] In fact, most of the rules of procedure and evidence, leaving aside extrinsic factors dealing with privileges and rights unrelated to truth-finding, make good sense once viewed from the vantage point of the practicalities of presenting facts to a body of twelve finders.[17]

The judge plays a needed, though much misunderstood, role to insure an orderly, not chaotic, presentment of facts to this jury. The judge "instructs" the jury and rules on objections to the evidence. Instructions are necessary, since jurors are not lawyers and are not supposed to be well-informed about the fine points of law. Few of them are acquainted with technical rules of order, process, or procedure.

The judge's role in ruling on objections comes, in part, from a need for culling evidence having minimal worth and, in part, from the nature of trial by party adversary presentment. Someone has to decide whether an offered and objected to item has enough connection with the case to warrant its submission to the jury. The objector role is inherent in the Anglo-American adversary system, which considers that truth will best emerge from the clash of parties reacting to each other under rules which attempt to motivate each party to best serve its own interest: most contests need a referee.

Under adversary procedure, the parties are adverse. At a criminal trial, the accused and the accuser—we the people, the surrogate of the victim and society—are separate from the judge and jury. The jury finds the facts, resolves credibility, and determines where the weight of evidence lies. The judge in his role is not to present evidence, extensively examine witnesses, or even to decide whom to believe. He is more of an arbitrator. It is not his function, except in most extraordinary situations, to try a case, substitute his theory, call witnesses for incompetent counsel, or save the state case.[18] It is not in the judge's ken to advocate. This could become his function, but such a development would drastically alter the roles of party, counsel, advocate, and the sitting jury empowered to conclude guilt or innocence.

Given the proclivity of humans to fashion the unknown in the portrait of the known, the inquest system (which combines in one personage investigation or discovery aspects of fact with the decision-making or the finding function) tends to develop the kind of early bias and prejudgment which impedes thereafter disinterested discovery of facts, especially those at odds with the earlier apparent picture. Inquisitions are nothing new.[19]

Recent empirical findings, however, indicate that client-centered adversary presentation and discovery procedures which, after all, help define a jury's *role*, motivate attorneys to greater effort in seeking more information than would an inquest or a mere court-oriented alternative procedure.[20]

It is precisely the late wait, wherein jury hears all the evidence presented to it by the parties, that constitutes insurance against (as surely sometimes happens in, say, police handling of a station confession investigation) a half-hearted prejudice for one result or another, occurring before all the evidence is in and before one is supposed to make the judgment.

EVALUATION OF THE JURY SYSTEM

How well does the jury function? Does it follow instructions? Is there a better way?[21] Perhaps the best way of approaching these questions is to analyze objections to the jury system.

It is said that jury trials are too expensive—a contention utterly belied by the facts. As one commentator recently pointed out, the amount spent on federal juries in an entire year would buy two jet fighters—"if they weren't too sophisticated."[22] As good an argument could be made that, given the typically low per-diem jury rate, the system saves money by comparison with the estimated cost of providing competitively priced judges, magistrates, masters, or experts on the roll to hear and decide the evidence.

It is said that many trials are "too complicated" for the jury. The answer to this is that expert witnesses are available whenever special knowledge, experience, and skill would render their views and opinions helpful to the jury. There is no rule of law which forbids the use of experts, called by parties or the court, on its own motion.

A trial may be too complicated for *counsel* who, busy in other affairs, takes insufficient time to adequately marshall and organize his case. That, of course, is not the fault of the jury.

Today, extensive pretrial discovery in criminal cases, together with pretrial motion practice, tend to make trials less complicated than ever. With two-way data access, opportunity for stipulations, partial dispositions, and pretrial hearings, the issues actually tried tend to be fewer and better framed than in the good old days of demurrer and common law issue-pleading.[23]

It is said in criticism of the jury system that, particularly in criminal cases, there exists too much plea bargaining and jury rights waiver. While there is surface validity to this line of approach, there is nothing intrinsically *fatal* in the practice of having checks, balances, and filters designed to separate the nongenuine from the meritorious controversies.[24] If advance data clearly indicate that a defendant is guilty, why should he not voluntarily plead guilty, thus tending to save victim and witness trial, trauma, and expense; enhance early release, rehabilitation, or sentencing; and save scarce judicial resources needed for other trials—the most complete trials required anywhere in the world.

A real argument could be made that only plea bargaining and a system of principled attrition in the twentieth-century crime metagopolis allows *anyone* to obtain, in meritorious contested cases, a jury of his peers.[25]

A defense attorney owes a duty to his client to recommend a plea, where the facts are very clear and the situation warrants it. Moreover, what a defendant in a criminal case will receive by way of negotiated charge or sentence represents, in great measure, the present discounted estimate of what a jury would do, were a trial conducted under adversary-oriented rules of evidence.

It is often the complaint that a jury trial takes too long. This is the delay factor. Most trials, however, take less than a day. It is submitted that much of the criticism about delay comes from those well-publicized trials involving political figures or a sensational and uncommonly complex trial having multiple parties, offenses, and issues.

Over-criminalization is not, parenthetically, the fault of the jury system. Furthermore, under any criminal law system, someone has to spend the time looking at the evidence and deliberating. Under the present system, a judge is at least spared deliberation time for other matters.

An argument could be made that trial by affidavit, brief, written motion or memorandum did yesterday, and would tomorrow, contribute more to delay and the consumption of judicial resources than jury trial delivery, by the parties. Trial by carta was attempted and found wanting centuries ago.[26]

Another objection to the jury system, sometimes voiced by jurors themselves, is the relative passivity with which the jury must sit "to hear the evidence." Why can they not get up and around, separate into special subgroups, take notes, ask questions, view the premises, or interview potential witnesses? They could do that, but the result would not be trial by adversary clash of party and interest; instead, the system would be transformed into a core inquisition procedure where the fact investigator (two parties, under the adversary system) becomes combined in personage with fact-finder.[27] The basic objection to inquest procedure is the tendency of finder-investigator to judge too swiftly in terms of the familiar, to shape the extent and scope of the issues, to conform the unknown to a priori data, and to develop a bias toward one version or another before all the evidence has been accumulated.

Recent studies validate the hypothesis that adversary presentation, which requires that a jury wait and hear all evidence presented to it by others, seems the only effective means to avoid prejudging a case and controversy.[28] An activist, encounter-oriented jury could develop the same bias and human prejudice; but this risk is at least ameliorated under the jury system by challenge practice at voir dire and by the communication rule (the principle that all evidence must be presented in court and the requirement that the jury avoid case-related extraneous contacts while deliberating).

Were the jury liberated, many more instructions and rulings by the court would ensue in order to insure some semblance of order and structure to the group's endeavors. Most critics of jury passivity would probably not be willing to accept the costs in bench interference and direction in exchange for reform in this respect.

A recurrent criticism of juries is that they do not follow the direction of the judge to disregard evidence or that they cannot disregard objectionable evidence once disclosed. This criticism is difficult to dispel because juries cannot be interrogated or their verdict generally impeached.

However, a body of law has developed in respect to what kinds of trial disclosure by counsel can be cured by instruction and those which, because inherently prejudicial, require, on party motion or the court's motion, a mistrial.[29] In addition, sharp practice by counsel may be the predicate of reversal on appeal. An opportunity for judicial review for harmful or prejudicial errors by counsel or the trial court is an important check and safeguard to make sure that verdicts are not based on bad evidence that a jury could not help but misconstrue. Surely it remains more reasonable to presume that juries follow instructions than to presume, in the absence of valid contrary data, that they do not generally do what they are told to do.

Kalven and Zeisel, in their study, *The American Jury,* found that contrary to voiced suspicion, "the jury does by and large understand the facts and get the case straight;"[30] that juries do not disagree with the judge any more often in difficult cases than they do in easy ones; and that close cases create the same degree of disagreement, whether tried by judges or judge and jury. There are other checks on capricious jury action. The present system requires the trial judge to direct a verdict if there is no substantial evidence or where the verdict would have to be based on mere surmise and conjecture. This is an important balance on the uninformed or runaway jury.

Sometimes the criticism is made that jurors cannot understand *purpose* in the law of evidence; and where an item is proper for one purpose, but improper for another, that jurors do not apply it for the qualified proper purpose, but, instead, use it improperly.

A favorite contention in this respect is that jurors confuse prior out-of-court inconsistent statements of a witness (which are classed in most jurisdictions as inadmissible hearsay) when offered substantively to prove what they say is true, but called admissible non-hearsay when the same statement is offered for the qualified purpose of contradicting what the witness says at trial (which is to say in *disproof* by impeachment and not affirmative proof). The rule distinguishing hearsay purpose from contradiction has been described as a pious fraud, because it asks for a distinction beyond the compass of ordinary minds.[31] When a witness at trial says defendant was not in Peoria, but told police, his neighbors, or a grand jury out of court yesterday that defendant was in Peoria, the jury ought to be able to choose which statement to believe in its entirety. This is certainly one point of view sanctioned in California[32] and under the first version of "Proposed Rules of Evidence for Federal District Courts."[33]

Many states, however, have retained the orthodox rule which allows an out-of-court prior statement merely to contradict or impune the credibility of positive trial testimony, but not to supply missing links or serve as affirmative evidence of a fact. These states have expressed concern about the impact system if a change occurred vis-à-vis "woodsheddery" occurring out of courts in order to obtain statements; calling hostile witnesses for a mere pretext impeachment with the real purpose to get an out-of-court jury;[34] or the policy against allowing men and women to be convicted on unsworn testimony of witnesses. Such practices run counter to the notions of fairness and due process on which our legal system was founded.

THE COSTS OF REFORM

Critics of the adversary jury system, as it presently operates, seldom analyze the cost of reform as a scale weight in evaluating how well the admittedly fallible present system works. There is, for instance, much criticism about restrictions on expert testimony and the artificiality of the rule allowing experts to convey impressions, opinions, and conclusions to the jury based on prior experience and knowledge, but disallowing opinions on ultimate issues[35] or phraseology in substantially the same form as is tended to the jury.

The result, however, of allowing experts to decide themselves what are the ultimate facts would be to emasculate the jury as fact-finder and to return to a much earlier, primitive period of sterilized oath-helping where the jury could believe or disbelieve witnesses, but was not free to find the facts. Moreover, there would seem to be no guarantee that trial by expert would not, in short order, develop the same infirmities of secrecy, bias, and bad judging habits stemming from repetitive ritual that today's juries are thankfully spared. Four centuries of Chancery jurisprudence were enough.[36]

Drastic modification in the rules of evidence occasioned by jury abolition would mean destruction of the fact-opinion rules, examination restrictions, cross-examination rules, impeachment methodology, and rules on collateral relevancy—all of which would undercut reasoned policy and deposits of sense from centuries of experimentation in achieving unit perception, collective memory, collegiality, and group decisions.

The burden of proof on the need for massive jury change lies with the critics, for adumbrations of the jury challenge fundamental democratic concepts.

There is, too, in criminal cases more involved in jury evaluation than the abstract desirability of swifter or more accurate methods of fact-finding. The Founding Fathers, well aware that there were in Mother England more than one method of trial and court procedure at the time of the Constitution, enacted the sixth and seventh amendments in 1791 to ensure that before life, liberty, or property could be taken by court process, a person's right to adversary jury would have to be respected.[37] The U.S. Supreme Court has held that states must accord, in any misdemeanor charge carrying a six-month sanction or more, a Magna Carta right to trial by a jury, fairly selected and without reference to race, sex, or creed.[38]

Juries have little or no influence with respect to crime and punishment or the prison system, but jury service does afford in a most visible manner a way for the citizen to participate directly in the work of the judicial branch of government.

Finally, the right to a jury springs in great measure from man's conscience, liberty, and historic quest to civilize himself. The institution cannot be lightly disregarded, especially in the resolution of issues in criminal cases.

SUGGESTIONS FOR REFORM

Can the jury system be improved? Several suggestions for reform are discussed below.

One of the most time-consuming aspects of a trial is voir dire jury challenge and selection practices. Though proposals permitting the judge to conduct the examination of veniremen to the total exclusion of counsel seems an over-drastic reform, proposals for better array and panel organization, use of written interrogatories to veniremen, and attuning counsel to the philosophy of obtaining a juryman fairly selected for impartiality and not necessarily one friendly to a side, will help shorten trials.

More lawyers should try cases—a development which would dampen wasteful paperwork, continuance time, and reduce trial docket backlogs. Newly awakened interest in criminal law and trial practice in the law schools promises in the near tomorrow a better trained or certified trial bar. This, in turn, means better organized, clearer, and more efficient fact transmission to the jury.

There are other ways of improving the system. More resort in criminal cases should be made to pretrial motions designed to eliminate, filter, or sharpen fact issues, where objections, stipulations, noncontested facts, and contested but collateral constitutional issues may be disposed of—e.g., the sufficiency of a search affidavit.[39]

One technique to shorten trial disputes, overrulings, and evidence is more resort to the motion *in limine*—a pretrial device to obtain a ruling, restrict opposing counsel, allow the introduction of a witness, or preclude various comments or objections. There seems, for instance, no reason why defense counsel should not find out before a trial begins whether the court will permit impeachment by a past criminal record.[40]

The trend toward experimentation with less than twelve jurors should be continued, at least at trials for lesser offenses (see note 4 below).

Nuisance crimes and victimless offenses should be taken from the purview of substantive criminal law or at least from busy jury docket addressed to crimes with victims.[41] More emphasis should be placed on devising trial or pretrial procedures based on the peculiar characteristics of offense, time, place, offender, and likely victim.

More is becoming known about patterns of crime, and appealable trial error in defined offenses.[42] Identification evidence is, for instance, a problem in short, hasty crimes such as quick street robbery, but it is not a factor in embezzlement. Perhaps trial or pretrial procedure could reflect the difference.[43]

A centralized witness bureau to expedite the calling of witnesses, booklets for jurors to help them understand procedures, and uniform policy with respect to the problem of early jury deadlocks are ways to improve jury performance.

The public needs more information and less critical rhetoric about the jury. Most jury trials, even those involving high officials, are not "political trials;" no man is tried because he is a politician, but because he is accused of having committed a proscribed offense. The jury trial is not the appropriate forum, neutral vehicle, or guerrilla theatre to protest extrinsic community injustice. It is, instead, an imperfect but—compared to the alternatives—the better way to collectively find truth for the ends of individual liberty in a society worthy of respect.

N O T E S

1. See, in general, 1 W. Holdsworth, *A History of English Law* 318 (1927); and Thayer, "The jury and its development," 5 Harvard Law Review 249 (1892). See also Bertoch, "The Greeks had a jury for it," 57 ABA Law Journal 1012 (1971).

2. The figure twelve has been most often associated with apostles or the tribes of Israel. The U.S. Supreme Court has upheld in criminal cases brought in state courts a six-man jury; see Williams v. Florida, 399 U.S. 78, 90 S. Ct. 1893 (1970).

3. See Haralson "Unanimous jury verdicts," 21 Mississippi Law Journal (1971); "Ryan less than unanimous jury verdicts in criminal trials," 58 Journal of Criminal Law, Criminology, and Police Science 211 (1967). The less than unanimous verdict was upheld in state criminal trials in Apodaca v. Oregon, 406 U.S. 404 (1972).

4. See, in general, *Selected Essays in Anglo-American Legal History,* by various authors, compiled and edited by the Committee of the Association of American Law Schools (1907); and *On Ancient Law; Maine, Ancient Law; A General Survey of Events, Sources, Persons and Movements in Continental Legal History,* by various European authors, Little, Brown (1912). Most standard texts discuss the *Development of Compurgation, Battle, the Ordeals and the Origins of the Inquest Jury* by Tracy; and *Handbook of the Law of Evidence* (1952). *The Maguire Casebook on Evidence* (fifth ed.) traces the court's power over juries by way of instruction and direction of verdict in the chapter entitled, "Burden of proof." See also "The changing role of the jury in the nineteenth century," 74 Yale Law Journal 170 (1964).

5. At the time of the growth and development of the adversary model in England, there were other "trials" sometimes called "ordeals of truth." There was, for instance, a practice of immersing suspects in cold water to discover the truth on a sink-or-float basis. There was trial by battle. Experience with informal trial procedures in England animated many a hasty trip to the New World.

6. In trial by oath-helping, battle, or compurgation—party, witness helper, or accuser were "aligned" as per sponsorship. Under that system the line between a civil action for contract of debt and a criminal proceeding made little difference in trial procedure. In trial by inquest, the parent of the modern "jury," there was no place for "sponsorship" at all, for all but inquirer were witnesses. The transition in the fifteenth, sixteenth, and seventeenth centuries from Norman inquest trial by government to adversary trial by a party system (albeit cum inquest jury) explains how, under adversary rules, government or people become parties. For a historical sketch, see Ladd, "Impeachment of one's own witness, new developments," 4 University of Chicago Law Review 69 (1936).

One is struck by the similarities of the adversary civil jury trial for damages to 1971 criminal trial procedure in rules of examination, credibility, and expert testimony. Surely the state was once more than mere party in criminal cases. The "people" should include victim and defendant. Historical development from adversary to inquest (1066-1640), and thereafter back to party adversary (1640-1688), may explain why criminal cases people are aligned as *party* in same fashion as private individual per civil party plaintiff.

7. By the end of the Middle Ages, a peer indicted for a felony by indictment procedure under pleas of the crown, "in pace Domini Regis," could be tried before either inquest or adversary-oriented tribunal—depending, it was said, on whether Parliament was in session.

He may be tried before a court in which all his peers sit as judges of both fact and law, presided over by a high steward who is but "primus inter pares"; on the other hand he may find that a high steward empowered "ad audiendum et terminandum" is his only judge, while a selected body of his peers summoned "ut rei veritas melius sciatur" plays the part, not indeed of a jury, *for they do not swear,* but of a quasi-jury charged to find fact but not to meddle with law.

See Matiland, ed., 1 *Select Pleas in Manorial and Other Seignorial Courts,* (1888), p. ixvii.

8. See notes and bibliography in Levy, *Origins of the Fifth Amendment* (1968), pp. 443-544. His chapter 1 is entitled "Rival systems of criminal procedure." Lord Coke of the seventeenth century ascribed fifteen branches to English law, each administered by its own judiciary; the branches included chancery, admiralty, ecclesiastical, and star chamber law.

9. The following comparative chart is taken from Burns, "Criminal justice: adversary or inquest? Did due process reform the wrong system?" 2 Loyola (Chicago) Law Review 249 (1971), pp. 252-253:

Adversary	*Inquest*
Civil and criminal proceedings alike	Same
Parties (or later their lawyers) asked questions	Fact-finder asked the witness questions
Accuser—private person; later (seventeenth century) state, people, or government	Accuser—government
Parties called and sponsored their witnesses	Trier called the witness
Party chief investigator	Fact-finder, chief investigator
Confrontation: the right to cross-examine accusers	No special "right" to examine accusers
A public trial	Mostly private
Friends, jury; later, judge and jury —finder of fact	Grand jury, judge, petit jury, king, prelate, commission probate, or chancellor —fact-finder
Bench defendant disqualified to testify for himself until 1870	All defendants treated like any other witness and encouraged to speak out or else . . . (today: contempt)
Defendant sometimes confessed his guilt out of court	Witness (defendant) sometimes confessed guilt at the trial proceeding

10. See 2 Holdsworth, *A History of English Law* (1923), pp. 178-187. Ecclesiastical courts were, of course, inquest in nature, before and after church and state became embodied in Henry VIII. For a series of articles on Norman-Saxon English trial development, see J. B. Thayer, "Older modes of trial," 5 Harvard Law Review 45 (1891).

11. See Moschezesker, "The historic origin of trial by jury," 70 University of Pennsylvania Law Review 1 (1921).

12. Goldstein, "Reflections on two models: inquisitional themes in American criminal procedures," Stanford Law Review 1009 (1974). See also the extensive discussion of models

and values in Griffith, "Ideology in criminal procedure on a third 'model' of the criminal process," 79 Yale Law Journal 359 (1970).

13. See Gideon v. Wainwright, 372 U.S. 335, 83 S. Ct. 792 (1963).

14. Walker, Thibaut, and Andreoli, "Order of presentation at trial," 82 Yale Law Journal 216 (1972).

15. See James, "Relevancy, probability and the law," 29 California Law Review 689 (1941).

16. Reeve v. Dennett, 145 Mass. 23, 28 11 N.E. 938, 944 (1887).

17. For some recent psychological-legal literature, see Marshall, Marquis, and Oskamp, "Effects of kind of question and atmosphere of interrogation on accuracy and completeness of testimony," 84 Harvard Law Review 1620 (1971); Walker and Thibaut, "An experimental examination of pretrial conference techniques," 55 Minnesota Law Review 1113 (1971). See generally Jurow, "New data on the effect of a 'death qualified' jury on the guilt determination process," 84 Harvard Law Review 567 (1971); and Lawson, "Experimental research on the organization of persuasive arguments: an application to courtroom communications," Law and Social Order 579 (1970).

18. See ABA Standards Committee, "Trial by jury: who should control criminal procedure?" 13, 1 American Judiciary Society 107 (1929).

19. See historical citations above in notes 1, 4, 7, and 8.

20. See Lind, Thibaut, and Walker, "Discovery of evidence in adversary and non-adversary proceedings," 71 Michigan Law Review 1129 (1973)—a study in confirmation of an earlier one entitled, "Adversary presentation and bias in legal decision-making," 86 Harvard Law Review 386 (1972).

21. "Note toward principles of jury equity," 83 Yale Law Journal 1023 (1974).

22. Janata, "Federal civil jury trials should not be abolished," 60 ABA Law Journal 934 (1974). It costs, for instance, $200 million to run the entire federal court system; of this sum, less than .09% is allocated for jury costs (PL 93-162).

23. There was no discovery or pretrial exchange of information between the parties; only vigorous didactic pleading served to filter triable issues. On the effect of discovery on the system, see Justice Brennan, "The criminal prosecution sporting event or quest for truth," Washington Quarterly Law Journal 279 (1963): "Discovery is the most effective device yet fashioned for the reduction of the aspect of the adversary element to a minimum" (p. 291).

24. The "united" profession in defense of plea negotiations is set out in Alschuler, "The prosecutor's role in plea negotiations," 36 University of Chicago Law Review 50, 51, 52 (1968). See also Underwood, "Let's put plea discussions-and-agreements on record," 1 Loyola (Chicago) Law Journal 1 (1970). Justice Burger stated in Santabello v. New York (404 U.S. 257, 92 S. Ct. 495 [1971]), "Properly administered, it is to be encouraged."

25. See, generally, Dash, "Cracks in the foundation of criminal justice," 46 Illinois Law Review 385 (1951). Dallen Oaks broke down the figures on the disposition of Chicago's reported 225,000 arrests in 1964 (the "hurdle-derby" versus transfers, prelims, nolo, S.O.L., D.O.L., bench jury, and plea) in Oaks and Lehman, "The criminal process of Cook County and the indigent defendant," University of Illinois Law Forum 584 (1966). See also the figures from the National Opinion Research Center's six-stage study from victimization to trial disposition (for the President's Commission on Law Enforcement and Administration of Justice) in *The Challenge of Crime in a Free Society:* of 2,100 incidents, there were only

50 convictions. See also ABA Foundation, *Law Enforcement in the Metropolis* (1967), p. 132.

Possible degrees of felonies, misdemeanors, counts, multi-offenses, attempts, conspiracy, and complex penitentiary release and probate possibilities form a veritable patchwork quilt. See, generally, Goldstein, "The state and the accused: balance of advantage in criminal procedure," 69 Yale Law Journal 1149 (1959); President's Commission on Law Enforcement and Administration of Justice, *Perspectives on Plea Bargaining* (1967), Appendix A, p. 118; and "Comment: the influence of the defendant's plea on judicial determination of sentences," 66 Yale Law Journal 204 (1956). The armed robbery indictment with 22 lesser pleas and combinations is discussed in Polstein, "How to settle a criminal case," 8 Practicing Lawyer 35 (1962). For tables classifying second to fourth offender by reduction, see Weintraub and Tough, "Lesser pleas considered," 32 Journal of Criminal Law, Criminology, and Police Science 506 (1941-1942); and Alschuler, "The prosecutor's role in plea bargaining," 36 University of Chicago Law Review 50 (1968).

If demands on lawyer's time is the chief constituent of his need for a continuance, the record, brief and proposed findings, and conclusions of law would—when required to be in writing—cause further delay ipso facto.

26. See discussion in 1 Jadine, *Historical Criminal Trials,* 436 (1832) 5 Wigmore Sect. 1364 (third ed., 1941).

27. See discussion of the decline of juries in Mannheim, "Trial by jury in modern continental criminal law," 53 Legal Quarterly Review 99 (1937); Casper and Zeisel, "Lay judges in the German criminal courts," 1 Journal of Legal Studies 146 (1972).

28. See note 20, above.

29. See for instance Burton v. United States, 391 U.S. 123, 88 S. Ct. 1620 (1968), where the Supreme Court reversed the conviction of a defendant inculpated by admission of a joint defendant's confession even though the jury was instructed that a codefendant's confession had to be disregarded in determining guilt or innocence.

30. Kalven and Zeisel, *The American Jury,* University of Chicago Press, 1971, especially chapter 11, pp. 149-181, entitled "The jury follows the evidence and understands the case."

31. Morgan, "Hearsay dangers and the application of the hearsay concept," 62 Harvard Law Review 177 (1948). See U.S. v. Desisto, 329 F. 2d 929 2nd Cir. (1964), but *contra* U.S. v. Brener 52 F. Supp. 54 D.C. Penn. (1943).

32. Cal. Evid. Code 1235 (1966) Section 770 merely required that the witness be given an opportunity to explain or deny the statement at some point in the trial. The section was declared unconstitutional by the California Supreme Court (People v. Johnson, 68 Cal. 2d 646), but was upheld before the U.S. Supreme Court in California v. Green, 399 U.S. 149, 90 S. Ct. 1930 (1970).

33. R 801 Applied to any prior statement; however, the revised version confines the admissibility to prior statements under oath.

34. See Douglas v. Alabama, 380 U.S. 415, 85 S. Ct. 1074 (1965). Some federal courts, concerned at the prospect of smuggled out-of-court statements, require a showing that impeaching counsel-party was surprised and/or damaged by the inconsistent trial testimony. Some courts say the preferred procedure in lieu of admitting for impeachment the outside statement is to permit the surprised party to withdraw the witness and strike his testimony from the record—e.g., U.S. v. Gregory, 472 F. 2d 484 (1973); United States v. Dobbs, 5 Cir. 1971, 448 F. 2d 1262, 1263; Thomas v. United States, 5 Cir. 1961, 287 F. 2d 527, 529;

Culwell v. United States, 5 Cir. 1952, 194 F. 2d 808, 811; Young v. United States, 5 Cir. 1938, 97 F. 2d 200, 206.

35. By ultimate issue, it is meant the very question or issues which the jury is to find or decide.

36. See Adams, "Origin of English equity," 16 Colonial Law Review 87 (1916); Hohfeld, "The relations between equity and law," 11 Michigan Law Review 537 (1923); Barbour, "Some aspects of fifteenth century chancery," 31 Harvard Law Review 834 (1918).

37. See note 8 above and 2 Holdsworth, *A History of English Law* (1923), pp. 178-187. The sixth amendment contains the party adversary trial package of rights to jury, proper venue, confrontation, speedy trial and process.

38. See Ham v. South Carolina, 409 U.S. 524, 93 S. Ct. 848 (1973).

39. See ABA "Recommendations for omnibus hearings and pretrial in criminal cases."

40. See, for instance, Proposed Federal Rule 609 which envisions that the trial judge should have discretion to exclude convictions if the probative value of the evidence of the crime is substantially outweighed by the danger of unfair prejudice. Luck v. United States, 121 U.S. App. D.C. 151, 348 F. 2d 763 (1965).

41. See Morris, *The Honest Politician's Guide to Crime Control* (1970).

42. See, for instance, the study on patterns of burglary by the President's Commission on Law Enforcement and Administration of Justice.

43. See note 11 above. See also Damaska, "Evidentiary barriers to conviction and two models of criminal procedure: a comparative study," 121 University of Pennsylvania Law Review 506 (1974).

9

FROM THE PRESS

GENE S. GRAHAM

The public's "right to know" directly conflicts with the alarmingly increasing number of closed-door trials and gag orders which have been issued by the courts, ostensibly to prevent newspeople and others from disseminating trial information. The courts contend that to release certain information either before or during trial would endanger the concept of fair trial proceedings.

This chapter focuses on the dilemma of the newsperson's responsibility to the public versus the constitutional right of the accused to an impartial proceeding.

The swelling tide of criminal appeals based on alleged prejudices planted by the news media attests to the fact that modern communication technology has become a serious challenge to the jury system. Jurists are aware that they can no longer conduct civil or criminal proceedings "in a sterilized courtroom before twelve men and women from whose brains the last ounce of pretrial information has been strained."

While this chapter examines the impact of politics and media upon ultimate verdicts, it also confirms that juries, at times swayed by public passion and prejudice, are generally able to "grow to the office," press notwithstanding, and that the jurybox presents to the world a collective profile in courage.

Chapter 9

FROM THE PRESS

GENE S. GRAHAM

Under the protocols of public debate, it is the historic duty of the negative side, having supposedly proven the ills or illogic of their opponents' case, to replace the system under dispute with one more viable or serviceable. In the case of the American jury system, this journalist-turned-teacher would have to join the affirmative and give the jury system a favorable verdict until someone devises something better. Despite its documented miscarriages of justice—a few of them regrettably to the detriment of criminally accused persons—our jury system is about as sound and just as any human institution might be.

There are those, of course, who would doubt the objectivity of any press (we include electronic) appraisal of a system which, in years past, has supplied so much grist for the mills of the media. Trials are dramatic, and the media dote on drama. So naturally, one might contend, the beneficiaries of a system will surely defend it. My own defense, however, is predicated more upon the protocol of debate mentioned above than upon the desire to preserve some institution popularly misconceived as one which sells many newspapers or fills empty hours on the gaping time yaw of television. Jury trials are not that large a bag of grist.

The truth is—and this is the most important matter—no one has yet been able to erect a system superior to trial by jury to preserve the rights of individuals accused by society of violating one of its laws. The system, as provided by the

Constitution, should also entail "speedy and public" trials, ingredients so conveniently overlooked by some attorneys who otherwise defend juries as if their legal lives depend upon them, as indeed they often do. "Speedy" trials were provided by Constitution drafters well acquainted with the Tower of London. The rights of habeas corpus and bail-bond were won for the accused with identical purpose: to assure that the government cannot imprison a citizen for unnamed cause or unreasonable period. But everyone familiar with the modern American system of jurisprudence well knows that criminal types—and perhaps more often at least one of two or more litigants in civil lawsuits— want no part of a speedy trial, jury or no jury. As evidence leaks away with court continuances while witnesses die, depart, or forget, the shibboleth, "justice delayed is justice denied," becomes ally of the culpable instead of axiom coined in defense of the innocent.

From the language of the Constitution, a defendant can offer a sharper argument for the closed-door trial; "public" trial appears his guarantee, and he can waive if he wishes to avoid publicity or embarrassment, the argument goes. While understanding this viewpoint, one who sees the issue in historic context can find nothing but long-range loss in it, even if that Constitutional reading is accurate—which many lawyers doubt. Star-chamber excesses prompted the demand for trial in the open—our new-found public "right to know" aside—and the hidden deals and hush money secrets unearthed from Watergate should underscore the danger of any turn back toward closed courtrooms.

I.

A proper perspective of our jury system, then, must overview the entire American judicial process, as we shall note again later. Perhaps the time will arrive when the justice of juries is worthy of more serious question, some time when the jet-speed of technology which brought about its most recent challenge will have accelerated even more. I simply do not see it yet; the glass is too dark. Futurists might forecast proliferating problems with ease. Solutions do not and never have arrived as quickly or with such grace. When "solutions" do appear, of course, it is axiomatic that they create more, often worse, problems.

That modern media technology has provided one of the jury system's most profound challenges is hardly a debatable point. Confirmation can be found with the swelling tide of criminal appeals based on some alleged bias planted in the minds of prospective jurors by the invading eye of television or its printed media counterpart reporting "in depth" from wire services and large metropolitan dailies, magazines, "advocacy" or muckraking underground sheets—actually as visible above the surface as below—and instant paperback bestsellers. While the advance in technology in the electronic media—radio and TV—is really visible to the public, there is equal significance in the more hidden advances in printing. Computers tied to electrostatic printing devices accelerate and cheapen production while reducing the word "press" to no more than a symbolic term; one can print today upon the yolk of raw egg without disturbing it.

Another confirmation of the growing tension between bar and press, centered on jury justice, is the alarming number of "gag orders" issued by the courts to prevent newsmen, public officials, or others making public pretrial information they possess, under threat of contempt. This outgrowth of the Reardon report (Reardon and Daniel, 1967-1968), which ostensibly referred only to judicial control over lawyers and law enforcement officers, was nevertheless quickly extended to the press by some judges. One of the first prior restraint attempts after Reardon involved two Memphis, Tennessee, reporters cited for contempt for publising what they had learned of the James Earl Ray assassination of Martin Luther King. But the citations were ruled moot when Ray pleaded guilty. After all, the reporters, though violating a court order, could hardly have influenced a jury where no possibility of a jury trial existed.

Though such "gag orders" involving the press have been overturned by the Supreme Court when cases reached that level, a very recent ruling has made newsmen tense. This was the high court's refusal to review a Fifth Circuit Court of Appeals' upholding of a district judge's contempt citation against two Baton Rouge, Louisiana, reporters although the Appeals Court acknowledged that the reporters had disobeyed an unconstitutional order. Disobedience, even of an illegal order, must nonetheless be punished, the high court thus ruled.

So the fair trial—free press debate rages on. Lawyers still argue whether Lee Harvey Oswald could have received jury justice, had he lived, following the absolutely essential media transmittal of the circumstances surrounding President John F. Kennedy's assassination in Dallas. The same basic argument, irony of ironies, has more lately been employed by President Nixon's former aides, fired as their Watergate involvements came to light. "Pretrial prejudice" was one of the defenses used, sometimes on the basis of official records the President himself released to the media in his own political defense.

No honest newsman can fail to recognize, therefore, that his trade is deeply involved in this problem of justice. But it is important to note that while the news media initiate their own involvement frequently, at other times they are used by politicians. At some times, the media deliberately inject themselves into the judicial dialogue through editorials and interpretive or investigative reporting (documentary and commentary are the radio-TV equivalents); at other times, the news trade is doing no more than reporting in the traditional manner the public events which transpire in the normal course leading up to and including a jury trial. It is the unsolved phenomenon of the TV camera which has so compounded the pretrial reporting problem with its live, slow-motion, instant-replay, stop-action murders. Jack Ruby and Sirhan Sirhan changed the dimensions of history, but those of judicial history most of all.

Mark Twain's cynical observation of jury membership in *Roughing It* (1872) was no longer entirely true in most courtrooms before Ruby took it upon himself to avenge President Kennedy. But it can never even remotely resemble Twain's characterization again:

> The jury system puts a ban upon intelligence and honesty, and a premium upon ignorance, stupidity and perjury. It is a shame we must continue to use a worthless system because it was good a thousand years ago. In this age, when a gentleman of high social standing, intelligence and probity, swears that testimony given under solemn oath will outweigh, with him, street talk and newspaper reports based upon mere heresay, he is worth a hundred jurymen who will swear to their own stupidity and ignorance, and justice would be far safer in his hands than theirs.

Sensible judges and lawyers no longer pretend that a criminal or civil trial can be conducted in a sterilized courtroom before twelve men and women from whose brains the last ounce of pretrial information has been strained. No longer, if ever it did, does an American jury box appear to be occupied by a dozen dimwits gathered at random. Indeed, in recent cases, juries have been handing down what would seem for many to be altogether astounding verdicts. Ms. Angela Davis, the young black radical and confessed Communist who had been accused of supplying weapons used by radicals to gun down a judge and other hostages while trying to free prisoners on trial, was acquitted.

And former Attorney General John Mitchell, one of those who claimed prejudicial publicity, was freed along with Maurice Stans, another former Nixon Cabinet member on trial for charges associated with campaign fund-raising in a spin-off of the Watergate case. Before trial, Mitchell's attorneys had submitted to the court a private survey by pollster Albert Sindlinger, showing that 75% of a national sampling who had heard of the Watergate cover-up considered the defendants guilty. In the District of Columbia, it appeared even worse: 84% thought them guilty; only 2% thought them innocent; the remainder were undecided. Yet both were acquitted.

Finally the President's "inner circle" was breached by a jury conviction of John Ehrlichman, though the charges were related to the break-in of the office of Daniel Ellsberg's former psychiatrist rather than Watergate. (Ellsberg had handed on the Pentagon Papers, first printed by the *New York Time*.) Ehrlichman's jury took six hours to convict him and three codefendants of violating the civil rights of Dr. Lewis Fielding, Beverly Hills psychiatrist, whose office had been broken and entered by White House "plumbers" on September 3, 1971. Ehrlichman was convicted of conspiracy in that operation, but he also was found guilty of lying to federal investigators.

In the Mitchell-Stans case, jurors were quoted after the trial that the contest was essentially one of credibility between the accused and the government's principal witness against them, former White House lawyer John Dean, who had confessed to perjury to save his own neck. This surely had a bearing on the outcome; weighing the worth of Dean's testimony, its intent and expected reward, was a totally proper jury process. But beyond such "proper" considerations, my own personal encounter with jurors indicates that far more than the traditional proprieties—"reasonable doubt," "innocent until proven guilty," and so on, go into a verdict.

Consider the handicapped railroad bookkeeper who supplemented his meager salary with an income tax advising service for a number of small business houses. Once a week, he testified, after the Internal Revenue Service had accused him of cheating on his own return, he drove his route of 100 miles or so to keep abreast of his clients' books. What he did not know was that an IRS agent was on his tail often enough to determine that his route was not that long at all; he was inflating his mileage to claim a larger business expense deduction.

To a reporter following the case, the precision of the IRS and its prosecution had him cold, though the criminal charge and the relatively minor amount owed seemed hardly worth the trial. But on the stand, the IRS agent was cross-examined by the bookkeeper's lawyer:

"How much did the government allow my client to deduct for the use of his private car in his business?"

"Seven cents a mile, sir." (That was the then allowable amount.)

"And did you use a government car or your own private car to tail my client?"

"My private car, sir."

"And how much did the United States Government reimburse you for the use of your car?"

The agent blanched. He knew he was had. In a low voice, he replied, "Ten cents a mile, sir."

"That is all," the attorney smirked. "Stand aside. The defense rests, your honor."

Shortly, the jury trooped out, but hardly had the last member retired before, led by the foreman, they trooped right back to deliver what was not entirely unexpected:

"Not guilty, your honor."

And this is the American jury system—not as described in the civics classroom, but as it more often actually works. The accused might well have been guilty. But the U.S. government, with all its power and weight, though hewing the line of the law's letter, had favored its employee over one of its citizens. The defendant had been unfairly treated. That was enough for the jury.

Almost any newsman and every federal prosecutor can tell you it is very difficult to convict on income tax evasion, for the most part, unless some prominent and well-heeled person without political influence stands trial on a violation so gross that its patent unfairness to honest taxpayers cannot be overlooked. In every jury of twelve, attorneys trust, there could be one or two chipping on their own tax returns. At the very least the likelihood is good that some sit there who are not quite sure of the complete accuracy of their tax declarations—IRS regulations and forms being about as decipherable as a Chinese puzzle. The juror who would lock up a peer of whom he can say, "There but for the grace of God . . .," is about as rare as the judge who will imprison a man for drunken driving the morning he is himself hung over from an excessive evening at the country club, from which he drove home.

There are those letter-of-the-law legalists, I suppose, who would disapprove of such jurors and lead us all back to Leviticus. But the very purpose of the peer panel without expertise is to assure that nuances, extenuations, value judgments, and a layman's sense of fair play (mercy?) be placed in the balances with the law books. This system may sometimes produce cowardly or over-leaning juries, bowing to the heat of public passion, but as often the jury box creates profiles in courage.

Consider the pressure on the lone, middle-aged black man who voted to acquit Jesse Hill Ford, the affluent white author of *The Liberation of L. B. Jones,* in the racial tension of Humboldt, Tennessee, after Ford had shot and killed a young black soldier just home from Vietnam.

The shooting occurred in the week Ford's violent novel, reduced to film, was shown at the local theatre. The novel was based on a fictionalized, but thinly veiled, actual case involving black and white sex and murder in the cotton plain "northern Mississippi extension" that West Tennessee is often called. Ford's local reputation was that of an eccentric liberal and "nigger lover," but the movie's realistic depiction of the blacks of the region was anything but complimentary and had members of both races boiling. The district attorney general chose to prosecute for first degree murder, and selecting an "unprejudiced" jury in such a climate was a long and tedious process. Ford's defense counsel was thrown into visible consternation when a black man's name was called for jury service. After much whispered debate along the tense table length, the defense (rather reluctantly, it appeared) accepted the juror. The state okayed him at once.

For this observer, assigned to make courtroom sketches (which one jurisdiction has now outlawed), there was never a doubt of Ford's innocence of first degree—premeditated, malicious—murder. Testimony was uncontroverted that the lives of Ford's family had been threatened and that his son, Charles, had not returned for the evening. The car in which the young soldier was slain had trespassed on Ford's property and had positioned itself to command a clear view of the driveway. Though it developed that he was parked there with a young woman, Ford testified he ordered the intruder away, then fired warning shots from the hip with a rifle. One of the shots, entering the rear window low, angling upwards, struck the victim in the head before tearing through the windshield above the steering wheel. Today, the lone black juror may be Uncle Tom to Humboldt's young blacks, but otherwise he is simply another citizen-juror who voted his convictions in circumstances that could never produce comfort for him, then or now.

The Ford case, too, produced much publicity, pretrial and from the courtroom, though it never came near rivaling such landmark affairs as that of Cleveland's Dr. Sam Sheppard (*Sheppard v. Maxwell,* 1966). A quick thumb-through of the centerfold exhibits contained in the Sheppard record would convince all but a tiny few that this indeed was a newspaper travesty. One can readily see how sustained, provocative editorial headlines could, as the Supreme Court concluded, unduly influence a jury. Even so, there is reason to speculate that the jury which acquitted him twelve years later may have considered, in view of the confused and scattered evidence in the interim, that a dozen years in prison was enough punishment in any event. Who knows what considerations filter through the brains of a dozen deliberators?

As one who has served a term on a circuit (civil) jury, I can attest that all does not show in a verdict, if, indeed, one can analyze his own final rationale for decision. In civil matters, if a case is not settled before it "reaches the courthouse door," as the lawyers put it, there are at least two good sides to the issue. This means that, when twelve minds reach accord on a verdict, the chances are that some of those jurors left the deliberation sessions still filled with doubts. There is usually compromise in the jury room, no matter how rigid the judge's charge.

How could one expect otherwise of laymen when so many Supreme Court decisions—justice as determined by some of the best legal minds in the land—fall out five-to-four so often? In the Pentagon Papers case, each of the nine justices wrote a separate opinion—so divergent were their reasons for individual decisions. Perhaps it is in recognition of the inevitability of divergence that some states have modified the unanimous verdict and allowed conviction on a vote of, say, nine-to-three or eight-to-four. This only produces an uneven hand of justice in the United States, however, and my own inclination is to cling to unanimity within the jury in the traditional notion that it is better for a hundred guilty to go free rather than to deny life or liberty to one innocent person. This notion seems to have fallen into question in some quarters recently, another indication of a growing lack of faith in the jury. My own experience has not indicated that "a hundred go free" of jury justice often.

For example, one of the textbook cases always cited when dealing with prejudicial publicity is that of *Irvin v. Dowd* (1961). But despite undoubted press excesses, the accused did not "go free." In this case the defendant was accused of multiple murders, and a frightened community—Evansville, Indiana— was alarmed the more by the type of media reporting. The presiding judge granted a change of venue, but only for one county removed, where the Evansville newspapers also had strong circulation. Since Indiana law permitted no second venue change, the trial was held there and the defendant sentenced to death. When the Supreme Court reversed, ordering a new trial, a second jury made the sentence life imprisonment. Irvin, clearly, was not one of the hundred to go free.

But this case is an excellent argument why the jury system must always be accompanied by judicial review. Here again, the jury cannot be isolated from the entire judicial process and condemned or upheld on its own. Of course, juries can be influenced and impassioned. Perhaps, as the Supreme Court ruled, it was an impassioned first jury which dealt with Irvin. The second jury did not change the verdict, only the degree of punishment. From a newsman's perspective, even such extreme cases as Sheppard and Irvin, involving media overreaction, provide scant evidence to undermine the integrity of the entire jury system.

II.

Neither the press nor the courts have yet managed to deal fully with the electronic marvel of the cathode ray tube. In the landmark case of *Estes v. Texas* (1965), the Supreme Court itself suggested that, while convicted swindler Billy Sol Estes was denied his fair trial rights by the presence of TV during one of his hearings (a jury was not involved here), the day could come when television is so thoroughly absorbed into the culture that its courtroom presence will not offend the Bill of Rights. Practitioners of the printed medium may have reason for cynicism regarding the court's optimistic observation in this regard. Despite the rather abolutist language of the first amendment, those who would put ink to paper have found themselves continuously in court since the amendment was drafted, and no small bit of that time has been spent in trying to convince judges that this free press process has not contaminated the jury guarantees of the sixth amendment.

As for TV, it is hardly likely that a medium of such capabilities can be kept out of court, and the efforts of prosecutors to subpoena film as well as the information gathered by men and women throughout the news trade only underscore an inevitability. Can one really, in the interest of truth or fairness, deny from a jury the evidence provided by such media? Sports buffs know that film can be slowed, stopped, backed up, repeated again and again instantly. They know it is subject to interpretation, too, and that varying angles create differing illusions. But eyewitnesses do not agree, either, and circumstantial evidence can mislead. Is not a jury entitled to every possible helpful means of providing justice to an accused person? Or to society?

This may seem professional heresy from a journalist during times of dispute about a "newsman's privilege," but we have no assurances in statutory or common law that supercede the Supreme Court's ultimate interpretation of the Bill of Rights, and each case must be judged independently. So will any case involving the validity of a newsman's privilege law when it reaches the Supreme Court. The court's decisions in the series of cases generally called "the Caldwell case" were, in overall effect, dangerously damaging not just for newsmen but for individuals and for society as a whole. But it is about as apt to stand, unrevised by future courts, as were the pornography decisions of the Warren Court. For newsmen to argue blindly that photographs they have taken, still or motion, cannot be utilized by a jury to help determine justice is irrational. The denials may as well be condemning an innocent man as aiding a culprit escape.

Trial television, taped unobtrusively with court permission or even on its order, could soon be one of the greatest aids to the jury process in the system's centuries of evolution. To refuse its proper usage by juries, simply because it is an innovation would seem as foolish as the hidebound folly Mark Twain deplored. As the mechanical shorthand machine replaced the quill, as the accurate recording device will one day totally replace that contraption in courts of record (though President Nixon's handling of the Watergate tapes might delay the day for a while), so eventually trials will be televised under auspices of the courts. Why not adapt, in the cause of justice, something as useful as is last week's gridiron film to a coach attempting to correct mistakes and improve strategy?

Law is often accused of bringing up the rear in the employment of modern means. By training in precedent and *stare decisis,* judges and attorneys are among the most conservative elements in our society, possibly for the best of causes. Since individual rights were purchased in blood, they should be guarded with a care that does not swiftly embrace every innovation in a world arriving at *Future Shock* (Toffler, 1970) almost before the author can cover his typewriter.

Jurors are charged to observe and consider the demeanor, as well as the possible motives, of those who testify. And one day jurors might replace their frequent requests for the judge to explain the relevance of testimony or to repeat some legal point he made in his charge or to resolve juryroom debate over precisely what some witness testified by ordering, "Send in this or that section of the videotape."

The press role will be greatly altered, of course, when and if these and other communications marvels are applied to the jury trial. This is particularly true with respect to the frequently noted prospect of making public trials truly "public" by televising them live on an expanding cable system. One must presume, first, that any public televising by cable would be broadcast by a public station and would resemble, if not duplicate, the undramatized record made for the court. It is the prospect of giving commercial stations similar courtroom rights, I think, that opponents fear—and not without some cause. With limited time for journalism, and the need for sponsorship, TV court coverage would necessarily center on the more dramatic occurrences of an otherwise bland day.

As for the direct effect TV coverage might have on jurors, one is inclined to consider it minimal. It would be a simple matter for a jury officer to insure that news programs are not seen by jurors, a device far more effective than delivering them newspapers with huge holes clipped out, an invariable tip-off as to the importantance accorded the court case they are deliberating by news editors. But there might indeed be a more indirect danger to the jury in that they are playing courtroom roles which might become difficult to separate from conceptions gained in living rooms or dens where "Perry Mason" or "The Defenders" has been watched.

It is not my belief commercial TV would greatly alter the behavior of jurors, since their roles in a trial are the most passive part of the procedure. Jurors seldom win camera angles, even on these clearly dramatic productions. One can conceive of some attention-attracting antic on the part of a juror or an unusually attractive female face which pulls the lenses like a magnet. But there is something very sobering about the juror role: trials are deadly serious business; and few miss the point that they are not sporting contests where silly slogans are trooped before the cameras, and grown men wave as if ten-year-olds when they suspect they are on the tube. Jurors, in my view, are apt to behave as jurors.

Like many elected public officials, jurors frequently "grow up to the office." One is hard put to explain this phenomenon, and I am certainly unable to do it with the "quantitative data" academics supposedly worship. Perhaps the explanation is to be found somewhere in those mercurial clichés of the Fourth of July: "our heritage" and "the nation's culture." Whatever the prompter, I have seen it occur; the town wisecracker, solemnly sworn, takes on a visage of attentive granite; the flightly housewife best known for bridge is ready to fight for deep convictions; the ne'er-do-well dons a clean shirt and tie; and the reputed bigot becomes a backward-leaner.

Sane arguments, common sense, and collective wisdom begins to flow from a dozen dissimilar brains, any one of which might have been termed scattered before its possessor assumed for the first time something he had not heretofore fully understood: public duty. Jury duty is as good for the citizen required to provide it as for the body politic; it is my conviction that the ills of our system of jurisprudence can be more profitably sought elsewhere.

More danger to justice lies in the temptation of witnesses, judges (notably, those elected), and lawyers to play the ham before an audience known to be larger than the traditional one behind the rail. One does not do the honorable legal profession a disservice by recognizing the obvious fact that lawyers, as professionals, are unable to advertise beyond hanging out their shingles; but as humans, some are sure to succumb to temptation when they are aware that well out of direct view are perhaps thousands of potential clients. The temptation upon them to "act," therefore, would be considerable. (As Mark van Doren once observed, one's mother exhorts him more often to "act" nice than to "be" nice.) Such excessive behavior could have a negative effect on jurors, however. Intelligent men and women are likely to recognize quickly the grandstander, and flamboyance is not always held in high esteem; that jurors are growing more intelligent over the years is something to which I can personally attest, without IQ proof, through twenty years of observation.

A footnote should be added, indirectly affecting the jury system, that TV cameras have already been put to monitor usage in some police "third degree" rooms in an effort to defend against the growing number of police brutality charges. One case, *Rideau v. Louisiana* (1963), has already involved police questioning before TV cameras. But the clear violation of the accused's rights in this case tells us only that law officers cannot obtain confessions worthy of stature as evidence by the ancient rite of calling in the press to publicize their own heroics in the solution of some case.

III.

During a lecture at the University of Illinois, John Chancellor once appraised television's impact on social and political matters as less influential in shaping than it was in reinforcing the viewer's conceptions. During the media's extensive coverage of the Vietnam War, he said the networks found that "the hawks got hawkier and the doves got dovier" by watching the tube. One can guess that the same thing happened during the 1968 Democratic Convention in Chicago: in deep Dixie posters were erected with the heroic image of Mayor Richard Daley by law'n'order partisans with standard haircuts, while the Walker Commission in Chicago labeled what happened there a "police riot" to the cheers of pig-callers coast to coast.

This polarizing effect of television is a fascinating insight which I believe to be true because it squares with one's own observations during the question-and-answer periods following numerous public appearances dealing with one phase or another of the news media and, particularly, television. In every group the media speaker inevitably encounters a polarity of persons who are either hostile or friendly toward practitioners of John Chancellor's trade, and this opinion trend was well under way before Spiro Agnew gave it a shove in Des Moines. This translates into what newsmen now gravely ponder in august conventions—their own "credibility."

Invariably, the hostile listener seems to be endowed with a certain conceit that everyone except himself is being brainwashed; the friendly soul is pleased as punch with the same reporting. The viewers are reversible, naturally, according to personal notions concerning the political or social issue being examined. To what degree media influenced each listener's initial notion is the old insoluble chicken-or-egg propostion. In either event there is a close parallel to Wilbur Schramm's earlier research on the printed medium—oversimplified: one is apt to read that with which he already agrees or about which he is already knowledgeable.

Even if it should seem to stimulate acting on the part of trial participants, TV coverage would be bringing nothing new before the jury. The trial has always been a drama producing laughter or tears, pathos, tragedy, misconduct, attorney trickery, and often judicial pompousness. This probably stems from an adversary system designed as a contest to sway the jury. Every city has its ambitious district attorney and its lawyer-stylists, though the louder and showier of the latter are not always the most effective. Some attorneys, in the quietest, most reasoned manner seem able to influence jurors with a sense of sincerity and persuasiveness which completely upstages emotional pomp or aggressive pageantry.

Long before the advent of the mass media, Shakespeare's *Merchant of Venice* attracted playgoers for the same reasons that today's juicy trial attracts authors, newsmen, photographers, artists—that is to say, the eyes and ears of the public. To argue that jurors, or even judges, are not influenced would be to deny that persuasion is the very purpose of communications, and beer advertisers might save their money. But to contend that all this will surely prejudice a jury beyond the point of honestly, fairly, and objectively weighing the evidence is an insult to the public's ability to adapt to the present and a surrender to the archaic fatalism of Twain.

Indeed, the necessity of adapting to present conditions could be, in the end, the most persuasive of all arguments favoring the jury. A generation of young people have been vaccinated with a black-and-white serum of criminal justice, most often administered from the automatic muzzles of televised detectives and private eyes. The real-life parallels are too painful to mention, though it is not always the bad guys who get it in the genuine streets. An increasingly violent nation and world must not be lured to the dramatized simplistic "final solution" of complex problems. For my part, I will choose twelve level heads unread in the law above the latest TV police or private-eye hero who knows how to evade it or the single cranium of a black-robed judge, however learned in the letters printed on a codified page.

One hopes he does not sound too much the cynic by recalling from personal experience with several legislatures how some laws get on the books. And the phrase "black hearts sometimes beat beneath black robes" is not one fresh from my own pen; it is borrowed.

On the civil side of the docket, it is not difficult to see where "law" is headed, and again I choose the jury for justice. Civil rights litigation may be in its waning days; but consumerism is on a hasty upswing, and America's economic fate at the marketplace is best placed with those "twelve good men (or women) and true." The division of wealth being what it is in this country, the most likely alternative would result in elitist decisions by those least familiar with everyday household budget burdens.

There are those, of course, who argue persuasively that a continuation of jury trials can only retain economic and social systems in regions such as Dixie, where racial prejudice often cancels justice. My news career, spent in the mid-South, has witnessed such injustice, but not as often as one might think; and the recent change there has been so swift as to promote George Wallace and Strom Thurmond to eligibility for a jury list. One cannot always be more confident in "de-facto" regions of a rapidly reshaping nation.

IV.

To defend the jury system as it currently operates without the slightest toleration of improvement would be, as justice is sometimes mistakenly presumed to be, totally blind. The traditional statue of Justice, blindfolded, holding those balances up before her, is a moving symbol. Symbol aside, the sculptor made monstrous presumptions. First, he assumed the lady had a perfect sense of touch and needed no aid from our most cherished gift of sight to reach her judgments. Second, under our jury system, the monolith-lady represents twelve wriggling, sometimes impatient women and men whose sight and hearing, far more than their touch senses, will be played upon by lawyers, the accused, their kin, witnesses from both sides, and even faces in the crowd during the courtroom tug-of-war.

The struggle to gain or distract the eyes and the ears of the jurors is often amusing and deliberately designed to prejudice those whose prejudices have already been thoroughly sifted and catalogued—prejudices rooted in heritage, religion and ethnic culture, social status, and line of work—prejudices often dating from infancy. Again, one is tempted to wonder what the media could do to such prejudices beyond, in John Chancellor's words, seeing that "the hawks got hawkier and the doves got dovier."

The media, therefore, may play only a minor role in prejudicing a jury; efforts to do so have been going on for years, largely through the adversary system of law, and there are all sorts of tricks of the trade. Legendary now is the story of how Clarence Darrow dulled the eloquent tongue of William Jennings Bryan in Tennessee's historic monkey trial in the 1920s. As the then aging "Boy Orator of the Platte" began his Biblical summation, it is said, Darrow lit a cigar in the steaming courtroom. While Bryan warmed to his subject Darrow puffed calmly, emitting large puffs of smoke from the defendant's table. The ash on his cigar grew longer and longer as Bryan spoke, but it would not fall; the longer Darrow's cigar ash grew the less attention paid by the jury to Bryan's plea. Rather, it stared, transfixed, waiting for Darrow's ash to drop and only later was it learned that the foxy defender had threaded a stiff wire through his stogie before he lit it. This had no bearing on the case's merit, but the jury's sense of sight was put to distracting use. Prejudice?

Some years ago, I was assigned to cover the murder trial of Earl David Bircham, then on the FBI's "Ten Most Wanted" list, for killing a Louisville, Kentucky, policeman and seriously wounding another. When the city's police chief took the stand, he referred at once to "the night of the murder," coming down hard on that unproven legal charge of murder. The defense objection was immediate and the judge, his dispassionate countenance that of a sleepy iguano sunning itself on a rock, quietly, "Sustained." Perhaps a half-dozen times during direct and cross-examination, the police chief laid down the murder charge, and each time defense counsel leaped to its feet, angrily objecting until the judge swayed forward in his swivel and kindly lectured the witness:

> Now, Colonel Heustis [in Louisville the police chief is so ranked], you know it is improper to testify in this manner and ladies and gentlemen of the jury will disregard any characterization of this matter as "murder." As I will charge you, that is a legal term and it is for you to decide if the defendant is guilty or innocent.

But as the California Supreme Court once observed, "You cannot unring a rung bell," and every lawyer and lawman knows how to ring them in court. Bircham, convicted, died in the electric chair at Eddyville, Kentucky, State Prison when all his appeals were exhausted. Without respect to feelings concerning capital punishment, I am satisfied that the jury's verdict of "guilty" was a correct one. This is certainly not to defend nor condemn such behavior as that of either Darrow or Heustis, but it is to suggest that juries can be prejudiced by court officers and lawmen within the courtroom more than the press has managed to do outside, though one must admit the media problem is growing. As J. Edward Murray (1968: 184) has written,

> by far the major single impediment to a just trial, to some semblance of rational justice, is the adversary system. Under this system, opposing counsel are openly engaged in prejudicing the jury in any way they can. That's the name of the game. The lawyers brag about it.

Murray quotes Oklahoma prosecutor Curtis P. Harris: "The legal profession can cut crime by 50 per cent overnight simply by telling the truth about their clients." Harris, Murray writes, related how when a nationally known attorney came to town and told the local bar how he used chicanery to free defendants, the lawyers stood up and applauded.

Under the adversary system, Murray claims, "the trial bears no resemblance to an honest search for truth, but is admittedly a sporting contest or game in which each side uses whatever tricks or surprises it can muster." Sporting figures have been known to become part of the tricks, in fact. The late Robert Kennedy told in his best-seller (1960: 57, 60-61) how the Teamsters Union acquired the cooperation and paid the expenses of former Heavyweight Champion Joe Louis "to come from Detroit to Washington and appear in the courtroom for two days" where he "publicly embraced Mr. (James R.) Hoffa" before a jury which "consisted of eight Negroes and four whites." Hoffa at the time was being tried for an alleged bribe in the famous Cye Cheasty case. But he went free.

Later, a similar stunt was undertaken but aborted in another Hoffa trial in Nashville, Tennessee, involving two popular ex-football stars from Vanderbilt University and the professional ranks. The pair approached, Bill Wade and the late Phil King, refused to cooperate. But this trial witnessed what has often been termed the greatest assault on the American jury system in history. Hoffa's efforts to fix several prospective jurors to assure a hung jury were uncovered and, formally charged with these efforts, Hoffa and a number of coconspirators, among them two attorneys, received sentences, again after jury trials. These cases won nationwide publicity, but this time the press was acquitted of "prejudice."

Nevertheless, one should not acquit the media at the expense of others who sometimes attempt to pollute the jury system. A newsman assigned to the courts becomes aware of many such attempts, from panel selection, manipulated sometimes by a foxy old jury officer whose duty it is to make up lists, through the not unimpeachable voir dire process, and finally throughout the trial drama. But I have witnessed no abuses one could call sure-fire. For how a juror might behave, having been solemnly sworn, still furrows the brow of expensive counsel, once that juror and his eleven colleagues hear all the evidence and retire to the secrecy of the jury room. As there are no atheists in foxholes, there are no interested parties to a lawsuit unconcerned while the jury is out.

"Two things are always uncertain in this world," a veteran police officer once told me, "the mood of a woman and the verdict of a jury." As long as American society can retain the assurance of those uncertainties, life will remain interesting and justice in reasonably safe hands.

REFERENCES

Estes v. Texas (1965) 381 U.S. 532, 553, 85 S. Ct. 1628.
Irvin v. Dowd (1961) 366 U.S. 717, 81 S. Ct. 1639.
KENNEDY, R. (1960) The Enemy Within. New York: Harper.
MURRAY, J. E. (1968) "Fair trial–free press: a dialogue." Colorado Quarterly (Autumn).
REARDON, P. C. and C. DANIEL (1967-1968) Fair Trial and Free Press. Washington, D.C.: American Enterprise Institute.
Rideau v. Louisiana (1963) 373 U.S. 723, 724, 83, S. Ct. 1417, 1419.
Sheppard v. Maxwell (1966) 384 U.S. 333, 86 S. Ct. 1507.
TOFFLER, A. (1970) Future Shock. New York: Random House.

10

ANOTHER VIEW FROM THE BAR

C. ANTHONY FRILOUX, Jr.

The author discusses the shocking theory that the right of trial by one's peers is increasingly in danger of becoming extinct. The current juror selection process excludes those individuals who would not serve the interests of either the prosecution or the defense. Both sides in the adversary system know well which geographic areas will produce the "favored" attitudes for either conviction or acquittal.

A random juror selection system would avoid the problem of eliminating one group or overrepresenting another. An entire spectrum of the population would thus emerge, producing a truly "fair and impartial" pool of prospective jurors.

There is a deplorable lack of community facilities to educate the public and teach the lay juror the basic philosophy of the criminal justice system. A tragic result of this misunderstanding of the function of the justice system occurs all too often when a jury unconsciously shifts the burden of proof from the state to the defendant who, constitutionally, is under no obligation to prove his or her innocence.

Despite these flaws, the author has found no viable alternative to the American jury system and the concepts of justice embodied by it.

Chapter 10

ANOTHER VIEW FROM THE BAR

C. ANTHONY FRILOUX, Jr.

Defense lawyers, civil libertarians and scholars intimately acquainted with the present status of juries in state and federal trials in matters involving violations of a criminal nature sense the magnitude of a growing crisis which, if unchecked, has the potential to destroy the traditional American guarantees of the "inalienable" right to trial by a jury of one's peers.[1]

The American jury concept, born in the crucible of rebellion against tyranny and enacted to stand as guardian of due process and bar to constitutional abrogations by over-zealous minions of the sovereign, is threatened with extinction. Harsh words, but nonetheless true.

The innovative concepts of a jury of one's peers, of a twelve-man jury, and the indispensable requirement of "unanimity" were the creations of a concerned nation, newly emerging in a world where the individual was usually a victim to the sovereign of the system, and justice was limited to the strong, the wealthy, and those in power.[2]

Lawyers and educators, as well as the lay public, have grown complacent and apathetic about the criminal justice system. Traditional safeguards, bought at such great expense, are under assault from many quarters in our complex democratic society. One of the potential victims of the catastrophic crisis in the criminal justice system today is the traditional "jury" in criminal cases.

I.

Of all the many aspects of the common law jurisprudence, perhaps the least understood—by the legal profession itself as well as by the lay public—are the value and the role of the jury in criminal trials. When this provocative statement is analyzed, the present crisis in the criminal justice system can be placed in its proper prospective.

Juries vary in complexion from neighborhood to neighborhood, from locale to locale. Methods of selection are as varied as the personalities themselves who serve in this most important role. Even in the federal courts, rules for selection, the method of selection, and the composition of the venire or panel vary considerably.

While in theory every man or woman who stands charged with a crime is entitled to a jury of his or her peers, this increasingly ceases to be the reality in the average criminal trial in many jurisdictions today.[3] The crisis in the system has left a marked imprint on the composition of the average jury, on its objectivity, and on its resultant performance. While certainly far from perfect, the most significant single safeguard against arbitrary and unlawful action by those in authority is the right to have a lay jury reach the ultimate decision on guilt or innocence.

The writer's experience with juries in various states and federal jurisdictions has led him to the conclusion that generally the American lay jury performs its function within the traditional expectations of the founding fathers' hopes and expectations. There can be little argument that some juries have been insensitive to their responsibility to remain objective and nonpartisan in carrying out their basic "fact-finding" obligation. But this can be categorized as the exception rather than the general rule. Every experienced trial lawyer quickly learns that certain geographic areas contain a population whose attitude is reflected markedly in the average jury's attitude toward citizens who stand before the bar of justice.

In a critical vein, the admission must be made by even the most partisan defender of the jury system (as we know it) that prejudice, passion, and sympathy *do* constitute human frailties which cannot be excised by the simple mechanics of being selected as a trial juror. It is in this atmosphere, with a conscious awareness that individual jurors are human, that the gravest challenge manifests itself to the criminal defense lawyer in a criminal case.

The role of the defense is to prepare properly and search out the extremes in those human personality traits relative to the individual juror. A competent trial lawyer realizes that many cases are literally won or lost at the very initial stage of a criminal trial: selecting the jury.[4] Experienced prosecutors know that their probable success in a given case is directly related to exposing, factually, then striking the juror who is basically concerned about the defendant as a person—the juror who displays compassion and a sense of understanding of human frailty. The second thrust of an experienced prosecutor is directed to locating those jurors who interpret their role as being a part of the law enforcement process, with the resultant probability of deciding against the defendant on the fundamental issue of "reasonable doubt."

One inherent weakness with the present jury system is the tragic assumption by many jurists, prosecutors, and, surprisingly, defense lawyers that the average juror has a sense of awareness of the relationship a juror must have with the totality of the criminal justice system. Indeed, the average juror is not likely to fully understand the "adversary nature" of our criminal justice system.[5]

In spite of these recognized deficiencies, trial lawyers overwhelmingly advocate retention of the jury system. In retrospect, the alternative to jury determination of "guilt or innocence" is judicial determination; and just as juries reflect human frailty, courts have understandably historically fallen into this category.

The essense of the philosophy of jurors sitting as fact-finders, rather than elected or appointed public officials occupying this vital role, was to create a crucible where the facts could be tested in an atmosphere of the greatest objectivity possible in an adversary confrontation.

In analyzing the present jury system in relationship to its responsiveness and attentiveness to rules of evidence, a wide divergence is readily apparent. Assume, arguendo, that the adversaries (prosecutor and defense counsel) have done a credible job in raising the appropriate evidence issues, and assume further that the trial judge has the capacity to relate to the jury the instructional directions. The writer is convinced that the average juror in criminal cases is motivated and capable of understanding, and placing in proper prospective, evidence rules and their relationship to the ultimate fact-finding responsibility.

II.

Many problems related to the role of the lay jury tragically rest with other components of the court, i.e., the trial judge and the adversaries themselves. It would be a disservice to the jury concept to overlook this truism. Indeed, much of the dissatisfaction concerning the resultant contribution of the lay jury is easily attributable to weaknesses in the trial, in the judge, the prosecutor, the defense advocate, and outdated, many times confusing, state statutes and procedural variances.

Before a lay juror can fully appreciate his role in the trial, he must understand the basic philosophy of the criminal justice system and the responsibility delegated to the jury. Community educational processes have provided little or no real assistance to the public in this very crucial public responsibility. The traditional bar associations stand indicted by their inaction and failure to provide leadership and productivity in this area. Belatedly, there is a growing realization that the quality of justice is impaired when jurors, the bar, and the lay public fail to understand these fundamentals.

In many jurisdictions in this nation, a long-overdue awareness seems to be surfacing, that instructions to the venire, and to the jurors selected, is a material prerequisite to maximum jury performance of their grave responsibility. The juror who enters his service in the trial of a case armed with an understanding of his responsibility, and of the vital role his participation as a juror plays in the effort to seek justice, will in most instances assure a just and productive deliberation at the conclusion of the trial. When a juror thoroughly understands the basic tenets of our American criminal justice system, he is then better equipped to render his contribution to the end that justice is served.

The district attorney or the trial judge who publicly criticizes the verdict of a lay jury does a grave disservice to the system itself.[6] A juror should be able to reach an unpopular decision without fear of public or professional criticism. To do otherwise would defeat the basic constitutional safeguards the jury was designed to protect.

Mass media exposure of police work, of prosecution of cases, and the strange role that television has assigned to the defense lawyer in far too many cases have tragically influenced many potential jurors. When one considers the instant news coverage of important criminal trials today and the leaks of vital evidentiary information from investigatory agencies and grand juries, the jury in the highly publicized trial would seem to constitute an entirely different problem than has historically been the case.[7]

One grave problem related to the crisis in the criminal justice system is the deterioration of the fiduciary obligation of judges, prosecutors, and investigatory agencies to protect the historic constitutional rights of the citizen who is the subject of the inquiry or investigation related to the "alleged" wrongdoing. One cogent lesson of the Watergate tragedy is inescapable: it is the dignifying of the philosophy that "the end justifies the means." Preindictment disclosure of rumored violations of the law by a citizen under investigation results in a pollution of the potential jury array. Persons unsophisticated in the law subconsciously form opinions, feelings, and conclusions all too often founded on inadmissible or simply nonfactual deliberate disclosures. This unfortunate predisposition is frequently carried into the jury box.[8] Whatever the motive, such conduct is reprehensible and must not, and cannot, be tolerated, if the right to a fair trial is to be successfully preserved.[9]

Jurors who come to the trial with open minds, unfettered by pretrial propaganda, are far more likely to arrive at a just verdict than jurors who have been bombarded with prejudicial pretrial disclosures before selection to serve as a trial juror (see *Shephard v. Maxwell* and *Irvin v. Dowd*).

In the field of expert testimony, the controversy over jury responsiveness, and its capacity to place such testimony in proper prospective, is a significant one. Experts are professionals in the field of their particular expertise, but they do not abandon their human traits of prejudice, partisanship, and interdisciplinary disagreement. For every psychiatric expert, for example, as all trial lawyers recognize, one can generally find an equally qualified expert to render a divergent opinion. The same is true in most disciplines.

Juries, for the most part, recognize this fact, and if it is properly presented by the adversaries during the voir dire and the trial itself, the jury will also recognize the proper posture of this type of evidence. Before allowing a jury to evaluate, test, and weigh the credibility of an expert who renders an opinion adverse to the defendant, a defense advocate must conduct a searching inquiry into the expert's background, his expertise, his relationship to the prosecution, his testimonial history, as well as his hidden partisanship and overt objectivity. When this has been capably done, the lay jury can place what weight and credibility, if any, it chooses to affix to the testimony of the particular expert.

There is a growing reliance on the use of expert witnesses by both the prosecution and the defense in today's criminal trials. Initially, the average juror will inevitably and instinctively accept the testimony of an expert more readily than that of the average lay witness. This responsiveness to expert testimony has a telling effect in many trials if the opinion of the expert, and far more crucial, the array of evidentiary facts upon which the opinion is predicated, go unchallenged by the defense lawyer. The same is true to a somewhat lesser degree when the expert is brought forth by the defense. The jury will generally evaluate the expert just as it evaluates a lay witness if, and only if, the advocate who challenges his testimony performs his cross-examination in a competent and professional manner.

Expert testimony, when reviewed, is a most crucial and important evidentiary tender. Many "experts" normally encountered in criminal trials are, in truth and fact, quasi-experts or trained paralegals. A graphic example of this type of "expert" is the breath analyzer technician who is a trained officer. He generally qualifies as an expert, but he is in essence a trained paralegal. He is vulnerable to defense attack, and most juries quickly recognize this fact. Experts who are employed by the police or other investigatory agencies are effective; but jurors, on the whole, approach their testimony in a guarded and understandably more concerned manner than the independent expert from a particular discipline whose trial involvement is more "disinterested" and limited to the particular case.

Too many lawyers, judges, and professionals tend to underestimate the capability of the average juror. His feel for the case and his ability to correctly place the expert in a proper prospective have been reflected again and again in criminal trials.

One factor which must be constantly borne in mind, is that law enforcement-oriented jurors place far more credence in experts employed by the state, than do jurors who have no innate partisan feelings for the prosecution. This is the defense lawyer's nightmare: to wind up with a jury or jurors who subsconsciously shift the burden of proof from the state to the defendant in spite of the instruction that the defendant has no obligation to prove anything, but rather has a basic right to demand strict proof by the prosecution, of every material element of the statute which the defendant is alleged to have transgressed.

A very important issue, when one considers the importance of the jury, is the jury's attentiveness and responsiveness to the rules of law which govern the conduct of the trial, and the testimony and physical evidence that is either allowed in the trial or restricted from the trial as a result thereof. Jurors who have not been properly advised initially tend to resent the advocate whose objection restricts an evidentiary tender. Aware of this basic fact of trial life, any defense lawyer worth his salt must convey to the jury that the trial is an adversary proceeding, that under the rules of law certain testimony and certain evidence is not proper (see note 4, below). Couple this message with the pledge that the defense lawyer will partisanly fight to keep out such evidence that he considers inadmissible, and the average juror can then keep a balanced prospective. In many instances he subconsciously applauds the effective defense lawyer fighting for his client. Unfortunately, the level of defense advocacy has been such that, in all too frequent circumstances, this vital tactical action is either overlooked or is ineptly carried out. Failure to instruct the jury places the jury in a position fraught with danger for the defense.

The greatest guardians of the quality of the jury is the trial prosecutor and defense lawyer, who after reasonable interrogation, observation and evaluation, exercise intelligent strikes to eliminate the most unfit jurors from their respective standpoints. If this selection process works, and the venire is selected in a non-controlled manner, insuring a representative composite of the community from whence the jury was drawn; then, the resultant panel, with all its many variances, is still the most productive fact finding device yet developed in the Anglo-Saxon system and the American Criminal Justice system which evolved from it.

III.

No brief analysis of the jury system would be complete without a summation of the most common problems that reduce the effectiveness of the role the jury plays in a criminal trial.

The most common problem confronting selection of the "ideal juror" is the all too frequently inadequate and haphazard method of selecting citizens from the general pool from which individual panels are drawn.[10] Selection which is random, where all segments of the society are represented, which has no built-in screening device to eliminate any group, or to insure inclusion of another, and which no individual can influence or control, is the ideal and necessary basic ingredient to the selection of a "fair and impartial jury."

The second area influencing the effectiveness of the trial jury is the instructional presentment by the court to insure that each juror fully understands his obligations, responsibilities, and the relationship of the jury to the other components of the system. Adequate instructions, coupled with timely advice by the trial court, generally cures this area of deficiency.

By far the most critical is the role played by the antagonists in the trial. They must seek out the unfit, the reluctant, the unqualified, or those with a predisposition to partisanship. Capable advocacy (assuming that selection from the general pool has been properly accomplished, and that the court's instructions have been delivered in a coherent and timely fashion) is the great purifier of the jury system. Proof of this fact is reflected by the record of the great trial lawyers, each having mastered the techniques of searching out and eliminating hostile jurors, which has resulted in their unusual success in winning difficult and complex criminal trials.

IV.

The anathema of a democratic society is to place the control of the life or liberty of an individual in the hands of a representative of the sovereign. The salvation of a democratic society is to insure an individual of a concerned judgment of one's peers drawn from the community in which the person charged with an alleged transgression personally resides.

Tragically, today the fate of a jury guarantee is in grave doubt. Many jurists, including those in the highest courts in this country and England, have questioned the need for, or the desirability of, the retention of the jury system as we now know it (*Williams v. Florida; Apodaca v. Oregon; Johnson v. Louisiana;* see also note 3 below). Various suggestions have surfaced which are proposed as alternatives to the jury in criminal cases. The crisis in the criminal justice system provides the environment for advocation of strange doctrines and theories.

To suggest, as has the Supreme Court of the United States, that the peer concept is a luxury no longer needed, that unanimity is outmoded, and that six- or four-man juries are just as capable of arriving at the truth as the traditional twelve-man concept is semantic hearsay.[11] It is reflected in part by an overreaction to the public impatience with the seeming inability of the justice system to meet the rising crime rate. Docket backlogs, mediocre jurists, poorly trained prosecutors, inadequate defense advocacy, and budget restrictions all play important roles in feeding the flames of discontent with our present system.

To the writer's knowledge, no viable alternative has been suggested which substitutes in the jury's stead some other procedure for sitting in judgment of one charged with a crime. The American criminal justice system and its concept of justice has been distinguished from other societies by one critical innovation —i.e., the American jury system. The American jury in criminal cases is conditioned to acknowledge the *right* of one who is accused of a crime to demand that the sovereign prove his culpability or guilt by "proof beyond a reasonable doubt;" and this right carries no obligation for the accused to testify or present any evidence, unless he freely elects to do so.

The trend toward "no-knock" intrusions into the privacy of one's home, the attack on the exclusionary rule,[12] the growing invasion of privacy by electronic listening devices—as in the Watergate case, the computerization of records containing harmful notations of suspicious arrests without disposition, preventative detention—all constitute twelfth-hour warnings that time is running out on a free society.

Students of human rights, of due process, and equal protection of the law recognize that anything less than a total commitment to preserve the jury in criminal trials, coupled with a searching concern to improve and strengthen it, will invite disaster and endanger the American dream of liberty and justice for all men under the law.

NOTES

1. Article III, §2, U.S. Constitution, "The Trial of all Crimes, except in Cases of Impeachment, shall be by Jury; and such Trial shall be held in the State where the said Crimes shall have been committed. . . ."

Amendment VI, U.S. Constitution, "In all criminal prosecutions, the accused shall enjoy the right to a speedy and public trial, by an impartial jury of the State and district wherein the crime shall have been committed, . . . and to be informed of the nature and cause of the accusation; to be confronted with the witnesses against him, to have compulsory process for obtaining witnesses in his favor, and to have the assistance of Counsel for his defence."

But note that the Constitution does not specifically provide the number of persons on the jury or that the jury shall be comprised of "peers." The tradition of English common law, set forth further in note 2 below, defined "peers" to be neighbors and fellow townsmen. Relatives and those involved in the dispute on trial were not allowed to serve as jurors.

2. Prior to 1194, jurors were gathered to vouch for the sincerity of the party from whom they were called. Later, jurors, who were also witnesses, were subject to extreme sanctions, such as forfeiture of their lands and liberty, for failure to testify to the truth.

In 1194, Richard I provided that twelve knights in the county (shire) should accuse and try criminal suspects. The knights comprised a combination grand jury and petit jury, but these responsibilities were divided in 1215 by the act of the Lateran Council.

By the end of the thirteenth century, jury trials in criminal cases had become common. An exception to the right of trial by jury, however, existed for cases of poisoning. The accused was required to defend himself by combat; if he lost his fight, he was deemed guilty. Additionally, it was later held that jury trials were required in all criminal cases, although the defendant might not want one because of the nature of the crime or because of his reputation in the community. By the thirteenth century, if a defendant refused to be tried by a jury, he was deemed to have confessed to his guilt. See Bloomstein (1968: 18-19).

3. Because of crowded dockets, many defendants enter into "plea bargaining" agreements with the prosecution, trading the defendant's guilty plea (and thus waiving right to jury trial) for a more favorable sentence (or probation, as the case may be). While a defendant may waive his right to a jury trial, his or her decision must be understandingly and intelligently made *(Adams v. McCann);* but, waiver of jury trial does not entitle a defendant to a right of trial by the judge *(Singer v. United States).*

Perhaps more alarmingly, the Supreme Court has held that the right to a jury trial does not mean that the jury must be composed of twelve persons. A Florida law provided for six-member juries; the Court noted that it could not find any intent of the Framers, the First Congress, or the states in 1789 to explicitly equate the constitutional sixth amendment guarantee of right of trial by jury. The Court noted that the size of the jury at common law generally was fixed at twelve, but "that particular feature of the jury systems appears to have been an historical accident, unrelated to the great purposes which gave rise to the jury in the first place" *(Williams v. Florida).*

The Supreme Court has further upheld a state constitutional provision permitting ten members of a jury to render guilty verdicts in noncapital cases. The sixth amendment, applicable to the state by the fourteenth amendment, does not require jury unanimity *(Apodaca v. Oregon).* In the companion case of *Johnson v. Louisiana,* the Court rejected defendant's contention that the standard required by "proof beyond a reasonable doubt" required by the fourteenth amendment meant that jury verdicts in state criminal cases must be unanimous. The state law involved permitted nine-to-three jury decisions for conviction. The Court noted that "nine jurors—a substantial majority of the jury—were convinced by the evidence. [D]isagreement of three jurors does not alone establish reasonable doubt, particularly when such heavy majority of the jury, after having considered the dissenters' views, remains convinced of guilt." But, it would seem logical that one could argue the reverse: that because three of the jurors voted for not guilty, "beyond a reasonable doubt" had *not* been established.

More recently, the California Supreme Court recognized that the "peer" concept, as applied to California state courts via California law, required that a jury be selected from the district in which the crime occurred *(People v. Jones).* See also, "People v. Jones—the jury must be drawn from the district of the crime" (1974).

4. The legal literature contains much on the importance of juror selection, ranging from the practical "how-to-do-it" type of material to the more general discussion of the selection process. For practical aides, for example, see Burnett (1973); "Selection of the jury" (1970); and Tessmer (1968: ch. 4).

For general discussion, see Kalven and Zeisel (1966: ch. 28); "Economic discrimination in jury selection" (1970); "Exploring racial prejudice on voir dire: . . ." (1974); Padawer-Singer et al. (1974); and Teitelbaum (1972).

5. Generally, the juror has received inadequate or no information about our criminal justice system's adversary nature either through the educational processes or through the mass media. What he has received, as a result, is a distortion through the media portrayals of the relationship of the components of the system. For example, Perry Mason's exposure of the guilty party (who is, conveniently, sitting in the audience) does not happen in a real courtroom. The jury has the job of unraveling the complexities of the evidence and judging whether or not the defendant is guilty. In the average state trial court, the judge's admonition to the jury contains very little to acquaint it with its unique role in the total aspect of the trial process—as the exclusive judge of the facts.

For a discussion of some of the reasons for differences between judge and jury disagreement over issues of fact, see Kalven and Zeisel (1966: ch. 14).

6. Bloomstein (1968: 17-18) tells how the attaint (subjection of the jurors to forfeiture of their lands for failure to render a proper verdict) caused one riot in 1670. One of the two English defendants on trial, from which the attaint charge arose, was William Penn.

7. Not only are the jury panel members subject to intense public interest in them as individuals, the jury must often undergo problems a "normal" jury would not—i.e., sequestration for frequently long periods from family and friends, absence from jobs, and having their reading and media viewing materials monitored. The mere willingness to serve as a juror frequently depends on duration of the trial; while some express interest in serving, they are often unable to serve a two- or three-month-long jury term and thus must exclude themselves from consideration. One might ask—if the right to trial by jury includes the concept of trial by one's peers—then is the resulting "peer" group, in the long trial, consistent with the minimum definition of "peers"?

In the case of *Shephard v. Maxwell,* the U.S. Supreme Court released Dr. Sam Shephard because of the publicity to which the jurors were subjected. The Court noted that the judge's "suggested" and "requested" directions to the jury not to expose themselves to the publicity, coupled with the celebrity status in which the jurors were thrust and the general "carnival" atmosphere, caused defendant Shephard to be deprived of that "judicial serenity and calm to which he was entitled."

8. In the Shephard case, the Court notes that it had set aside a federal conviction where the jurors were exposed, through news accounts, to information not admitted at the trial. In *Marshall v. United States,* the Court held that the prejudice from such material may be greater than when it is part of the prosecution's evidence because such evidence is not then tempered by protective procedures. In *Irvin v. Dowd,* the Court said that jurors are not required to be totally ignorant of the facts and issues involved in a particular trial: "it is sufficient if the juror can lay aside his impression or opinion and render a verdict based on the evidence presented in court." The Court further noted that "the influence that lurks in an opinion once formed is so persistent that it unconsciously fights detachment from the mental processes of the average man." Therefore, the Court continued, where so many persons so many times "admitted prejudice, such a statement of impartiality can be given little weight."

9. As a cooperative effort between the nation's media representatives and the bench and bar, the American Bar Association has published its *Standards Relating to Fair Trial and Free Press* (1968) in which guidelines for the judiciary, the prosecution, the defense and the media are set out.

10. The ideal juror may be defined as one with no predispositions to either side, no knowledge of the facts prior to trial, free from prejudice for either state or defendant, and who possesses an awareness of his responsibility and the importance of rendering a verdict based solely on the facts—free from reliance on intuition, feelings, or prejudice, regardless of the popularity or consequence of the verdict.

11. Ashman and McConnell (1973); Rosenblatt (1972); Zeisel (1971); and "Effect of jury size on the probability of conviction: . . ." (1971).

12. The exclusionary rule essentially states that illegally obtained evidence by the police cannot be used, i.e., is "excluded" from use, in the trial of the accused, even if such exclusion results in acquitting a guilty defendant. The rationale is that of deterrence: law enforcement officials should be deterred from unlawful searches and seizures [the fourth amendment] if the illegally seized, although sometimes trustworthy, evidence is suppressed often enough and the courts persistently enough deprive the police of any benefits they might have gained from their illegal conduct.

In his dissent in *Bivens v. Six Unknown Named Agents,* Supreme Court Chief Justice Burger said, "I do not question the need for some remedy to give meaning and teeth to the constitutional guarantees against unlawful conduct by government officials." However, he said, "Some clear demonstration of the benefits and effectiveness of the Exclusionary Rule is required to justify it in view of the high price it extracts from society—the release of countless guilty criminals." The question becomes, what happened to the presumption our Founding Fathers seemed to adhere to—that all persons are presumed to be innocent until proven guilty by the State? Granted that today's sophisticated police procedures probably garner more "guilty" persons than innocent, but does that mean that we are to discard this basic presumption?

See also *United States v. Calandra;* Sevilla (1974—and Editor's Note following); and Baada (1974: 646).

REFERENCES

Adams v. McCann (1942) 317 U.S. 269, 63 S. Ct. 236.

American Bar Association (1968) Standards Relating to Fair Trial and Free Press [approved draft].

Apodaca v. Oregon (1972) 406 U.S. 404, 92 S. Ct. 1628.

ASHMAN, A. and J. McCONNELL (1973) "Trial by jury: the new irrelevant right?" Southwestern Law Journal 27: 436.

BAADA, H. W. (1974) "Illegally obtained evidence in criminal and civil cases: a comparative study of a classic mismatch II." Texas Law Review 52.

Bivens v. Six Unknown Named Agents (1971) 403 U.S. 388, 91 S. Ct. 1999.

BLOOMSTEIN, M. (1968) Verdict: The Jury System. New York: Dodd, Mead.

BURNETT, W. (1973) "Voir dire examination." For the Defense 8 (March): 4.

"Economic discrimination in jury selection." (1970) Law and Social Order 474.

"Effect of jury size on the probability of conviction: an evaluation of Williams v. Florida." (1971) Case Western Reserve Law Review 22: 529.

Exploring racial prejudice on voir dire: constitutional requirements and policy considera-tion." (1974) Boston University Law Review 54: 394.

Irvin v. Dowd (1961) 366 U.S. 717, 81 S. Ct. 1639.

Johnson v. Louisiana (1972) 406 U.S. 356, 92 S. Ct. 1620.

KALVEN, H., Jr., and H. ZEISEL (1966) The American Jury. Boston: Little, Brown.

Marshall v. United States (1959) 360 U.S. 310, 79 S. Ct. 1171.

PADAWER-SINGER, A. M., A. SINGER, and R. SINGER (1971) "Voir dire by two lawyers: an essential safeguard." Judicature 57: 386.

People v. Jones (1973) 9 Cal. 3d 546; 510 P. 2d 705, 108 Cal. Rptr. 345.

"People v. Jones—the jury must be drawn from the district of the crime." (1974) Hastings Law Journal 25: 547.

ROSENBLATT, J. C. (1972) "Should the size of the jury in criminal cases be reduced to six?" Prosecutor 8.

"Selection of the jury." (1970) Goldstein Trial Technique. New York: Callaghan.

SEVILLA, C. M. (1974) "Remapping the exclusionary rule: an alternative suggestion." For the Defense 9: 4.

Shephard v. Maxwell (1966) 384 U.S. 333, 86 S. Ct. 1507.

Singer v. United States (1965) 380 U.S. 24, 85 S. Ct. 783.

TEITELBAUM, W. (1972) "Voir dire: another view." American Journal of Criminal Law 1: 274.

TESSMER, C. W. (1968) Criminal Trial Strategy. Dallas: John R. Mara.

United States v. Calandra (1974) 414 U.S. 338, 94 S. Ct. 613.

Williams v. Florida (1970) 399 U.S. 78, 90 S. Ct. 1893.

ZEISEL, H. (1971) "And then there were none: the diminution of the federal jury." University of Chicago Law Review 38: 710.

11

FROM THE JURY BOX

EDWIN KENNEBECK

This chapter traces one thoughtful individual's confusing and often frustrating experiences with the American jury system from the initial summons and voir dire for a major, dramatic criminal trial to the denouement of a "minor" and less pressurized civil case.

Through his experiences, not only are we acquainted with the explosive drama of a Black Panther trial, but we are also made aware of the too frequent occasions when an "ordinary" participant (layman) in the court process is neglected by legal officials and is not made properly cognizant of what is taking place around him.

Careless lawyers, blasé judges, witnesses whose Facts and Truths have wasted away to only shadows of Recollections and, lastly, the author's niggling self-doubts—all these aside, this chapter attests to the tremendous personal impact of participating in the justice system.

Chapter 11

FROM THE JURY BOX

EDWIN KENNEBECK

I thought of beginning with an apology for not having experienced jury duty in wide variety, until I realized that most people do not have a great deal of such experience. The juror's job, unlike that of an attorney or a judge, is only a sideline. Like plaintiffs or defendants, jurors often are, in a sense, strangers to the system of justice. But I was a juror in the case of the New York Black Panther 13—originally the Panther 21 case and officially *State of New York v. Lumumba Shakur et al.*—for eight months. With fifteen companions in the jury box (there were four alternate jurors), I watched six defense attorneys, one judge, and two prosecution attorneys contend in the trial of thirteen members of the Black Panther Party accused of conspiracy to blow up Manhattan subway tracks and department stores and to murder policemen, among other things. The case covered more than two years: the first arrests were made in April 1969, jury selection began in September 1970, the trial began in October, and the swift verdict of acquittal came in May 1971.

This became the longest trial in the history of New York State, costing about two million dollars. Three books about it have appeared (including my own), as well as a magazine article by another juror. The trial has receded into history; the cry of "Black Power," with its exhilarating magic for some and its depressing menace for others, has lost its original force, whatever new connotations and values it may have taken on. The Black Panther Party, whose existence gave the trial its political flavor, no longer makes headlines. And the murky wonder of secret-police surveillance—an important part of the case—has become an almost banal horror; Watergate and other filthy tricks have brought into plain daylight what were once dire radical accusations.

I had been summoned to jury duty several times before that trial, without ever serving in the jury box; and a year and a half after it, I anticlimactically had jury duty in civil court and helped to pass judgment in two cases of traffic accidents. It was almost amusing then to find myself in a small courtroom, with no spectators or guards to speak of, only five fellow jurors, and a very low reading on the drama scale. Those experiences, nonetheless, gave me some small insights into the major one.

I.

"Mr. Kennebeck, sir, . . ." So the assistant district attorney who was prosecuting the Black Panthers began questioning me at the voir dire; and, as I look back, I can try to compare my vexing dilemma then with that of a prospective juror in any trial. But whereas the average juror is going to give only a few hours or days of his time to a case, I was—it turned out—going to give more than half a year.

Some questions I might have asked myself then rose only part way toward my consciousness, preoccupied as I was with trying to give the D.A. the right answer. I might have wondered how I would like sitting through hours of often boring testimony, not to mention the long summations at the end of the trial and the judge's own rundown of the evidence. Some citizens worry about being away from the job for even a routine two-week period; what would my employer think of my taking so much time off? Who would absorb the work that would pile up in my absence? Another problem that could have arisen, but did not, was whether the jury would be sequestered. More seriously, could I take on this responsibility of sitting in judgment on people who lived in a world tragically different from mine? There would be black jurors as well as white ones like myself; would racial differences impair my perceptions and theirs? Could I face the black defendants day after day with a clear sense of being one of their "peers?" How wisely would I be able to articulate my viewpoint to the other jurors when the time came, and give it the force of persuasion?

Even the large questions often, in some form, confront the citizens summoned to jury duty; and, like the small ones, they can affect his or her feelings about participating in this aspect of the American system. For most people, jury duty, no matter how undemanding, is notoriously inconvenient, and nearly everybody agrees that it is inefficient.

The miseries, which have been described frequently, must be fairly similar in most parts of the country. Often a prospective juror is taken from his job and salary to an uncomfortable place, for a purpose that is sometimes boring, sometimes frightening. The varying fees for jury duty are ludicrously low. I do not know how it feels to be picked up on the street by policemen for jury duty, as has happened in some communities when the regular rolls did not meet the demand, but it must be more distressing than exciting. Whatever the circumstances, seldom does a sense of civic responsibility compensate for a juror's "sacrifice."

My first summons, quite a few years ago, made me resentful and somewhat apprehensive. Although the company I work for does not suspend salaries during jury duty, I answered the summons with strong reluctance. I wanted to postpone the chore and was relieved to learn, when I got downtown to the central jury room, that I would have no difficulty in doing so. On my appearance in front of the designated desk to ask for postponement, the clerk himself said to me, "Business reasons?" and I said yes.

Sooner or later, however, the time usually comes for the week or two of discomfort. Nearly everyone who has done such a stint knows the dreary hours of waiting around, very likely in a stuffy, ugly, smoky room, for one's name to be picked from the squirrel-cage lottery machine or other device. New York City used to show prospective jurors an interesting short film in which E. G. Marshall made it acceptably clear that our presence by itself was helping the cause of justice. I am sure many of us felt better about the "wasted" hours after we understood that a judge and the contending parties can often expedite the resolution of a case simply by having a potential jury available. At any rate, since seeing that film, I have not felt useless as I sat squirming in the central jury room. I agree, nonetheless, with those who complain about having to wait too long on the premises. There is often no need for such tedious sitting around.

Other juror problems can range from missing important business calls to discovering that there are not enough available parking spaces in the neighborhood of the courthouse. When the judge or some other authority acknowledges the parking problem by advising prospective jurors to leave their cars in illegal areas because tickets will be "taken care of," the juror is likely to take a dim view of what the law means. He or she might also be dismayed to learn that certain professional people are never placed on jury lists. And some of those professionals who are summoned may be doubly resentful at having to go through the mill despite the fact that they (newspaper reporters, for example) are scarcely likely to be chosen for any jury.

The several attempts to keep us amused—with free coffee or tea (no such thing in New York City), or with bad commercial-plug movies, such as reporter

Tom Gavin (1974) described in a witty article about his jury days—may indicate some concern for the poor citizen. I have sensed this concern among the city employees in the New York jury rooms, a respect and sympathy that flourishes as best they can in poorly financed, inadequate surroundings. These employees have no more delusions than do jurors about the quality of the court environment. I have found that they do their best to keep from adding to the tiresomeness and frustration.

II.

The tedium is broken, of course, when the prospective juror hears his name called and lets himself be led to a room where the voir dire takes place. Now, at last, we face more direct and absorbing concerns. It may not be a pleasant experience, but it is what we have patiently been waiting for.

My first experience of a voir dire I found dismaying. I felt challenged, as if I were unwillingly participating in a competition that I needed to win. Somehow I felt that once I was, so to speak, in the jury box, it would be a humiliation to be excused from it by either party.

In an abortion case some years ago, I deliberately got myself excused by telling the judge that I had strong feelings about abortion which would probably hinder me from reaching a fair verdict. I could not easily have explained in detail how my feelings went, and the judge did not ask me to explain further. I suspect that it was my fear of "getting involved" rather than a firm sense of principle that made me ask to be excused. And my request was easy to make because the judge had allowed quite a few jurors to do the same thing. If he had made it more difficult to beg off, I and some others would probably not have done so with such rapidity. It seemed clear afterward that we were being "used" by the judge and the contending parties in a way different from the obvious and usual one. Needless to say, several of us nonexperts surmised that an out-of-court settlement had been the judge's desire. But—another of the unchosen juror's frustrations—we never learned how the case did turn out.

In other cases where I have been excused, I left the room with the strong egotistical desire to tell the attorneys that they had misgauged me, that I could indeed give a perfectly fair verdict. One comfort comes from the understanding that sometimes one side does not *want* a fair verdict.

I was encouraged to see, during my more recent civil court experience, that voir dires were held without a judge—the attorneys apparently being able to keep an adequate check on each other's questioning, suspending the process when necessary to ask a judge somewhere for a ruling when they did not agree. Here, at least, is one step toward releasing judges for, presumably, more urgent duties.

Despite my several degrees of resistance to jury duty, I found myself, in the Panther case in September 1970, surprisingly interested and—though nervous—less apprehensive about the responsibility that this job could bring. Like many people, I had come to feel that the question of Black Power did impinge on my life, even if other serious public matters aroused my concern much less. And this particular public matter was being set before me, so to speak. I was being invited, tentatively, to enter into the heart of it, whereas I was not invited, say, to give a direct and immediate verdict on the Vietnam War.

I could not help feeling astonished when the invitation became concrete. Professional people were, in effect, saying to us lay men and women, "All our expertise is now being exercised for your sake. We can try to make sure that you hear all the proper evidence in the case, and that the court explains clearly the laws that will apply, but you with plain common sense are the ones who will make the final decision." Later I came across G. K. Chesterton's essay, "Twelve Men," in *Tremendous Trifles,* which comes to this conclusion:

> Now, it is a terrible business to mark a man out for the vengeance of men. But it is a thing to which a man can grow accustomed, as he can to other terrible things; he can even grow accustomed to the sun. And the horrible thing about all legal officials, even the best, about all judges, magistrates, barristers, detectives, and policemen, is not that they are wicked (some of them are good), not that they are stupid (several of them are quite intelligent), it is simply that they have got used to it.

> Strictly they do not see the prisoner in the dock; all they see is the usual man in the usual place. They do not see the awful court of judgment; they see only their own workshop. . . . Our civilization has decided, and very justly decided, that determining the guilt or innocence of men is a thing too important to be trusted to trained men. . . . When it wants a library catalogued, or the solar system discovered, or any trifle of that kind, it uses up its specialists. But when it wishes anything done which is really serious, it collects twelve of the ordinary men standing around.

So the court clerk who pulled my name from his squirrel cage and summoned me to be interrogated before a microphone in the witness box (as was done in the Panther case, with many spectators and reporters present), was potentially bringing me, one of the "ordinary men standing around," into a more intimate relation with a more serious public problem than I had ever known (except for bombing missions I participated in as a B-17 radio operator over Germany near the end of World War II). Certainly my habit of writing letters to newspaper editors and my willingness to vote in most elections were instances of social concern at a great remove. Maybe city authorities ought to give greater emphasis and publicity to this sense of participation, even in less important trials, in order to make the job more appealing. Most citizens have a sense of "public spirit" when they know how to implement it, when they know that it will be taken seriously and will be effective.

This voir dire was another competition that I expected to lose; I was inclined to agree with friends who said that prosecuting attorneys were usually wary of "liberal" editorial types. The assistant district attorney who was prosecuting this case did not press deeply with his questions. Apparently he was so sure of his case that he felt he did not have to screen his prospects very closely. He would have been wrong to challenge me—I, of course, believe— because I know that I and my fellow jurors were scrupulously fair in our judgment.

There came a moment, however, when I thought I might "lose;" the D.A.—after ascertaining that I was chief copy editor in a publishing house, and other commonplace facts—said,

"If you felt, sir, that someone believed in a cause and therefore did some actions that were illegal as a result of that, would you think that would absolve them from wrongdoing?" I hesitated over my answer, so he said, "You've heard of Robin Hood, I take it?"

I said that I had.

"And you've heard of robbing from the rich to give to the poor?"

I agreed that I had.

"But nevertheless it's robbery. You understand that, don't you?"

At about this point, the judge intervened with "Please ask a proper question."

But the D.A. continued, to my surprise (we amateurs learn, or mislearn, some court rules quickly). "I may have one more question in that area and I'll go on to something else. Do you have any reservations in your mind that if Robin Hood were indicted for robbery, that you would convict him of robbery even though he might have wanted to give to the poor?"

I did not immediately recognize that the question was confusingly hypothetical, based on a legendary figure with no relation to the thirteen black defendants before us. The intervention of the judge should, I suppose, save the prospective jurors from such "trap" questions, but at this point the judge said nothing. Fortunately, I had the presence of mind to say, "I'd have to hear the evidence. The answer is no"—meaning that I would not acquit a robber merely on the basis of his good intentions.

The D.A.'s next question, as he concluded his interrogation of me, was one that I presume most lawyers ask or imply. It underlines a problem that every juror faces in a complex way:

If you were in the jury room and the vote was eleven to one and you were the only minority juror, would you continue to reason with the rest of your fellow jurors to try to reach a verdict or would you just say, "I've made up my mind. I'm brighter than the rest of you fellows and let's not discuss it"?

A question like that could lead a prospective juror to complicated self-analysis under other circumstances, but here it seemed more of a reminder than an inquiry, because the form in which the D.A. asked it practically dictated the answer. A willing prospect would hardly want to say, "I'm sure my own opinion will be more carefully thought out and wiser than anybody else's, and I certainly will not discuss or debate it with the others if they don't agree with me." I gave the proper answer.

The D.A. apparently wanted to make doubly sure that my college credentials had not given me a superiority complex. "And just because someone didn't have the experience and background that you might have," he asked, "but might have some common sense, would you also listen to that type of person?" I could only answer, "Certainly."

The defendants' attorneys were far more interested in probing into my opinions than the D.A. had been. Since in those days the name "Black Panther" evoked strong feelings, the six defense lawyers (only one was black) obviously wanted to take as much care as possible to find jurors without notions or feelings prejudicial to their case. Only two of them interrogated me. Would I have any problem, they wondered, if I knew that the defendants were opposed to the Vietnam War? Could I be fair and open in thinking about Black Panther Party members despite all that I had read about the organization? Would I be prejudiced by the fact that there were undercover agents in the case? Would I be likely to take the testimony of an undercover agent over someone else's word, just because he was a policeman?

The black attorney probed specifically into the matter of color. "Do you feel, sir, that you might in any way, conscious or unconscious, be affected by some prejudice or bias that might interfere with your passing judgment upon thirteen black men and women who are charged with a serious crime?" This was another question that a psychologist or philosopher might probe for hours; but I said no. He asked me whether I had ever been the victim of a crime, and I told him that my apartment had been burglarized twice. "Is there anything about the fact that you have been the victim of a crime, that, perhaps unknowingly, might affect you in passing judgment upon thirteen men and women who are accused of a crime or crimes?" To that, also, I answered no.

Finally, on the matter of my education again, with a hint about a possible touch of ivory-towerism:

Do you feel that, as a result of your educational background and as a result of your experience and perhaps being somewhat removed from some areas of life, that you would have difficulty in passing judgment upon thirteen men and women, some of whom have not been so fortunate as to receive as much education or to experience some of the experiences that you have had?

Since the D.A. objected to the question, and the judge sustained him, I did not have to answer.

A few moments of suspense followed. I was surprised to hear the D.A. say that he had no objection to me. By this time, I found myself accepting fully and eagerly the formidable obligation. The defense lawyers, after consulting with the defendants, whose evaluating gazes I had myself been trying to evaluate, said they did not object, and the clerk thereupon led me over to the jury box, where I became juror number four. I was told to look upon the defendants, they were told to look upon me, and I swore that I would do my utmost to judge them fairly.

It was a moment of intense drama for me. Even the most trivial case has its elements of theater—contending forces, conflicts of character and of recollection as far as the case is concerned, along with conflicts of personality between amd among attorneys, plaintiffs, defendants, and judge, and among jurors, too. This case made front-page headlines and had national repercussions. A new kind of responsibility, clearly defined and pointed and weighty, was descending on me. It was softened somewhat by being shared with eleven other citizens.

Far from wary of "editorial" types, the D.A. chose two others of that category on the same day—another book editor and a man who edited television news tapes. The sixteen jurors who were at last chosen after six weeks of voir dire constituted a fairly good cross-section of modern city life. Two women (one an alternate), both black; six black men; one Puerto Rican; seven white men. Postal clerks, city employees, teachers, a retired longshoreman, a building superintendant—we came from "ordinary" life into the center of civic storm.

III.

The voir dire lasted six weeks (the judge did not hold court sessions on Fridays, in response to some defendants' requests as Muslims), and I heard all but the first week of the extended interrogations. The defense attorneys frequently asked prospective jurors the familiar "You understand, don't you, that a real trial is different from a Perry Mason television show?" It may seem an obvious point to people with courtroom experience, but it is helpful to amateur jurors to be reminded that defendants are under no obligation to prove their innocence, that jurors cannot expect to walk out of the courtroom at the end of a trial with a clear and total picture of what did happen.

Lay people are used to the patterns of television shows, detective novels, and movies that offer the obligatory explanation of the whole case, with the guilty parties unequivocally identified. Indeed, the criminals often oblige us by confessing everything just before the close of the story, if the camera (or narrator) has not already shown us events that policemen and judges cannot have seen for themselves. Audiences are grateful to be saved from reading about, or seeing, the protracted detention of the suspect, the tiresome legal discussions, bail hearings, a perhaps boringly drawn-out trial, and the like—the very material that a jury *will* confront.

These entertainments also insulate us from the ambiguity of justice; people who watch a Perry Mason show never disagree about what happened, never have to reach a compromise verdict. I think of Enid Bagnold's sage and delicious play, *The Chalk Garden,* where a woman who has served a jail sentence for murder says, "Truth doesn't ring true in a court of law." Someone asks her, "What rings true then?" and she replies, "The likelihood. The probability. They work to make things fit together. What the prisoner listens to there is not his life. It is the shape and shadow of his life. With the accidents of truth taken out of it."

One of the major insights, I am sure, that many people get from jury experience is precisely this ambiguity, this necessity of dealing with shapes and shadows. Not only fictional crime stories but so-called objective news media habitually reduce complex situations to a few issues easily grasped. It is not difficult for even a fairly liberal-minded person to decide, almost inadvertently, who is guilty in a crime he reads about in the newspaper, which is most likely reporting insufficient evidence. The distinction between "suspect" and "perpetrator" is hard to keep in mind. Widely publicized cases raise the question of whether it is possible to find jurors who have not been influenced toward an opinion. Nonetheless, I think this problem is often exaggerated by those who underestimate how effectively a trial can pare away the inessential elements of a case and focus on the evidence and the law—provided that fairly competent judges and attorneys are at work. In addition, although of course a juror's mere claim to being open-minded is not enough, presumably other questions can establish the nature of his experience and temperament and perspicacity.

So, in the courtroom, the juror comes to see how Truth is reduced to Fact and Fact often reduced to Recollection. Sometimes Truth, Fact, Recollection, Opinion, and Justice itself appear to be functions of six or twelve personalities, as they have been formed by experience.

And what about those personalities? In recent years we have read about lawyers who try to choose juries on the basis of professional psychological —sociological?—evaluation. Whether this method is any more effective than the intuition and instinctive judgment of a seasoned lawyer can never be proved.

Besides the jurors' attitudes toward the principal parties in the case, their relationships with each other can obviously be important.

I do not suppose many attorneys have the opportunity to consider how the jury members might evaluate each other; I recall thinking facetiously during the Panther voir dire that we who had already been chosen ought to have some say in who our fellow-jurors would be. This was absurd, of course, but jurors do have to size up and deal with those varied strangers (and, in small communities, friends and acquaintances and enemies), regardless of their mutual opinions. Who are the other five, or eleven, or whatever, men and women with whom I will be trying to make sense out of the ambiguities? Already the voir dire has given me a few clues—maybe as many as I am going to get—about how they think and otherwise function. Intelligent, dull, stolid, high-strung, defensive, aggressive; wise guys and know-it-alls; cool operators with subtle ways; clear-eyed innocents; confused neurotics, maybe easily swayed. . . . Meanwhile, they are doubtless trying to size me up, and I am trying to give them a certain impression: I am friendly, but not the type to join a clique; open-minded, but wary of tricks and gimmicks; experienced in chicanery, but not a cynic. . . .

A long trial gives jurors more opportunities to evolve factions and antagonisms than the brief traffic trial, for example, that will be decided probably by a group of strangers. In the seven months of the Panther trial, we all remained remarkably friendly. We took care to avoid talking about the case, as the judge frequently "admonished" us to do. We sorted ourselves out into lunch partners or groups; to a small degree some jurors saw each other socially at other times. We became used to the strange custom of walking from stormy scenes in the courtroom to our own jury room, then settling ourselves down without comment, to read or brood in silence, to do office work, or to make remarks about the weather or other matters unrelated to our most immediate concern. Probably more than most juries in more ordinary cases, we were successful in our attempt to avoid giving signs of our reactions. Toward the end we may have begun to sense that most of us considered this case of undercover spies against revolutionary rhetoricians to be weak. But even then, there were no overt remarks about it, and until deliberations were well under way I feared that there could be fierce contention.

The most notable and upsetting episode came one day midway in the trial, after the judge had delivered some particularly harsh comments against the defendants and their attorneys. His Honor allowed the D.A. to present us with speculative testimony by police chemical experts on how much damage certain explosives might do. Since the major charges were those of conspiracy, the judge was allowing some witnesses to say things that could be taken "subject to connection" and applied if we later decided that there had been a conspiracy.

Whatever the legal justification for this, even though the prosecution had not yet "laid a foundation"—had not come to the stage of trying to corroborate charges that the defendants had possessed dynamite and other explosives—the police experts were allowed to give us examples of what various kinds of bombs could do to innocent bystanders.

The defense attorneys objected repeatedly to these statements, since not even the D.A. was charging that such explosions ever took place. The judge was denying their objections with obvious impatience, frequently in tones of anger (which are not, of course, recorded by the court reporter). When he granted us a brief recess we filed, as usual, silently into the jury room, prepared to keep our thoughts and feelings to ourselves. One of the jurors, however, let his indignation burst out. "He's railroading them," he said. "I want to quit!" We calmed and comforted the man, reminded him that he would get his chance to make his feelings known at the time of deliberations. He was mollified, stayed with us to the end, and learned that we had been sharing his reaction. Whether the fact that he was black made a difference in his reaction, I do not know; there did seem to be times when the impatient judge was inadvertently making it hard for all of us to keep our minds open to the prosecution's side.

Prospective jurors terrified at the responsibility that may fall upon them can take heart from a comment in Thomas Griffith's book *How True:*

> The true relationship between a journalist's beliefs and his reporting is something like that of a juror's desire to reach an impartial verdict. Jurors are not required to be empty minds, free of past experience or views; what is properly demanded of them is a readiness to put prejudices and uncorroborated impressions aside in considerating the evidence before them. . . .

IV.

Most trials are milder, less complicated, less strained by public pressures. A summons to jury duty, nevertheless, is seldom welcomed, and many people may be distressed more by relatively trivial difficulties than by any worry over jury psychology. Perhaps if city authorities took the process less for granted and gave more thought to the hesitations and confusions that some of us endure in answering our summonses, and perhaps if they offered us more simple information about what they are asking of us, we would be happier about doing it. Likewise, if there were more explaining during the voir dire and the trial, jurors might come to feel more intimately and importantly associated with the system.

This taking-for-granted is a natural part of every repetitious enterprise.

Doctors, teachers, lawyers, and such all have their routines and their jargon, and are so grooved or tracked into the invariables of their work that they forget how alien much of it may sound or look to an outsider. To many a juror, "relief" may have something to do with relaxing in an armchair or getting out of tight shoes; "remedy" suggests aspirin or a Band-Aid. Even "plaintiff" and "defendant" can become interchangeable in a layman's mind, especially in some of the more hasty and sloppy cases he might have to listen to.

There are other technical matters that many of us would like to understand better. In the course of a long trial, we may begin to learn some of the pitfalls that a good lawyer has to avoid, but many of them remain obscure to us; and in short trials we never get a chance to comprehend the subtleties fully. An attorney may ask what sounds like a fair and helpful question, but to our bewilderment his opponent says, "Objection," and the judge says, "Sustained." During one of the more heated moments of the Panther trial, one of the defendants—she was acting as her own lawyer—demanded that the judge instruct the D.A. to cooperate in conducting a fair trial. To this the judge responded, "Request denied," causing many of the black spectators to laugh scornfully, and—as we learned after the trial—upsetting one or two jurors. The irony of the judge's answer did not seem quite as strong to me, since I thought he could well have meant only that he did not feel it necessary to give the instruction. Unfortunately, he had already indicated that his sympathies lay with the prosecution, and his "request denied" sounded harsher than perhaps it really was. Whatever the question, when it is the form rather than the substance of the question that is faulty, the juror may wonder at the objection. Unfortunately, it is not possible for him to ask for an explanation.

When I was serving in civil court, I had the luck to be drawn for a trial in which an unusually articulate judge presided, a man also unusually sympathetic to the average juror's unfamiliarity with the routine. He spoke with vigor, and emphatically acknowledged that the jargon of the courtroom might be confusing for jurors. With agreeable enthusiasm, he carefully told us just what such-and-such meant, what we could ignore, whither we should direct our major attention. It was a joy to have this man in charge. When the minor traffic accident case was ready for our deliberations, we knew exactly what we could find, what specific questions we would have to decide.

In contrast, the judge I encountered in another traffic case was old and weary; he read his greetings and instructions to us in a droning voice from a printed card, making (thank heaven) no pretense that he was speaking extemporaneously. When we went into deliberations, we were not entirely sure of the issues; but because of my experience with the judge of the previous day I was able to assure my fellow jurors that we not only would be asked to indicate the person whom we had found against, but would also have to account for the three other parties involved. It all came out clearly enough eventually, but it took longer than it need have.

It was the "good" judge who said something like, "Ladies and gentlemen of the jury, the verdict is now up to you. My job here is only to see that you get as much proper evidence as possible. As to the disposition of the case, I assure you I am totally indifferent. After you have delivered your verdict I will put the entire matter out of my mind. . . ." Somehow, if this had come from the other judge it might have sounded callous; from this man it sounded admirably right.

We cannot demand that every judge have a sense of humor and unflagging vivacity, but we can be grateful when those blessings appear, not only because they help to keep our attention alive.

Another minor revelation of the two civil court cases had to do with the nature of lawyers. After watching eight lawyers in the Panther trial who knew their sides of the case thoroughly, and who kept their passion and verve at high pitch for the seven long months, I observed a couple of their civil court counterparts with a feeling of letdown. Granted, these cases were relatively unimportant. It jolted me, nonetheless, that in one case neither lawyer gave any indication that he had visited the intersection where the automobile collision took place. Both had the name of the street wrong, and the judge had to correct them.

Doubtless, this is par for the course: a lawyer with many small cases can hardly keep tabs on all details. But it adds to my realization that minor cases may get minor treatment, which also simply means that justice is not always given first-rate, complete attention.

I was equally dismayed by one lawyer's attempt to impress us with histrionics. He was representing the defendant, whose car allegedly sideswiped the plaintiff's. The plaintiff, a young man with Hispanic accent and an incomplete knowledge of English, told us how long he thought the block was in which his car had been traveling. But the defendant's attorney, in cross-examining the young man, rather puzzlingly got him to estimate a quite different length for the same street. It was clear to me and (as I later found out) my five fellow jurors that the plaintiff was simply confused, but the cross-examining attorney went on to say, "Were you deliberately misleading us, then, when you said the street was XXXX yards long?" To which the befuddled young man mumbled, "Yes." (This raises the question of whether some people should have the right to an interpreter in the courtroom.)

The histrionics came when the defendant's lawyer gave his summation on the following morning. He now held before us a paperback edition of Dante's *Inferno.* He had planned to read to us, he said, the passage that described the punishment of perjurors, but then had decided to spare us the recitation. Later, when the plaintiff's lawyer, during his summation, came to the matter of his client's discrepancy the other attorney, seated at his table, pointedly lifted the book in his hands and pretended to be reading. In our deliberations we commented angrily on this transparent attempt to influence us. Ironically, we did find in favor of the defendant, and I cannot help fearing that the lawyer thinks his Dante ploy had something to do with our verdict. (It is disheartening to imagine him polishing his courtroom tricks in the hope of further triumphs.) Despite my feelings about jurors as laymen wanting and needing explanation of the technicalities, I do not believe that many of them are charmed or duped by attorneys who are bad actors.

I also know of instances where lawyers have harassed prospective jurors during voir dires; whatever purposes are served by this, in the way of "instructing" or warning other jurors, it is one more condition that can make jury duty appear unsavory.

But careless lawyers, blasé or misguided judges, unreliable witnesses—these stumbling blocks can be dealt with by jurors who have common sense, and who are at least willing to "serve the cause of justice" to the best of their ability. Whether the average citizen will ever embrace jury duty eagerly and with pride, rather than with the usual sullen recognition that it has to be done, is a difficult question.

How could that eagerness be cultivated? One minor suggestion frequently made is to let the juror remain on call at his home or office. This is done now to some extent, but in this age of computers and quick telephone connections the practice could surely be widened. And what about the employer who will not pay salaries to employees on jury duty? Any business that lives in the system, on the system, off the system, ought to be willing to contribute to the functioning of that system. An employer, in fact, ought to be happy to encourage his workers to answer their jury summonses willingly.

Some kind of "ombudsman" to provide a liaison between the courts and the employers might be valuable to all parties. Most companies have people who are relatively "indispensable," and such a go-between could help to adjust schedules when such people are called—if they are valuable to the employer they are probably valuable in the courts. An ombudsman could likewise see to it that the employee is not penalized by having to work extra hours to make up the time "lost" to the business. Is it naive to imagine a time when employers will look on jury duty in a positive way, even to the point of encouraging their people to take part?

I can see other ways in which a city "juror coordinator" might function. He could, in some cases, provide transportation. He could provide diversion for those who have to wait—tours of the courtrooms, perhaps? He could arange to let jurors know the outcome of cases they have been partly involved in. He could see to it that jurors receive as much information as possible about their rights and obligations and privileges, the value of their work, the nature of the trials they might participate in. He could provide literature explaining some of the important technicalities of the law—including a glossary for those jargon words and phrases. He could create a public "image" of jury duty as something desirable and, yes, noble. He could perhaps even do a little "buttering up" of the citizen who has been jolted out of his usual schedule and realm of concern.

Tom Gavin, in the newspaper article mentioned earlier, writes:

> Robert T. Kingsley, presiding judge of the Denver district . . . says we're going to sit, sit, sit, and he's sorry but it can't be helped. Judge Kingsley says wry things about jurors' wages. . . . He says if we were some sort of voting bloc the Legislature would elevate the pay, . . . but so far as legislators are concerned we are not an interest group, we are nobodies.

Since we do not constitute a power bloc, we jurors are a body without a voice, so to speak. I see no easy way to remedy this; any impulse toward making jury duty less unpleasant will probably have to come from other quarters. My own limited jury service has given me a tremendous respect for this part of the system—at least for its potentialities. The community does need, as Chesterton said, the voice of the lay person in these terrible matters of shaping human justice, the voice of the defendants' "peers." Most trials do not have the fascination that the Panther trial had and do not put the juror into such dynamic confrontation with large public issues. But whatever form the responsibility takes, surely the community's officials should help citizens to come to it with eagerness and interest and pride. To treat us casually, routinely, with accommodations derived from minimal budgets, is a mistake that can affect us and, therefore, the quality of justice.

REFERENCES

BAGNOLD, E. (1956) The Chalk Garden. New York: Samuel French.
CHESTERTON, G. K. (1968) "Twelve men," in Tremendous Trifles. Philadelphia: Dufour.
GAVIN, T. (1974) Rocky Mountain News (August 4): 4-5.
GRIFFITH, T. (1974) How True. Boston: Atlantic-Little, Brown.

ABOUT THE AUTHORS

ABOUT THE AUTHORS

ALLEN H. BARTON is Director of the Bureau of Applied Social Research and Professor of Sociology at Columbia University. Dr. Barton's recent research includes participation in studies of ethical behavior of New York City lawyers, effects of disasters on communities, opinion-making elites in Yugoslavia and the United States, and effects of administrative decentralization in New York City.

PHILIP H. CORBOY is an attorney with the firm of Philip H. Corboy and Associates in Chicago.

MICHAEL FRIED is affiliated with the Prosecuting Attorney's office for the City of Detroit.

C. ANTHONY FRILOUX, Jr. is an attorney with the firm of Friloux, Smith, Woolf & Abney in Houston. He is also 1975-1976 Regent, National College Criminal Defense Lawyers and Public Defenders.

GENE S. GRAHAM is Professor of Journalism at the University of Illinois, Urbana. Since January, he has served as editorial commentator to Station WILL, the PBS station on the Urbana campus.

HAROLD M. HYMAN is the William P. Hobby Professor of History at Rice University, Houston, Texas. A specialist in American constitutional and legal history, his latest book is *A More Perfect Union: The Impact of the Civil War and Reconstruction on the Constitution* (Knopf, 1973).

CHARLES W. JOINER is United States District Judge for the Eastern District of Michigan.

KALMAN J. KAPLAN is Associate Professor of Psychology at Wayne State University.

EDWIN KENNEBECK is on the editorial staff of the Viking Press and is the author of *Juror Number Four: The Trial of Thirteen Black Panthers as Seen from the Jury Box* (Norton, 1973).

[253]

JOAN B. KESSLER is Assistant Professor of Communication Arts at Loyola University of Chicago. Her current research interests include the examination of the effect of litigant appearance and sex of litigant on mock juries. Dr. Kessler also conducts communication seminars for criminal justice personnel.

KATHERINE W. KLEIN is associated with the Psychology Department of Wayne State University.

RITA JAMES SIMON is Professor of Sociology and Law, and Research Professor of Communications, at the University of Illinois, Urbana. During the 1974-1975 academic year, she was Visiting Professor on the Faculty of Law, Hebrew University, Jerusalem.

ALICE M. PADAWER-SINGER is Senior Research Associate at the Bureau of Applied Social Research, Columbia University. She is President of the American Psychology-Law Society and recently organized and chaired a National Workshop on Decision-Making in 6- Versus 12-Member Juries and Unanimous Versus Non-Unanimous Decisions.

COOKIE STEPHAN is Assistant Professor of Sociology at the University of Texas, Austin.

CATHERINE M. TARRANT is a constitutional and legal historian and resides in Houston, Texas.

EMILY S. WATTS is Associate Professor of English at the University of Illinois, Urbana. She is the author of *Ernest Hemingway and the Arts* (University of Illinois Press, 1971).

NOTES

NOTES